THE PURPOSE OF GOD

(As Seen in the Old Testament)

BY

CLAUDE CARSON TAYLOR, A.M. B.D.

Professor of Historical and Systematic Theology in the College
of the Bible, Phillips University

CINCINNATI, OHIO

THE STANDARD PUBLISHING COMPANY

To my parents and my wife,

this book is dedicated

in grateful affection

3

PREFACE

CHRISTIANITY is a static religion; that is, its object of faith, Jesus the Christ, the Son of the living God, is forever fixed. Its rule of faith and practice, found in the New Testament Scriptures, is revealed once and for all. The ritual there given is for the church for all subsequent ages. Progress lies in the improved efforts to interpret what is given in thought and action. "Spiritual things are spiritually discerned;" hence the mind must be prepared more and more to see the things revealed.

The book of nature is a system of fixities. The same laws that are functioning to-day functioned in the earliest day of man's experience. Therefore progress is a term used to describe man's discovery of these laws and their application to his own welfare and happiness. God's system of physical things on the one hand and that of the spiritual on the other are analogous in that the part God performs in each has been given to man in a fixed and stable form, while man is given the task of approaching the standards in an ongoing series of progress.

On the physical side of this question I take it all are agreed: that the same physical laws obtain from age to age; that when once man has found, for instance, the chemical combination that makes up any substance, then that element of knowledge is fixed. When he finds the relation of the planets their future movements may be determined. If a drug is found to have certain effect upon the body, he may rely upon that as a law. It is upon this very principle of the fixity of nature that man finds stability in life, and that which furnishes him with faith for future plans and activity.

When, on the other hand, we come to religion many are ready to say that there is no fixity. Oh, there may be as to the nature of man, which seems at all times to have been religious, but no fixity as to content. Yet others will admit that the object of faith in the Christian religion is fixed; that God is the "same yesterday, to-day and forever," and that Christ is unchanging in His being. But when we approach the Bible they are ready to raise many objections as to its furnishing a fixed standard. Therefore the battleground of Christianity with its opponents to-day is over that Book which has given to the world the story of Jesus, and which has carried Christianity forward through nineteen hundred years, and made it the leading religion of the world.

For the last two hundred years the nations of the Occident have been in the midst of the most intensely scientific era the world has ever known. To consider as a passing panorama what has been attained through scientific investigation since Bacon introduced the method of induction, makes one dizzy. It even leads men to predict that no such advancement, similar in time and content, can ever be made again. Now, the effect of all this is, that just as men were one-sided in their thought in the age of scholasticism, looking back and interpreting everything in terms of preconceived standards, so now men are tending in the opposite way to develop a one-sided view by rejecting all the old in terms of the new. There must be a happy medium in which the truth is to be found.

That this scientific age should develop a certain type of mind is perfectly natural. Science is a process of experimentation and demonstration. As men are trained in that atmosphere, they come more and more to want a demonstration for everything and to take a skeptical attitude toward that which does not, in their opinion, conform to their notions of law. In comparison with the scientific research of the last two centuries previous eras make but a poor showing, and most of the thought prior to the eighteenth century has had to be revised. This has tended to make the scientific type of mind skeptical about all the writings, profane and sacred, produced in earlier times.

The question of the authenticity and the credibility of the Bible is one of absolute vital importance to Christianity. If the Bible account be unreliable, then we have no authentic account of God's dealing with man. We have no God-man as a revealer of truth and the "way of life." With no Christ, Christianity collapses. Here we reach the crux of the whole matter.

It is within the province of every teacher of apologetics to make a diagnosis of the thought of his time. Since apologetics is a defense of Christianity, it is incumbent on the teacher to know, if possible, against what thought or systems of thought he is to make a defense. Since this book is an apologetic interpretation of the Old Testament, I have made the foregoing brief statement that the reader may have an idea of my diagnosis of the present situation.

The subject-matter of this book was gathered while lecturing upon courses that come in my department. It was put into form as a part requirement for the degree Bachelor of Divinity.

It was thought by some of my friends to have sufficient merit to justify its publication, and at their suggestion it is given to the press.

I here express my gratitude to my colleagues, Dean F. H. Marshall and Prof. Harry D. Smith, for the efficient help they rendered in reading the manuscript and in making valuable criticisms.

My desire is that those who read this humble work may have their faith in God strengthened and their insight into His plan made clearer.   C. C. TAYLOR.

ENID, Okla., Apr. 28, 1925.

CONTENTS

BIBLIOGRAPHY

Anderson, Sir Robert: "Daniel in the Critics' Den," "The Bible and Modern Criticism."

Ames, Edward Scribner: "The Psychology of Religious Experience."

Bible Commentary.

Begbie, Harold: "The Proof of God," "Twice-born Men."

Bruce, A. B.: "Apologetics."

Bryan, William Jennings: "In His Image."

Bowne, Borden P.: "Theism," "Theory of Thought and Knowledge," "Metaphysics," "Principles of Ethics," "Immanence of God."

Bonney, T. G.: "The Present Relations of Science and Religion."

Ballard, Frank: "The Miracles of Unbelief."

Barton, George A.: "Archæology and the Bible," "The Religions of the World."

Beckwith, Clarence A.: "The Idea of God."

Campbell on Debate: "The Evidences of Christianity."

Conley, John Wesley: "Evolution and Man."

Coriat, Isadore H.: "Abnormal Psychology."

Driver, S. R.: "An Introduction to the Literature of the Old Testament."

Driver-Kirkpatrick: "The Higher Criticism."

Drawbridge, C. L.: "Common Objections to Christianity."

Davidson, A. B.: "The Theology of the Old Testament."

Drake, Durant: "Problems of Religion," "Problems of Conduct."

Fairhurst, Alfred: "Theistic Evolution," "Organic Evolution Considered."

Fairburn, A. M.: "The Philosophy of the Christian Religion," "The Place of Christ in Modern Theology."

Galloway, George: "The Principles of Religious Development," "The Philosophy of Religion."

Green, William Henry: "The Higher Criticism of the Pentateuch," "General Introduction to the Old Testament—the Canon."

Hastings: "Dictionary of the Bible."

Jevons, Frank Byron: "Introduction to the Study of Comparative Religion."

Jones, Ilion T.: "Is There a God?"

Kidd, Benjamin: "The Science of Power."

King, Irving: "The Development of Religion."

Kyle, M. G.: "Moses and the Monuments," "The Deciding Voice of the Monuments in Biblical Criticism," "The Problem of the Pentateuch."

Kirkpatrick, A. F.: "The Doctrine of the Prophets."

Leuba, James H.: "A Psychological Study of Religion."

Lodge, Sir Oliver: "Life and Matter," "Continuity."

McGarvey, J. W.: "The Authorship of Deuteronomy."

McCann, Alfred W.: "God—or Gorilla."

Mauro, Philip: "Evolution at the Bar."

Orr, James: "The Problem of the Old Testament," "The Christian View of God and the World."

Ormond, A. T.: "The Philosophy of Religion."

Osborn, Henry Fairchild: "Men of the Old Stone Age."

Price, Ira M.: "The Monuments and the Old Testament."

Pratt, James: "The Religious Consciousness," "Matter and Spirit."

Paulson, Friederich: "Introduction to Philosophy," "A System of Ethics."

Prince, Dr. Morton: "The Unconscious," "Disassociated Personality."

Raven, John H.: "Old Testament Introduction."

Rogers, Arthur Kenyon: "A Student's History of Philosophy."

Sayce, A. H.: "Monument Facts and Higher Critical Fancies."

Smith, Henry Preserved: "Old Testament History."

Smyth, Newman: "Christian Ethics."

Stevens, George B.: "The Theology of the New Testament."

Streeter, and Others: "Immortality."

Weidner, R. F.: "The Doctrine of Man," "The Doctrine of God," "Biblical Theology of the Old Testament."

Wood, William Hamilton: "The Religion of Science."

Zollars, E. V.: "Hebrew Prophecy."

And in thy seed shall all the nations of the earth be blessed.—*Gen. 22: 18.*

In those days, and at that time, will I cause a Branch of righteousness to grow up unto David; and he shall execute justice and righteousness in the land.—*Jer. 33: 15.*

This is the purpose that is purposed upon the whole earth; and this is the hand that is stretched out upon all the nations.
—*Isa. 14: 26.*

INTRODUCTION

IN making a study of the purpose of God as seen in the Old Testament, we could assume the existence of God and take for our guide the Scriptural picture of Him; we could assume the inspiration of the Scriptures and then follow the revelation given to man, basing our whole conclusion on these premises alone. But when looking into the purpose of God in relation to man as being worked out in a material world, we find that we are really in the process of forming a philosophy which includes, to some extent at least, a study of the being and nature of God, the origin of matter and its relation to God, together with the origin, nature and destiny of man.

There are three distinct forms of reality in the world: the rock embodies one, the tree two, and man embodies them all. They are matter, life and mind. These three are closely associated, but can not be reduced to one so far as this world is concerned. Of course, any system of philosophy which attempts to unify all existence in its last analysis will assume that all three forms of reality have a common source. But scientific analysis, which has to do only with the phenomenal world, can get no further than this threefold division.

For the reason, then, that it is well to have a somewhat broader background of meaning for our particular course of thought, it seems best to take time to lay this more comprehensive foundation. Then, because our source of information (the Old Testament) has been brought into question as to its historicity, because of the rejection by some of its claim of inspiration, that question will be first considered; not exhaustively, of course, but in a manner which it is hoped will help to strengthen faith. The question of the inspiration of the Scriptures is of vital importance to the theme in hand. If God did inspire men to write and we have those writings in the Bible, we may there study and come to some intelligent conclusion as to what God's purpose is. But if He did not inspire men to write, then we are altogether in the dark as to whether or not God has any purpose at all.

When we start a study of the Scriptures we meet in the very beginning with Him who is declared to be the creator of all things. In watching His work we can gather the meaning by and by, but as we watch the acts of men and know better what they are trying to do if we know the men, so it seems likewise helpful, in our study of the meaning of the acts of God, to take into consideration the being and nature of God. For centuries and centuries men have speculated on this subject, and we can hope to bring nothing new, but the purpose is to gather of what is before us that which best answers the demands of reason and which will best fit the facts of existence. Then, with what seems to be the best portrait of the Almighty, we are better able to judge the meaning of His activities in the world. In the study of God we come nearest to the nature of mind, one of the three forms of reality.

Since we have been passing through an intensively scientific age, we have had emphasized in an extreme way that form of reality called matter. Men, in their desire to know more and more about the material world and how to subject it to the use of man, have in some instances held matter so close to their eyes that they could scarcely see anything else; hence there has come to be quite a materialistic trend to thought. This movement has been aided by the growth of our purely secular institutions of learning, also by the influences of the commercial type of mind that has come in America because of her financial prosperity.

Because of this materialistic trend of thought, it is important to make a study of the relation of God to the material world, and in that study form a theory of ultimate reality and the relation of matter to it. If God is eternal and man is like Him, while, on the other hand, matter is only a form of reality which is therefore temporary in its being, it will make all the difference in the world as to our judgment of the place and importance of each in our system of meanings.

The materialistic trend of thought noted above has had much to do with the study of the origin, nature and function of man. This materialism, when combined with Darwin's theory of the transmutation of species, has made man the product of a blind system of causes pushing on from behind no one knows whither. This not only does away with the purpose of God, but eliminates God Himself. If the transmutation theory be coupled with God, in what is called Theistic evolution, it restricts God to that method of creation, although contradicting His word, and really takes the meaning from man and puts it into the system of transmutation.

If, on the other hand, we hold that man is the product of the special act of God, the entire meaning is centered in man. The nature of man is then traced directly to the act of God, and not to some genetic influence in the long list of his biological ancestry. As instance of this, the American school of psychologists, who accept the Darwinian hypothesis, are continually looking into the nature of animal life to find explanation of the nature of man. When they seek to discover the origin and nature of religion, they go to the so-called primitive man and his animal ancestry for the answer. On the other hand, for him who believes in the special creation, the answer to the question of the origin of religion is in the act of God in constituting man just what he is, neither good nor bad morally, but a being potentially religious from the beginning. Thus it seems necessary also to go into the question of the nature of man. This also necessitates a study of the

2

religious side of his nature, for this matter relates itself
especially to the question of what purpose God is
working out in man in this present life.

We find the true significance in the moral acts of
man, since here is the interest of God found to be
pre-eminent, then it behooves us to make a more careful study of sin. Around this subject gathers much of
religious philosophy, for with sin is associated those
facts of supreme importance, life and death. Here,
too, we come to the search for the true relationship of
law and sin. For to accept a God as ruler of the universe is to attribute to Him law, and if sin is the transgression of law and the wages of sin is death, then
what is the nature of that law the transgression of
which brings so much misery and woe? For these
reasons a study will be made of the nature of law and
why it is so related to life.

In this connection arises the question, What is of
supreme value to man, and why? What is the true test
of value by which a definite standard of right and
wrong may be had? Man is ethical, seeking to know the
right, but how shall he know that he has reached the
ultimate standard? Surely to think a thing to be
right does not make it so, nor does the opinion of the
majority constitute it such. Then what is right? This
question will also receive incidental consideration to
the extent that it bears on the main theme. And this
in turn brings in the question of immortality, which in
itself is closely related to, if not in fact co-ordinate
with, the goal of this thesis—the answer to the question, What is the purpose of God?

When we have made a brief study of the being and
nature of God, the origin of the material world and its
continuous relation to God, and the nature of man, we
have, in a small way at least, gotten at the primary elements of the world—matter, life and mind. Without
this background it seems impossible to get finally at
the meaning of anything. For this reason the reader is
asked to be patient in taking what might otherwise be

counted a roundabout process. Many discussions are not clear becaus᷒ of failure to bring into view plainly a definition of the main terms that are used. If one shall hold one idea of God while the writer is using another, and so on with the other main terms in use, only confusion can result.

Having reached the point when we shall consider the claims of revelation and inspiration to be not only possible, but probable; when we shall see that these mental activities are in harmony with some of the so-called natural phenomena of the experiences of mind to-day; when we shall see that the most reasonable explanation of the cause of all things is an intelligent, personal God who is all-wise, all-powerful, holy and good; when we shall also come to the conclusion that matter, life and mind are but different forms of the manifestations of God in His ultimate being; when we come to view man as an intelligent being like unto his Creator in his moral and intelligent nature, created by God in a special specific act with a moral and religious nature from the beginning—then we shall be ready to take up the narrative of what God has said and done with the possibility of giving that account a just interpretation.

The reader is, then, asked to follow in a brief survey of the legal, the historical, the prophetical and the devotional elements of the Old Testament in the search for an answer to our important inquiry. While each element has its particular function to perform toward some particular task, yet it will be found that each has its place in the plan as a whole, and therefore plays its part, whether great or small, in the consummation of the one great purpose. This predictive element is true of the Old Testament history as it is of no other. Here only do we find the doings of men and of nations, lives and institutions, with a double meaning. The event has a meaning for its own particular day and a significance for a time to come. Previous events in history thus give a greater significance to the ones that follow. The present is read in the light of the past. This, of course, embodies the miraculous element, which is the dividing line between Christianity and its foes.

Holding this general plan in mind as a background of thought, and keeping in mind the true definition of terms, we shall be better able to interpret each special act of God. Without a view of the general plan in mind, it is easy to interpret this or that act of God as biased or partial in relation to certain individuals or nations or as having in itself no moral worth. For this reason the reader will find the conclusion often anticipated in the language of the early chapters that the value of viewing the particular from the standpoint of the whole may obtain. This method is found valuable and necessary in almost every search for truth. The scientist starts his investigation and research with an assumption in mind. In the process of investigation he proves his assumption to be true or else finds sufficient evidence to discard it. Men first hold in imagination the new discovery or invention and work toward its realization. The difference here is that in the interpretation of history a writer uses the conclusions to which he has already arrived in guiding the reader in his study, just as the builder of a machine explains to an observer early in the demonstration what came to him only after the study was made.

The writer will try not to be dogmatic in his position or statement, and yet from the nature of the study many subjects must be treated in such a brief form that it may cause some of the argument to appear blunt. But any such statements may be tested by the reader's own further investigation.

CHAPTER I.

REVELATION AND INSPIRATION

IN any general study of the Bible the question which seems to arise first for solution is whether or not the Bible is the word of God. Did God give directly to man some of the information and direct him in gathering such other material as was needed? And, further, was man directed in the process of writing? Such, then, is the problem of revelation and inspiration, and it seems practical and natural to consider this subject first. In the light of one's attitude toward this subject will he judge the contents of each book, and by it will his conclusions be colored. In other words, if a man start his study of the contents of the Bible with the notion that there has been no special revelation, then will his conclusions be formed accordingly, and *vice versa*. Revelation is generally considered under two heads or divisions—natural and special. Natural revelation is that message man obtains in his study of nature, while special revelation is the message received directly from God in whatever manner He has chosen to convey it. In this latter sense revelation will be used in the following study.

1. *Limitations of man when unaided.*

A first thing to be considered in our study is the limitation of the mind of man to discover some things unaided. It is not presumed that it is within the purpose of things for man to comprehend all things. But it is claimed that man has the ability to know some things which, unaided, he has not the ability to discover. For instance, man has the ablity to know and understand what occurred among the various peoples of the earth in prehistoric times, but, having no record of their doings, he is forced to remain in ignorance. Memory, that power of the human mind which lays hold of the fact and makes it available for the present, is limited to the realm of human experience—that of ourselves or of others who have left to us their records. Reason, that power which makes deductions and inferences, can be relied on only to the extent that such inference may be verified in the realm of experience. As we observe sandstone forming to-day so we may infer sandstone formed in the prehistoric ages. But outside the realm of experience verification is impossible and our inferences may be but the wildest speculations, though the theories were spun by some of the wisest of minds.

Among the things impossible for man to know without revelation, we will consider, first, beginnings: the beginning of the world, of life and of man. Man's curiosity has ever probed into the question of beginning. He wants to know the whence of himself and of the things about him. To say that an answer to such questions will not add to his ability to feed, clothe and shelter himself, does not dispose of the matter; for what is of such fundamental interest to man is important, and does matter. The child stops his play to inquire who made the world, and the question stays with him until it is answered. Since man, with all his acquired ingenuity in the great physical laboratories, has never been able to construct anew one grain of sand, he has never been able to verify any theory he has devised as to the origin of matter. True, he sees matter broken up by the forces of nature and altered by his own hand as he applies the chemical forces to it. He stands and views a world of incessant change, but by his own law of the indestructibility of matter he admits he is unable to add to or take from the total bulk. Or, if he is forced to relinquish this law and admit there is loss of energy he admits it is from nature itself, and not from anything he is able to introduce that is transcendent to existence.

Again, man has been unable to introduce life. Sir Oliver Lodge says: "Many have been the attempts to generate life *de novo* by packing together suitable materials and keeping them pleasantly warm for a long time; but when all germs of pre-existing life have rigorously been excluded the attempt hitherto has been a failure; so far, no life has made its appearance under observation, except from antecedent life."[1] Here also man is without verification in the field of experience for his theories of the origin of life. He may talk learnedly of "spontaneous generation" or the transference of life from other spheres, but his inferences are projected outside the realm of observation and remain classified as pure speculations.

Now and anon some scientist breaks out with the prediction that soon they will be able to generate life in the laboratory; but since they are not able to produce matter which is considered lower in the scale of existence and can not even tell us what life is, we should look upon their predictions with considerable skepticism.

If man has been unable to bring into existence one new atom of matter or to make one addition to the animate existence, how much less is he able to add, other than through the natural processes, one human being to the total of human life. Here many turn face about, and, instead of claiming they can initiate human life, as they claim they will be able some day to do, they claim that neither God nor man started human life, but that man evolved from the lower species. If lifeless matter can be animated, then why not make a man as well as an amœba? The bulk should not matter, as there is plenty of material always at hand. It isn't a question of quantity, but one of quality, of labor. Second, among the things impossible for man,

---

[1] "Life and Matter," p. 171.

unaided, to discover is the purpose of things, himself included.

The question, "What for?" has also been ever present with man. While it is proper in the wisdom of God's economy to leave man to search out many things, as the author of Proverbs says, "It is the glory of God to conceal a thing, but the glory of kings is to search out a matter"[1] (for man would be pauperized if everything were furnished him without effort on his part), yet we find he is limited in his search for the purpose of the whole. He can see, in the nature of things, how the mineral kingdom supports the vegetable kingdom, how in turn the vegetable supports the animal, and all contribute to his own well-being. But why does it all exist anyway, and why should man be here for a brief span of threescore and ten years?

No one knows so well the purpose of a thing as he who made it, and if the world be without a maker then it is without purpose. With such conclusions entering our minds, all becomes chaos and all our anchorages are loosed. But purpose is to be read in all about us; that is, purpose as to immediate use. All things speak of a mind back of them, and the mind in us longs to read the mind that made us, so that our purposes may be made to accord with the purpose of God.

The great field of science, aside from discovering the true nature of the material universe, is to discover its use. What is it good for? What will this or that contribute to the welfare of man? In answering these questions science has made a wonderful contribution to human comfort and happiness. But when all this is done what may be said of man? What is he for? To this point man diligently travels only to find that the trail eludes him. What a sad commentary on the knowledge of man if he were able to tell the purpose of all about him, but must confess to

---

[1] Prov. 25: 2.

ignorance when asked as to the purpose of his own existence.

How easy it is, too, for man to become engulfed in the search for the use of things about him and forget to inquire concerning himself, taking himself as a matter of course. With his mind on the thing at the big end of the telescope, he fails to consider the one at the small end. Yet of how much greater importance is the mind that sees than the thing that is seen. As, for instance, a man stands before a cage of monkeys. How much more important is the one outside looking in than the one inside on exhibition.

Is man to seek the existence of himself at whatever cost and thus run society into individualism, or is the individual to be absorbed in the interest of the state and establish collectivism? Or what is the proper mean between these, and why?

The world has waged many wars trying to solve these problems, and yet finds them unsolved so far as the theories of men go. How long will man wander in darkness and the maze of his own theories? While infatuated with the contemplation of his own wisdom, yet he is brought to face the fact, time and again, that he has blundered, and that his blunder has cost thousands of precious lives. Why not be willing to look up to Him who made us, for the answer which man can not give, and in response to the will of God meekly say, "Not my will, but thine, be done"?

How foolish it is for man to wander stubbornly where he can not know the way, when there is a guide to be had. On the other hand, how dark a picture to think of man wandering in darkness, driven hither and thither by blind chance, and no one to know, much less to show, the way.

The last item to be considered among the things man can not know unaided is the end or destiny of things. As man naturally conceives of a time when the world had a beginning, of a time when life first appeared, and of a time when the first man made his appearance, he likewise thinks of a time when things, as they are, will cease to be. At almost every great catastrophe man has shuddered with the idea that the end was approaching, if not already at hand.

One thing he is sure of, and that is that life in the individual comes to an end so far as this world is concerned. He sees death about him on every hand and follows in a ceaseless procession his own fellows to the tomb. Yet this invariable experience has not exterminated the ever-present question, ''If a man die, shall he live again?''

Here, again, is ability to know without the power unaided to discover the knowledge desired.

2. *The Influence that Lack of Revelation Would Have upon Man.*

Assuming that man has not had a revelation, that he has been groping unaided these many centuries, let us speculate as to the influence a lack of such aid would have upon man.

One thing that man seems ever striving to get away from is uncertainty. That which disturbs the business world and has often helped to bring on the financial panic has been uncertainty and its accompaniment, distrust. Uncertainty begets distrust among nations and leads to war; it causes the same grim monster to arise in the home and destroy conjugal happiness.

Why are we afraid in the dark? The answer is to a large degree uncertainty. Hence man has stood trembling in the presence of death because of the uncertainty of the beyond.

In every field of human activity man strives to eliminate the element of uncertainty, by removing the cause of fear and distrust. Thus he stabilizes his life more and more and adds to the sum total of his happiness.

Man's life is filled with the struggle between truth and error, light and darkness as portrayed in the temptation of Christ—a battle between the ifs of Satan and the certainties of Christ.

Suppose each new generation had to begin and continue its life and activity with all its questions concerning the past unanswered. Certain it would be that life would be robbed of much of its joy, to say nothing of its being crippled in efficiency. Then, shall we assume that the power that made us would withhold from us that which we desire to know, and yet are unable to discover?

The conclusion is, then, that without revelation man would be surrounded with so much uncertainty as to keep him in a state of more or less dread, terror and superstition. He would be deprived, further, of the true means of interpretation of knowledge, and hence could not obtain the true meanings of things.

3. *The Necessity of Revelation.*

Seeing, then, that man is surrounded with so much of the unknown, which, strive though he will to penetrate its opaque depths, yields not to his efforts; and that this limitation of knowledge cripples him in his thought and leaves him to misdirected action; and, further, that it robs him of peace, joy, and the light of truth which alone can truly satisfy—we conclude that revelation is a necessity, and agree with the sage[1] of old that there must come One from above to make known those things to man.

Man's realm of knowledge is, first of all, made up of his own individual experience; then through the experience of others the horizon of the unknown is pushed further back; but, as has been said, as the island of the known enlarges, the shore-line of the unknown increases apace. Beyond human experience man can not go, and from there on must have revelation.

Another reason commonly given for revelation other than man's need is, that it is a necessity from the very nature of God.

Taking for granted now the existence of God, and leaving to another chapter the discussion of reasons for

---

[1] Plato.

such belief, we proceed to consider what must of necessity be His attitude toward man. Being the creator of all things, God must be endowed with omnipotence, and among the things He is able to do, it is reasonable to assume, is to make Himself known. Further, we must assume that God is just, and, being responsible for man's existence, He by His nature must deal justly with him. But in turn justice demands that if God can reveal Himself and give to man the knowledge he so much needs, He ought to do so. Therefore, if God can and ought to make Himself known, then He will. And if He has, it is most reasonable to believe that His message is found in the Book of books—the Bible.

Having considered why it is necessary for man to have revelation from a higher power, it is now logical to make a study of what the message of revelation ought to be. What in the nature of things is necessary to the happiness and well-being of man here and hereafter that, unaided, he can not obtain?

In the first place, it is necessary for man to be provided for physically, and this a beneficent Creator has done for man as for animal in the way of instinct. Until the mind has time to develop and take charge of action, intelligent direction is furnished by God in what we choose to call instinct. This is never fully supplanted, but in the main in adult man it is overshadowed by the individual's own intelligence. Thus man's intelligence, supplemented by instinct, is sufficient to secure for him that which is necessary to physical existence; yea, more, to add the comforts and luxuries which the earth holds in store for him who is diligent in the application of his ingenuity.

As before mentioned, it is a wise plan that the hand of necessity is here laid heavily upon man, that by the sweat of his face he should earn his bread. Forced by the desire to maintain physical life, aided by curiosity, and spurred on by pride and ambition, man searches out the hidden things of nature. By so doing he climbs to higher and higher heights of physical and social comforts. Should God reveal to man, without effort on his part, all the secrets of nature, man would be pauperized and reduced to a state of monotonous existence.

Next we turn to the realm of intelligence. Here we find ourselves in the field of controversy, since it is maintained by some that man has evolved intellectually. It is claimed that his ideas gradually evolved in the process of adjustment to environment, and that his speech was developed from the animal cries of his primitive ancestry. On the other hand, there are those who contend that man must have ever had a teacher, and therefore the first man must have been taught by God —hence had revelation. Alexander Campbell said: "Many experiments have been made upon the deaf who have been restored to hearing, to ascertain whether by the other senses, and all the reasonings which the mental powers were capable of, they had acquired any idea of God; and all have concurred in attesting the utter impossibility of acquiring such without the aid of revelation."[1] The contention is that the imagination can construct ideas out of the material furnished by the senses only, and since the characteristics of God would not be available without revelation, the mind, unaided, could not formulate the notion or idea, God. This controversy can not be settled by demonstration of either position, but the experience of man goes far to show the reasonableness of the view that the idea God was derived by the communication of God with man, and that in turn the idea was disseminated by passing from man to man.

While the question of his physical life is primary, and his intellectual life is of great value, man, being moral in his make-up, has another side of life not less in importance, that of his spiritual nature. Were each of us a Robinson Crusoe on a lonely island the problem

---

[1] "Evidences of Christianity," p. 145.

of human conduct would scarcely arise. There would be merely questions of how to procure food, shelter and clothing, and our contact would be with nature alone. What is good would be determined in terms of physical life, that action being right which led to some bodily comfort.

We are not Robinson Crusoes, but gregarious beings choosing to live in ever more and more congested groups, as our metropolitan cities attest.

When it comes to living with our fellows, it is not only a question of procuring the necessities of life, but how we shall procure them and how use them— our freedom being defined in terms of the freedom of others. But the question may be asked, Can not man be left here also, as in the physical realm, to his own ingenuity under compulsion of necessity to work out his own system of government, morals and religion? Man being moral, we grant he is striving after the good and seeking for the right; but what is good— good for what? Left to himself, man must use his brief span of life in contributing to the endless experiment to solve this perplexing problem. For the sake of argument, let us suppose that some millenniums hence man will have discovered the true standards of conduct which we must assume will make for his greatest happiness. How about the countless millions who have been sacrificed in the process of experimentation? Did they not have as much inherent right to know as the others, and to enjoy the fruits of that knowledge? This smacks too much of the German theory of the "superman," which ignores the rights of the many and makes its contribution to the few.

In the foregoing assumption two vital issues fail to have consideration, and without them it seems to the writer no adequate system of ethics can be constructed. They are the source of man and the destiny of man. These are so interrelated as to be treated together. If man is but the product of blind force through a physical process of evolution appearing as a mere individual portion of animated clay to continue for a few years and then pass forever out of existence, then is his conduct to be determined in the light of his own physical needs, limited only by the restrictions of his fellows—limitations which he can not avoid. On this basis, why not chloroform the aged, the feeble-minded and the insane? Why take a man out of the death-cell, as was done recently at Sing Sing Prison, to oper-ate on him for appendicitis in order to save his life, when in but a few days that life was to be taken? If this life be all and there is no intelligent Creator to whom we are answerable, then why not cut off the dependent, the deformed and the deficient? Many such are not only a burden to society, but to themselves as well.

Then, there is the stoical view of doing right for right's sake. This may be a sufficient reward for a few of the sophisticated, but the common people de-mand something more tangible and concrete. Whether conscious of it or not, we work in terms of self-interest, not that narrow form commonly called selfishness, but toward the end of the ideals of self we hold as our model. Human nature is so constructed as to labor for reward and to avoid its opposite, punishment. That reward may be approval of self as in the case of the Ethicist; it may be the goods obtained as with the Utilitarian; it may be the pleasurable of life as with the Epicurean; it may be the abnegation of the Bud-dhist, or the heaven of the Christian; all alike work for some reward, the idea of which is set up by self, in-herited from others or revealed from God.

On the other hand, if man was created by God and given a life that is to continue indefinitely, this physical existence being but the incubation period, then what vistas of interpretation open up in the consid-eration of human conduct. How we are awed and humbled by the thought of our responsibility to the great Author of our being! How we are stirred with the contemplation of spending an eternity in a

closer fellowship with Him and with those who have
chosen to do His bidding! Then life is no longer
measured in terms of earthly longevity, but in ideals;
no longer weighed in the balances of physical comfort
—in eating, drinking and sleeping—but in truth, virtue and righteousness.

Again, He who made us for another life will have
so fixed our nature as to make the plan of preparation
for another existence fit best into the economy of things
here below. Hence when life functions normally he
who is to be happiest yonder will be happiest here; but
when conflict arises man should decide for the greater
value; that is, in terms of spiritual life. Accepting
as fact that man is here as the purpose of a beneficent
Creator, and that this life is only the vestibule to a
greater existence, we are confronted again with man's
inability to guide himself. How can he please a God
whose will to him is unknown? How can he prepare
for a condition about which he knows nothing? We
answer in the words of the Ethiopian officer when
asked by Philip if he understood what he read: "How
can I except some one guide me?"[1]

On this basis the only conclusion is that God must
make known to man his beginning and destiny and give
to him a plan of preparation adequate to the demands.
This plan must be in harmony with right law in the
promotion of human society or else it will run amuck of
man's gregarious instincts; it must run parellel to right
law in the physical realm or it will tend toward the
extinction of the human race. But since God is the
Author of all, it follows that these will harmonize.

One other matter needs consideration before we pass
to the discussion of the content of revelation, and that
is, What is the purpose of God that is being worked
out in the world?

First, from the estimate of value man puts upon
things we find that he holds human life above all else;

---

[1] Acts 8: 31.

in himself he values character more than physical life, as instanced in the pilgrimage of our forefathers; in such statements as that of the illustrious Henry, "Give me liberty or give me death;" in the profligate expenditure of men and money in war that some principle may be conserved. The shores of history are strewn with the wrecks of nations who have turned in on themselves in the greed of selfish avarice, while others have struggled upward by the rough, but heroic, path of unselfish devotion to noble ideals. Some one has well said that the greatest thing in the world is man, the greatest thing in man is mind, and the greatest thing in mind is morals.

On the other hand, we find this estimate of values confirmed by the word of God. As His crowning act of creation, He brought into existence man, stating he was created in the image of God. If man, in contradistinction from all other life, was created in the image of God, then that image consists in man's ability to think the thoughts of God, to contemplate His handiwork, and glorify Him by his righteous acts. He also says man was made a little lower than God,[1] and that to him was given dominion over everything upon the earth.

But not only did God give to man His image, but He demands that that image be developed; hence it is godlikeness or righteousness that He requires. With all due respect to the omnipotence of God, righteousness or virtue is one thing He could not create. He could make it possible, but must have the co-operation of man, since virtue is the product of the action of a free moral agent directed by his own choice and will.

Now, having thus briefly considered the purpose of God, and having arrived at the conclusion that it is the development of righteous character in man, and, further, having seen that this end can be obtained only by the co-operation of God and man, we conclude,

---

[1] Authorized Version—Angels.

3

as a matter of course, that it is incumbent upon
each to perform his part. Without man's effort it is
impossible for virtue to obtain; without God's part—
revelation—it is impossible for man to know the way;
but with the efforts of both working in harmony success is assured.

In conformity with this view we must ever keep
in mind this law, that God does not do for man what
man can do for himself, else the purpose will be defeated by depriving man of that individual responsibility and activity which are absolutely essential to
his spiritual growth and character. God furnished the
image, man must develop it and God must give him the
necessary information to make that development possible.

Among the things to be revealed it is of first
importance that God reveal Himself, and this He is
represented in Genesis as doing in His conversation
with the first pair. Next of importance man wants to
know of the beginning of things, himself included, and
with this the early narrative deals. Some complain
that the account is too brief and that it is not scientific. Again let us remember that man must be left to
use his own effort where that is adequate, hence the
word of God is not given as a scientific text-book on
any material subject, but is concerned with revealing
to man that which is necessary in helping him toward
the end and purpose of all things—a righteous character. As to whether the creation account is scientific
will be left for future discussion; but suffice it to say
here that until we have a truly scientific account with
which to compare the Mosaic description, it behooves us
to withhold such judgment, especially in the light of
the fact that the Bible has withstood the criticism of
centuries.

From the creation story the narrative passes quickly
to man's moral nature, to the beginning of sin, and the
beginning of religion. God unites the first pair in holy
wedlock and tells them not how to build a house, but

how to build a home; not how to make a living, but how to make a life. God did not tell Abel how to shear sheep, but how to bring an offering acceptable unto Him. God did not tell Cain how to cultivate grain, but how to cultivate a soul. God did not tell men how to build cities, but He did give them such instructions as to their relations each to the other as would enable them to build social structures. By implanting in man the right principles of conduct toward God and his fellows, man would be able by his own ability to formulate such systems as would be needed for carrying them into group life and activity. There were special cases where it was necessary for God to give more minute directions to man in order to the fulfillment of some divine purpose.

Contemporaneous with God's revealing to man his lost condition because of sin, the promise of salvation was made known. Thus man was not thrown into the slough of despair, but consoled with that hope inspired by the promise of God. Not only was this promise given in the remote reference to the coming of His Son as in the language "He [Christ] shall bruise thy head [the serpent]," but God made it possible for man to worship and serve Him acceptably from the beginning.

He could bring an animal offering, only typical, of course, of the true offering—Christ Jesus—but, nevertheless, a covering for his sin.

It was necessary that faith and obedience to God be preserved among men, and to this end God kept in communication with a portion of the race, keeping up an unbroken succession of at least approximate faithfulness to Him. When God revealed Himself to a part of humanity it was possible for that part to take it to others, thus preserving intact that responsibility which belongs to man in this partnership.

Since the purpose of God was to develop a righteous character in man, and since man separated himself from God through sin, thus bringing himself into a state in which, unaided, he could not rise morally, it became necessary for God to furnish the plan of salvation and make it known to man.

Keeping in mind that it is not the work of God to explain the material universe, to make known to man ways and methods of agriculture, manufacture, commerce, art, etc., but to guide him spiritually in paths of moral truth which to man are unknown, and without revelation are unknowable, then may we rightfully expect the content of revelation to be in accord with this purpose and plan, and that the Bible as a whole will be given over to that consideration of man that has primarily to do with his spiritual nature and its development, to the end that man may become a righteous character.

Having made this general statement as to the content of revelation, there will be left to future consideration such particular parts of the revealed message as the nature of this discussion demands; hence we pass on now to the third main point of interest, the method of revelation.

4. *The How of Revelation.*

The forms or methods of revelation are, according to the Scriptures, direct communication, visions, dreams, and supernatural illumination. Let us take these up in order. Is it reasonable to believe that God could speak, and has done so in audible words to man? Are we to take as literal fact the account in Genesis of God talking to Moses at the burning bush? Granting for the present argument the belief in God, we must concede that God is the author of all being; that this material world is the expression of His power. Now, that which the human mind interprets as sound, and out of which it constructs words as signs of ideas, is in the material realm first of all just wave motions of the atmosphere. Then converted into nerve force, it goes to the seat of hearing in the brain, and there is translated by the mind into ideas. Now, shall we say that the power which was able to create the atmosphere,

the nervous system, and the mind, would not be able
to cause such wave motions of the air as, when reaching
the ear of Moses, would be interpreted by him to be his
own name? Fancy the personification of a group of
phonographs, unable to see the man who had made
them, saying one to another: ''There may be a being
who made us and so constructed our mechanism as to
enable us to talk, but that same being can not talk
or make himself known in audible sounds such as we
make, because we do not see him in the form in which
we exist. Reason seems to demand the very opposite;
that is, that he who can transmit to others any power
or ability must have that power or ability himself.

Moreover, except God appear to man in some manner by which man can lay hold of Him through one
or the other of his senses, He remains unknown and
continues to be a subject of speculation. But that
is to throw man back into the state of uncertainty,
doubt and despair. Man wants not the proof of God
which may be found in abundance in the philosophical
treatises of scholars, but he wants to know God, and
he can only know Him as he knows anything else, by
the regular process of mind. Not only does the Scripture represent God as speaking to man, but it says also
that His heavenly messengers have appeared and have
been seen by man. Thus we have further demonstration of the existence of superhuman beings.

Again, the fact that the Bible makes no effort to
prove the existence of God, such as may be found in
the theological works of man, goes to show that what
man knew to exist needed no argument, and while all
would not have the knowledge, the testimony of those
who did would be sufficient for others.

But some one says, How could God formulate
words? How could a purely spiritual being make
himself known to a human being? Suppose a man
should say to me, after thirty days of a certain diet,
''I have added ten pounds to my weight,'' shall I reject
his testimony because I do not understand how food

taken into the stomach is transformed into nerve tissue, osseous tissue, and globules of fat? Or shall I deny the testimony of scientists as to the various actions of electricity because I do not understand what electricity is? But one says: "We observe the actions of this and that force mentioned, but we do not observe these actions claimed for God." Neither is there virtue in accepting what is forced upon one, and in the realm of religion there must be a larger place reserved for faith, for in the exercise of one's own choice is there the possibility of virtue. I quote from Isaac Errett's "First Principles" (p. 64): "We can easily conceive how the evidence could be made more abundant and demonstrative than it is. We can see how it might be made so completely a matter of demonstration that it could not be resisted so as to leave no election to us whether to believe or not. But the moment that was done, all the moral element of our faith would be eliminated. It would no longer be our act—the choice of our hearts; and it could, of course, serve none of the moral purposes in regeneration which it is now designed to serve."

If this can be said of faith in Christ, it is altogether reasonable to apply the same principle to faith in God. What were the credit to us if at every step God spoke to us, telling which particular path to take, guiding and directing us in all the petty details of life? Rather is man put forward by his own choice and initiative, having been given, once and for all, his spiritual direction, the guide-book which he may study and learn for himself.

Next to be considered is the vision. It is said, in Gen. 15:1, that the word of Jehovah came unto Abram in a vision. Now, the Hebrew word has as its main idea that which is in the English word "vision," the act of seeing. Hence it is right to conclude that one evidence to Abram of the presence of Jehovah was through his sense of sight. What did Abram see? The narrative does not disclose the answer, but if we are to accept it

as true we must conclude that what Abram saw was to
him conclusive evidence that he was in the presence of
Jehovah. Further testimony was had in the fact that
Jehovah spoke to him, which message was the purpose
of the vision, and the whole was consummated in the
smoking furnace and flaming torch passing between the
pieces of the offering which Abram had set over against
each other.

It is a common experience with man that through
illusion and hallucination he sees things not comform-
able to the laws of nature, yet, nevertheless, he truly
sees them—as, for instance, the mirage. And may not
God, who made the eye, the light, and the object, so
dispose them that man may see what He would have
him observe? But does this not open up the way for
all kinds of fanatical claims as to visitations of God
through hallucinations to the setting aside of verified
knowledge and the laws of nature? The answer must
be yes; for the genuine is always counterfeited, but
the counterfeit is an evidence of the genuine. The task
for man is to provide himself with the means of dis-
criminating between the true and the false, and God
has furnished the means of verifying the truth of His
revelation.

It may be laid down as a law that God has not
asked man to believe a single thing for which He has
not given him as much proof and as reliable testimony
as man requires from his fellow. This has been sub-
stantiated again and again by some of the best legal
talent the world affords.

Whether God operates by His omnipotence on the
mind of man to bring about the vision, or brings, as
facts, the material objects to be seen, it is one and the
same to the writer. For if God made the machine—
the mind of man—He must be able to operate it to the
end and purpose for which He made it. Can not the
man who made the engine control its actions? Can not
the watchmaker cause the watch to run or stop at his
bidding? Then, on what ground dare we deny to God

the power to direct the forces He has brought into being?

In Matt. 1:20 it is said "an angel of the Lord appeared unto Joseph in a dream." In this dream the Lord made known to Joseph His message concerning Mary and the birth of Jesus. Again we see the message is of first importance.

Dreams, though strange phenomena, are the common experience of mankind. Psychologists generally agree that they are caused by some physiological disturbance, and that their content is made up of irrational and oftentimes gruesome combinations of elements of thought derived from the waking consciousness. This explanation may not always fit the circumstances, but in general may apply. As to what the consciousness is and its relation to waking consciousness, there have been many theories propounded; but of one thing we are sure; that is, we dream; our dreams are a reality. Since we can repeat with accuracy our dreams, it follows that if God directed man's thought in the dreamland and through it gave to him His message, man could obtain and retain that message. Only the question remains, How could God direct the mind in dream? If such an insignificant matter as eating too much at the evening meal, or partaking of a portion of food difficult to digest, can cause man to dream and the course of his waking, conscious thought determine the content of the dream, may not God, who knows the secrets of why and how we dream, communicate to man His message through this medium? But how? I can not tell. How do I dream? I do not know.

There is left to us of the methods of divine impartation of knowledge mentioned above that of divine illumination. By divine illumination is meant that process by which God imparts information to man apart from and different to a direct verbal expression of thought; but through some form of direct contact with the mind He causes man to know His message.

This contention is also met by the question, How? It is not the purpose of the writer to answer this question directly, for we can not see and detect immediate causes even in our own experience. We must be content to cite facts in the world known to man, which, though not understood, must be accepted, and, being accepted, must lead the way to acceptance of analogous occurrences.

What is the power of mind upon mind in human experience? In answering this surely we may throw some light on the question of what is the influence of the divine mind upon the human. In the last quarter of a century much has developed in the study of the phenomena of the human mind under such so-called abnormal activities as hypnosis, telepathy, crystal gazing, disassociate personality, automatic writing, etc. In hypnosis it is a scientific fact that mind does the bidding of mind, and that, too, while the subject is unconscious to the normal state. Even suggestions given during hypnosis are carried out with accuracy in the waking state. In telepathy it is well established that mind conveys to mind its message when distance intervenes and all the ordinary and known means of communication are wanting. In automatic writing the hand writes down a message unknown, or, at least, undirected, by the normal consciousness. These facts are now generally recognized.

How are these things done? Psychologists are trying to explain by some theory of a subconscious mind or subliminal self, but the answer to the question is not yet forthcoming. Then, shall a man who accepts the existence of a God deny to Him the power to give His message directly to man when he must accept as fact that man does exert such power with his fellow-man? But one may ask, How can I know that the message is from God? Just as human telepathy may be verified, so may the message from God. And just as there are false claims of human telepathy, just so are there false prophets. Man is always burdened with the responsi-

bility of exerting effort on his own part to obtain the
truth. He must separate the wheat from the chaff.

Thus it seems there is no middle ground; one must,
if he believes in a God at all, accept the claims of
His power to make known by word orally, by vision,
by dream, or by divine illumination, the message He
desires man to have. Or, on the other hand, he must
deny the existence of a God altogether—a very dangerous and illogical thing to do.

Now, having given attention to the subject of revelation, we pass to its kindred topic, inspiration. Granting the existence of God and the claim that from His
very nature and because of the needs of man He has
revealed Himself, then the question arises, Has He
inspired men to give His message to others?

Having accepted as a law, and for good reasons,
that God does not do for man what man can do for
himself, we next draw the conclusion that God will
not become directly teacher for every man. Instead,
He will call upon man to instruct his fellows. This
involves not only revelation that man may know what
to teach, but inspiration that the message may be properly presented. From these conclusions the following
definition logically follows. Inspiration is that power
of God exercised over the mind of man for the conveyance of His message to others, and revelation is
the process by which God makes His will known to the
individual with whom He is dealing. As in New Testament times, the baptism of the Holy Spirit is not for
the sake of the one so baptized, but for the sake of
others to whom Spirit-filled messengers shall take the
Word. So God revealed to Moses at the burning bush
His will that he should lead His people out of Egyptian
bondage. Later He inspired Moses to speak to Israel
and to Pharaoh. His message called on Israel to move
out of Egypt, and on Pharaoh to give his consent.

Unless God is to speak to each man as he did to
Moses, it will necessitate His putting into the mind of
man His message, and that in such a way as that this

message may be properly made known to others by the mouth of the prophet.

On the assumption that man is to be used as the agent to make known to others the divine will, it must not be assumed that the individuality of the agent is entirely lost. If so, God might just as well speak directly to man. On the other hand, it can not be left wholly to the mind of the agent, else it will fail to be God's message. In 1 Pet. 1:21, it is admirably expressed: "For no prophecy ever came by the will of man; but men spake from God, being moved by the Holy Spirit."

Then, what is inspiration? Pres. E. V. Zollars once directed a class in Christian Evidences (of which class the writer was a member), to present each his definition of inspiration. From the various definitions offered by members of the class, an eclectic summary was made in the following statement: "Inspiration as applied to the Scriptures of the Old and New Testaments is such a divine illumination and guidance of the mind of the chosen agent as enabled him to reveal past history otherwise unknown, to select from existing material that which is true and suited to the divine purpose in revelation, to reject from material at his command or from parts in his own knowledge such things as were not germane to that purpose, to stimulate memory, to recall necessary truth that otherwise would have been lost, and to communicate new truth necessary for man's salvation, and not discoverable by the natural, unaided powers of the human mind." The foregoing was then condensed into the following brief definition: "Inspiration is a special illumination and guidance of the mind of the chosen agent, enabling him to communicate the divine message, whether historical, legal, didactic or prophetic."

This definition indicates how closely related are revelation and inspiration, and how a comprehensive definition of inspiration includes revelation. While technically they may be held distinct, and may have

distinct purposes as before stated, yet in a general
sense the above may be used as a practical and work-
able definition of inspiration.

On the side of divine illumination it was necessary
that God make known certain facts which were otherwise unobtainable, such as the beginning of things, yet
of such importance as to be the requisite ground for
the true interpretation of life and one's relation to his
fellow-being. How did Moses come by the account of
creation? Either God made known directly to Moses
the information, or else had given it to others before
him, from whom Moses obtained it. He then so guided
him in the gathering of the material as to give to
mankind the true message. It would not have been
easier to give it to Abraham, to Noah, or even to
the first man, Adam; for, if given at all, it was a
revelation, and therefore the supernatural element
was present. Since there is no account of the creation
story preserved among the Israelites prior to Moses, it
may as well be assumed that it was given first to him.
It is true there was among the Babylonians such a
story. And if it seems necessary to suppose an earlier
revelation to account even for the polytheistic story of
the Babylonians, then well and good; but the claim of
liberalists that Moses obtained his account from the
Babylonians is being pretty generally discredited by
scholars on the ground that there is not sufficient reason for believing that such polytheism could so soon be
purified into the outstanding monotheism of the Mosaic
account. Furthermore, it is claimed by the Scriptures
that God not only made known past events, but gave to
man knowledge of that which had not yet come to pass;
notably, in Isa. 44:28, where the Lord is represented
as saying, "That saith of Cyrus, He is my shepherd,
and shall perform all my pleasure; even saying of
Jerusalem, She shall be built; and of the temple, Thy
foundation shall be laid," but some scholars claim that
chapters 40-66 were not written by Isaiah, but by some
other one during the Babylonian captivity who at-

tributed his work to Isaiah, and hence the verse quoted is not prediction, but history. It must be remembered that the critics who divide Isaiah begin their study and manipulation of the Scriptures with the assumption that there is no such thing as miracle, which is the very issue at stake, and, of course, the issue can not be granted in the beginning of the argument, else there were no discussion at all. This from James Orr as to the attitude of the critics: "For now it becomes apparent—there is, indeed, not the least attempt to disguise it—that to a large and influential school of critical inquirers—those, moreover, who have had most to do with the shaping of the current critical theories— this question of a supernatural origin for the religion of Israel is already foreclosed, is ruled out at the start as *a priori* inadmissible."[1] Of course, to him who denies the supernatural there can be no revelation either of past or future events, but that is the contention to be proved before the Scriptures are to be thrown aside or so manipulated as to be practically of no value.

The second outstanding element in the definition of inspiration is the divine guidance of the mind of the agent enabling him to give the message of God, whether historical, legal, didactic or prophetic. If man is to be used as the agent of God to carry His will to others, there must be a guarantee that it is the message of God, and not the think-so of man. Man's mind, no matter how highly developed, can not be depended upon to hold and convey truth to that degree of approximate infallibility as would insure successful transmission. Honest people are forever garbling that which they hear, with the result that after it has passed by word of mouth several times the story can hardly be recognized, as is strikingly illustrated in "The Story of the Three Black Crows."

Next, some one asks, Have we then word for word the language of God? The answer is, No; for, keep-

---

[1] "The Problem of the Old Testament," p. 12.

ing in mind that man is used as an agent, the human element is allowed to enter in, but not to the extent of causing to be lost the real message of God.

With all the minor discrepancies that may be found in our present Bible, not one vital theme is impaired, not one hindrance to the man who is sincerely seeking to know God's will.

Granting that there is a God, then why should it be thought a thing incredible with you that He should reveal Himself to man and inspire man to carry His message to others?

Man, unaided, can not know many things which are of vital importance to him; he can not, by striving, find the history of beginnings; he can not, unaided, determine the destiny of things; much more then, without this knowledge, is he unable to tell the purpose of things. This leaves him in darkness as to the true state of things and uncertain as to his true relation to others.

Not only does this constitute a great need demanding revelation, but the very nature of God Himself demands it. How can a just, merciful and loving God place man here on the earth and then leave him to his own blind wanderings?

A God who can, ought to make Himself known. That He can is evidenced by man's power over his fellow and by God's power over nature. If He ought, and He could, then He did, and His message is to be found in that most wonderful of all books, the Bible.

CHAPTER II.

"IN BEGINNING GOD"

WHEN man opens the first book of the library of the Almighty the words that first meet his eye are the ones put at the head of this chapter: "In beginning God." How fitting the phrase! How fraught with meaning! What harmony they bring to one's ear! How naturally one turns to the first book, first chapter, first verse, because he wants the beginning. Then with what satisfaction he reads, "In beginning God!"

The Hebrew does not contain the article, and whether or not it is to be inserted so as to read "In the beginning God"—as is usual in our texts—is a matter of interpretation, and not of translation.

The difference is whether the statement is a metaphysical one concerning time and material existence, or whether it is a historical statement of the first act of God relating to our own universe. It is the hope of the writer to cover both interpretations in the discussion which follows, hence the issue involved will be set aside for the present.

As previously stated, the Bible makes no particular effort in the way of argumentation to prove the existence of God. It takes for granted—what seems to be true—that it is the natural thing for man to believe in a God, and begins with a historical statement as to His activity, yet some men go contrary to the rule and even deny such existence; while the writer, recognizing the difficulty of convincing the unbeliever, thinks it worth while to give due consideration to the question to the end that faith may be strengthened, that belief may be made more intelligent, and that an answer may be ready for him who asks for a reason for the hope that is in him.

Is there a God? How much of human happiness or sorrow, how much of hope or despair, how much of confident endeavor or purposeless drudgery, hangs upon the answer to this question. Whether answered or not to the satisfaction of any individual or group, man seems unable to rid himself of the question. And amidst the endless caravan that follows mournfully his dead to the tomb, he asks the kindred question, "If a man die, shall he live again?"

In our discussion of the subject let us take up first some of the theories of the opponents. Atheism is that form of unbelief which takes the position that the arguments for the existence of God are insufficient and unsound, hence the theist's position is untenable. The atheist disclaims making any affirmation of the non-existence of God, for he, if wise to his position, knows the impossibility of proving a universal negative. But to disbelieve in the existence is to argue for a non-existence of God.

First of all, by his own admission, the atheist is engaged in the work of destruction, not construction; he would take from man, but give nothing in return. If the law of common barter were applied to him, he would be cast out because he would take something for nothing. Illogically, he claims that the failure of the theist to prove his position is a proof of his own. The earth was just as round when man had no proof for its rotundity as it is to-day, with all the proof we have at hand; and granting for the sake of argument that there was absolutely present with man no proof of the existence of God, his existence would not be altered by that lack of proof. Otherwise God could not have existed until he had created man and given to him full proof of His existence, which is absurd.

Grant again that there is no proof, in what better condition does man find himself in unbelief? It may bring some satisfaction to the esoteric circle of those who take delight in their ingenuous sophistry, but to the common people who must face the stern realities of life there can come no comfort from such a barren, lifeless philosophy. How many times are the atheists called upon to stand beside the tomb and shoot their poisoned darts at the fundamentals of religion? How often are they called to the bedside of the dying to cast their shafts of scorn and satire at the belief in another life? "Do men gather grapes of thorns or figs of thistles?" "By their fruits ye shall know them." No! men are asking for the presence of those who have something to contribute to their well-being, and not for those who come only to rob and destroy.

Of the two positions, man, if he face the question at all, must accept one or the other; there is no alternative. To refuse to face the issue seems to admit one's mental lassitude or spiritual cowardice. But for him who seeks intelligently his highest interests, there can be no mistake in accepting the side of the theist, since, if death ends all, he is yet equal to the atheist, but if there be a God and an after life, the atheist is found unprepared; he has all to lose and nothing to gain.

Next, we shall consider briefly—and it is not the purpose here to enter into an exhaustive study of these antitheistic theories—the theory of agnosticism. The position of agnosticism may be stated thus: Theists can not prove the existence of God; atheists can not prove the non-existence of God; and since it is irrational to believe anything without proof, they neither believe in God nor disbelieve in Him, but are wholly in the dark upon the issue. They do not know whether there is a God or not. First of all, we must look for fallacies in the definition of terms. What does the agnostic mean by proof? Evidently he means demonstration. But are we to accept nothing until it is demonstrated? Even demonstration must often, if not always, be preceded by faith. Had Columbus been required to demonstrate the earth's rotundity in order

4

to secure sailors, he would have sailed alone. Worse yet, he could not himself have made a start. Scientific investigation begins with hypothesis, or the unproved, and proceeds toward demonstration. The Wright brothers believed that a heavier-than-air machine would fly; scientists said it was impossible; the agnostic would have said it lacked proof, therefore he would have let the matter rest. But the men who had faith pressed on to fruition.

The same may be said of all great inventions and discoveries, which shows conclusively that the human race has been led onward and upward by the men and women of faith, and not by the agnostic. Men of business put goods on their shelves when there is no proof that the goods will ever be sold. Men spend their time and money sinking the shaft for gold and silver whose existence has not been demonstrated. The patriot fathers threw off the yoke of allegiance to the mother country and started an untried form of government which, of course, could not have the form of proof called demonstration. Agnosticism would not have acted so.

Again, it is impossible to demonstrate to the satisfaction of idealists the existence of material being, as instanced by the crude form of that philosophy held by the followers of Mrs. Eddy. Then, what shall we accept as demonstration, and where will our search end? If carried to its limits, we are left in solipsism—the belief in the existence of self alone. To ignore a thing is not to make it non-existent. Out of mind, out of being, will not do, else one must think of self continually to maintain existence. If man repairs to such philosophy, then why should he laugh at the poor ostrich with his head in the sand?

Some agnostics reason that in the very nature of things God is so different from anything we know, that therefore He is unknowable. Because we can not know Him fully, we can know nothing about Him. But that is to deny all knowledge.

We do not know all there is to be known about anything. Because a child does not know all that an adult knows about some one thing, does it follow that the child knows nothing of it? To ask the question is to answer it. We can know something about the cause, therefore can we not know something about the cause of the universe? If that cause be God, can we not then know something of God? Who is most apt to gain a knowledge of things about Him, the man who says "I do not know and I can not know," or the one who believes and presses on for reasons to support his belief? "I can" has climbed the hill, while "I can't" was sitting still.

One of the most formidable adversaries of theism in our own times, in the judgment of the writer, is materialism; not because of its more convincing tenets of belief, but because the influence of the scientific age through which we have been passing lends popularity to its cause.

Again, it is the material world with which we come first into contact. When we open our eyes in infancy it is the constant sense of the stern objective reality of things about us that makes its indelible impression on the mind. So about the last thing we take cognizance of is our inner spiritual self. Even then, with all the consciousness of our mind's reality, it seems such an intangible something; it can not be seen, felt or grasped by any of the senses; yet how easy it is to accept the existence of the stone which we pick up and throw away. So man, deluded by thinking that he saw with his eye, felt with his hand, and heard with his ear, admitted the existence of an objective world, and denied the existence of the very thing with which he saw, felt and heard; namely, his mind. True, he admitted a mind, but it was only the functioning of the brain— not a spiritual entity manifesting itself through a physiological activity. How exceedingly strange that man should believe in the existence of all things about him and yet deny his own spiritual self. Figuratively speaking, everything is at the big end of the telescope and nothing at the little end.

Materialism is that system of philosophy which undertakes to explain everything in terms of matter and motion. There is no such being as spirit. Matter first, then come life and thought, both of which are but forms of energy in the material universe. Given matter and motion, the materialist starts his world off in the blind process of becoming, bringing into existence life in ever higher and higher forms, culminating at last in an intelligent being called man. How is this accomplished? By resident forces through a process he elects to call evolution. What guides the process? Nothing, nothing but chance.

Let us give the materialist matter and motion—which, to say the least, is no small donation—then it must be some particular motion or system of motions at some particular point of time. Now, let us apply the materialist's own law: "That matter put in any particular motion will continue in that motion indefinitely unless acted upon by some external force." But there is no external force, since all that is given (matter and motion) is included. Then, how will he ever get change into the system? If he does not start with life, he can not obtain it. If he does not start with intelligence, he can not secure it, since these call for a change. But the rankest materialism will not claim that life and intelligence were in the beginning.

But if we refuse to grant the materialist matter and motion, how will he secure them? Perhaps by saying he has as much right to posit matter and motion as the theist has to assume a God to begin with. Let us see. It is true we must begin with an uncaused cause; but is matter a sufficient cause even if we assume its existence to begin with? In fact, is matter a cause at all? Certainly some will say, "Do we not see the tree moved by the wind, the soil carried by the water, and all about us the direct evidence of matter being a cause? It is true that matter for us in the uncritical consideration of things is a mediate cause, but, as we look into the situation scientifically, we find that when one thing happens, another thing happens in contiguity of time, but why, it is not known. And in the search for the reason the "why" simply recedes step by step before our investigation, until at last we must say we can not determine why. In other words, we do not discover cause in matter and motion. Then, let it be repeated, matter is the mediate, not the immediate, cause. To illustrate, suppose a clock will not run, and the housemaid moves it and it runs. She says it ran because she moved it. The clock-tinker says it ran because she loosed the pendulum; the physicist may say it ran because a proper equilibrium or relation to the law of gravity was established. But what is gravity? No one knows. It is, therefore, only a name to help systematize knowledge of relations, but it gives us no insight as to cause. We pass in regression from solid to liquid, to gas, to elements, to molecules, to atoms, to corpuscles, electrones or whirls of ether. Then, what makes the ether whirl? But to ask such a question is similar to the one, Who made God? Just so; and since we must have a beginning—or turn our backs to thought as do the agnostics—that beginning must be an uncaused cause. The question, then, before us is, Which will answer the purpose better, unintelligent, inanimate matter or a living, intelligent personality such as we conceive God to be? If we start with matter, we must obtain from the lifeless, life; from the unintelligent, intelligence, and from the non-moral, morality. This would be but to establish claim for the absurd proposition that out of nothing something comes.

In the definition given of materialism it was mentioned that mind is not an entity, but a function of the brain; and when the brain ceases to function as in death, mind also ceases to be. Let us test this portion of the theory. In pain the first element is physical force, as when a finger is being pressed; this is taken up and translated into a nerve force and conveyed to

the brain; there it is translated into a mental force
or energy known as idea. In reverse order the mind
initiates its own thought or idea, this is translated by
the brain into nerve force, and is conveyed to the
muscle, where it becomes muscular force for the moving
of the hand, which, in turn, counteracts physical force.
Can the materialist explain these various stages of transition. Are physical, muscular, nerve and mental
forces identical? If not, how are they related to each
other as cause and effect? Sir Oliver Lodge says:
"The brain is the link between the psychical and the
physical, which in themselves belong to different orders
of being."[1] If the mind be but the function of the
brain, then why not the same effect produced in each
person by the reading of such a message, "John is
dead"? There are the same words for each, the same
visual image for each, the same brain process of
receiving the message. But John is one's own brother,
while for the other he is a mere acquaintance. This
personal element mere material elements can not have.
No matter if one grants the unreasonable contention
that physical impressions on the brain account for memory, and therefore bring in the fact of the relation;
still there is no meaning to the relation such as we
hold by the word "brother."

Why is a certain amount of pain sufficient at one
time to cause one to remove the suffering member
while at another one will continue the suffering indefinitely? The answer can not be found in the material
realm. It must be sought for in the sphere of mental
activity, where meanings dwell and reasons are produced. Drawbridge, an able English apologist, in
opposition to the materialist's contention, shows the
relation of mind to body in the following language:
"The supremacy of (a) the self over (b) the apparatus
which it normally employs in the process of perceiving
physical things, is to be seen in the well-known facts

---

[1] "Man and the Universe," p. 91.

of hypnotism. For instance, if a hypnotist places powdered sugar on the tongue of the person whom he has hypnotized, telling the latter—or merely suggesting to him silently—that it is cayenne pepper that he is placing in his mouth, the hypnotized person will cry out with pain; he will feel an intense burning sensation, and, further, his tongue will become much inflamed. Conversely, if cayenne pepper be placed upon the tongue of the hypnotized man, and if it be suggested to him by the operator that it is sugar only, the subject of the experiment will taste the flavor of sugar only, and his tongue will not be inflamed. If the hypnotist tells the person whom he has hypnotized that an empty bottle which he is smelling contains ammonia, the patient's eyes will fill with water, and he will suffer pain; if it be then suggested that the empty bottle contains rosewater, he will enjoy the 'scent' of roses, a scent which exists only subjectively."[1]

Such instances may be multiplied indefinitely, not only in the state of hypnosis, but in the waking state. A man's friends agree to play a joke upon him. Each one greeting him that day remarks how bad he looks. After several have thus pronounced upon his looks he succumbs to the suggestion and goes home to take his bed.

The experiment has been tried of suggesting to the patient that he was to be bled. Unseen by him, the surgeon scratches his arm or other part of the body, and a stream of tepid water is caused to flow over his flesh. Soon the patient begins to grow pale, and gives every symptom of the loss of blood. A prominent surgeon in the British Navy has used this principle— and successfully, too—for the diagnosis and treatment of shellshock produced in the World War.

The materialists assert that we are much more certain of the objective existence of matter than we are of the ego or self. One is reminded here of the

[1] "Common Objections to Christianity," p. 151.

procedure of Descartes, the great thinker with whom modern philosophy begins. It is said of him that he resolved to strip himself completely of all that he had formerly believed, and start *de novo*. He would then admit only that which was absolutely certain, in order to see if on this basis a system of philosophy might not be erected which should escape the uncertainties of the old. What became his starting-point? *Cogito, ergo sum*—I think, therefore I am. It was the undeniableness of consciousness.

Whether the objective world exists or not depends for the individual on his belief or unbelief of the mind's testimony. But as to whether one thinks, there is no choice, for even in his assertion, "I do not exist," he asserts the existence of the I or ego.

The last antitheistic theory that will be considered is ethicism. This is given place, not because there are organized societies of such in this country—for there seems to be none—but because the doctrine of ethicism is often found to color, at least, the mind of him we call the moralist.

Ethicism is that theory that holds righteous conduct in this world to be of supreme importance, and that, too, without regard to whether or not there is a God and another life. Representatives of this faith contend that belief in a God and another existence not only does not help, but often hinders one in living the righteous life. They claim that the Christian acting in terms of the favor of God and through "other-worldly" motives is unethical and selfish. Their slogan is "right for right's sake," or for the welfare of this life. This all sounds good, and may strike some as very heroic in its ideals. But let us take a closer view. "Distance often lends enchantment to the view," while oftentimes a closer view exposes many errors that are not noticed by the casual observer.

Before discussing further the proposed system of ethics or right conduct, let us ask, What is right? Once an opponent told the writer that his religion was to do right; but *that* also is the Christian's religion, the issue being, What is right? Since the term is used only by morally responsible beings and applied to the acts of such beings only, we are justified in saying, then, that right is a term applied by morally responsible beings to the acts of other such beings which result in good.

But, in turn, what is good? Good for what? What, then, is the true standard of right? This the ethicists fail to answer. To show their inconsistency at this point, Mr. Drawbridge cites the fact that in the formation of a "Union of Ethical Societies" in England some years ago there was incorporated as the eighth article of the beliefs the following: "The acceptance of any one ultimate criterion of right should not be made a condition of ethical fellowship."[1] Thus, they who stress so strongly the right, confess the astounding fact that they have no standard as a test of membership. Any one may be admitted, no matter what his standard of right may be. Surely it would be going to a goat's house for wool to knock at the door of the ethicists asking for a standard of right. By their actions they disclaim any possession of such standards, and thus eliminate themselves from leadership in this realm of thought.

Counting out God and immortality, what are some of the answers to the question: What is good? One says happiness. But what may be happiness to one may be misery and woe to another. So there can be no common standard. Again, the epicurean says pleasure. But we are left in the same predicament. What is pleasure to one may be pain to another. A little boy beats his drum, and to him it is pleasure, but to the sick in the house it is the opposite. Another says utility: what is useful is good. Again we face the same trouble. The rain that makes the crops of one man grow and increase destroys the crops of another. The tariff that protects one man in his business

---

[1] "Common Objections to Christianity," p. 96.

may bring higher cost of living to others. Where
is there common ground? It must be found in that of
common value to all and that of highest value to all.
What man prizes most is life, and this is common to all.
Nature, through instinct in the individual, strives for
life. Man by his intellectual power strives to live.
Then, in the physical realm we may define that act
to be right which makes for physical well-being. Yes,
but one says, Have you not the same difficulty there,
that an act which makes for the physical well-
being of one is detrimental to another? True, and this
leads us on to say that life must next be considered
in social terms. What a child does at one time, seeking
his physical well-being, he refrains from doing later
because of the adverse opinion of his fellows. He is
now defining life in terms of social well-being as well
as in terms of physical welfare. When these conflict,
the normal person chooses the social as the one of
more value. Here the ethicist would stop, but is the
system complete? There is the same difficulty present:
that what may be to the social welfare of one may
injure the social well-being of another. And so man,
being spiritual in his being as well as social and physical, goes on to define life in terms of spiritual well-
being. Now, can the difficulty we have met hitherto
apply in this case? Can the same act be for the spiritual well-being of one to the detriment, spiritually, of
another? It is not so with Christianity properly interpreted as the spiritual system. Paul said: "I could
wish that I myself were anathema for Christ for my
brethren's sake, my kinsmen according to the flesh."[1]
This was a wish impossible of fulfillment, since the
very desire of sacrifice for others could only enhance
his own interest in the eyes of the Lord. Note some of
the principles of Christianity as cited in the Scriptures:
"Love the Lord thy God, and thy neighbor as thyself."[2] "Whatsoever ye would that men should do

[1] Rom. 9:3.
[2] Matthew 22.

unto you, do ye even so unto them."[1] "As ye have done
it unto one of the least of these my brethren, ye have
done it unto me."[2]

Now, what about the position of the ethicist who
leaves out the spiritual realm? When a parent is
old, decrepit, and in pain, no longer useful to himself
or society, is it not right—this world being all—to
apply the anæsthetic in order that he may be relieved
of suffering and society rid of a burden? The natives
of East Africa take their parents out into the woods
and leave them to die or to be eaten by wild beasts.
Can the ethicist deny that this is right? Would he not
admit such a one to membership in his society, since
no individual standard of right is to bar any one?

Again, since society's mandate is the highest in
ethicism, what shall deter one from committing any
deed provided it can be kept from the notice of others?
A returned missionary from Japan stated as the Jap-
anese view that when a man tells a lie the evil, if any,
is not in stating an untruth, but in being caught in it.
Just so; if a man could steal a fortune and men be
none the wiser, he could make himself comfortable
physically, and his money would in many places be a
passport to the highest social circles; yea, it might
bring him fame and renown in office. On what ground
will the ethicist deny it is right?

Mention was made above of the impossibility of
man, unaided, to learn the real meaning of life, since
he would not know its beginning or its end. For this
reason he would be unable to make for himself a true
system of right and wrong. He could not evolve a true
system of value, without which his efforts to formulate
a standard of conduct would be futile. It is a note-
worthy fact that, with all the progress made by ancient
Greece, the philosophers failed to get a true perspec-
tive of life. Plato, in his "Republic," advises that

[1] Matt. 7: 12.
[2] Matt. 25: 40.

when an unlikely child is born, it should be spirited away and disposed of by the midwife, and that no questions should be asked. Until the coming of Christ there was no proper estimate of the value of individual life, especially in the case of a child or a woman. But with Christ's interpretation of life we have learned to give it more and more its true value, whether in the new-born babe, the weaker sex, or the dependent and the deficient. Noticeable it is that with Christianity have grown up the eleemosynary and benevolent institutions. Evolution may decree the survival of the fittest, but Christianity decrees that the unfortunate shall be provided for and helped to survive.

What a low and contemptible thing it is for man to borrow his notions of right from God and then turn about and deny Him; to take and appropriate all the blessings that the gracious One has bestowed upon him and then turn Him out. Yet every one who has grown to manhood in this country has gathered from the influences of the teachings of the Bible his code of ethics, if it be worthy of the name "ethics." If he could cite us to one people who, aside from any influence of the teachings of the God of the Bible, has developed a code of morals surpassing those of any Christian nation, it would be time to listen to his moralizing. But until then we may well turn to him a deaf ear.

Let us turn to a constructive view of the question of the existence of God. First, the mind must have some point at which to rest. It can not run on in an infinite regress as did the mind of the Persians of old, who had the world to rest on the back of an elephant, the elephant to stand on a turtle and the turtle on something else, and so on and so on. Hence we must begin with an uncaused cause. How can that be, some one may ask. I do not know. But since in all forms of intelligent activities faith must have its place, so here. What we can not understand we accept on faith, but let us have the most reasonable grounds for faith; that is, let us support faith as far as possible with logic and facts.

Now, this first cause must be as any cause, an adequate one. And an adequate cause is one which is sufficient to explain the effect. The effect to be explained here is matter, design, order, life, intelligence, morality and religion. Will God as first cause adequately explain these? And, if so, what must He be?

The two forms of existence known to us are matter and spirit. The latter we know by what it does, but we are unable to arrive at what it is. Matter we find in various forms; and by chemical processes it is changed, and may be reduced from one form to another. While a solid body has such characteristics as to make it seem very real, on closer study we find it may be changed into a liquid form. By the application of certain chemical processes it may in turn pass into the gaseous state. Still, this is not final, for it may be further resolved into elements. These in turn are conceived by chemists to be made up of molecules, and these in turn by atoms. In recent years scientists are insisting on a subdivision of the atom: "The atom is to be conceived as a complex planetary system in which negative electrons and positive a particles, or some other form of positive electricity, revolve about each other with enormous speed."[1] Now, the tendency in this process of analytical subdivision toward ever more and more infinitesimally small particles is a movement toward a point where division must inevitably become impossible. Therefore what *is*, ceases to have extension, and, consequently, is no longer matter at all. As to what it then is, whether it be called energy, electricity, ether or spirit, it is one and the same so far as the nature of being is concerned. Hence it seems that man's investigation of the nature of matter is leading him more and more toward spirit; but the study of spirit does not lead toward matter; it leads away from it. The conclusion is, then, that by the very trend of investigation and study spirit is found to be a better

[1] "Beyond the Atom," Cox, p. 76.

answer for the ultimate being of things than is matter. Matter may thus be assumed to be a form or manifestation of spirit, but in no instance is the opposite found to be true.

Again, the manifestations of spirit or intelligent energy are self-initiated activity, cause, order, design, intelligence, morality and religion. On the other hand, there is no case of self-initiated activity on the part of matter. It was but a wild speculation when men spoke of "spontaneous generation." There is no fact to bear out the claim. Matter, as said before, is seen as mediate cause, but not as immediate, for such causes are not seen. Therefore matter is only relatively a cause. Order and design are not manifestations of matter. They are found in the material world, but only mind can anticipate and arrange activity toward a certain end. Of course, matter can have no direct relation to morality and religion. Since these are in the world, and are found not to be manifestations of matter, but of mind or spirit, how can we but believe, if we *must* begin with one, that that one must be spirit or intelligent energy? The most reasonable and adequate cause is the one which will best explain the effect. And since God is spirit, God, and not matter, will best answer our demands for an uncaused cause which is also an adequate cause.

This leads up to the consideration of the being of God. We have just noticed that, to answer the demands of mind for an adequate cause, God must, in the nature of His being, be spirit. What is spirit? Here again we are baffled for an answer; but as in the physical world, we must think and speak of electricity in terms of what it does, and not what it is—likewise with gravity, life and mind—so must we consider spirit. Just, then, as one man can not obtain first-hand knowledge of the mind of another either by sight, taste or smell, but must be content with the manifestations of mind in speech and other actions of the body; so must we be content to accept the existence of God by His activity. One form of His activity we call nature. The special evidence He has given of His existence we call miracle. Spirit may be thought of on the one hand as pure energy, on another as intelligence. It may also be thought of as personality. It is that pure being which, existing back of all things, is invisible, ultimate and eternal. This spirit essence, being self-existent, is not dependent, is not limited by time or space or any of the categories of human thought.

Again, God in being is ultimate. In the last reduction of all things there is God, God the uncaused cause of all things, the Alpha and Omega, the first and the last. Not only is He the One beginning all things, but the One sustaining all things. As Paul said to the Athenians, "For in him we live, and move, and have our being."[1]

Perhaps the outstanding problem of metaphysics is how to reconcile permanence and change. This problem engaged the earliest school of Greek philosophers. Heraclitus disposed of the difficulty by the simple denial that any such thing as permanence exists at all. There is no static being; change, movement, is lord of the universe; everything is in a state of becoming.

Now, this contention, it seems, may be easily shown to be fallacious by the fact that movement is relative, that the motion of one object is such in its relation to another. For example, the writer, his desk, the building, all seem to be motionless, but in reality all are moving with the earth at the dizzy gait of over one thousand miles an hour. But all things about me are moving at the same rate, hence all remain seemingly still. For the recognition of a stream there must be one on the bank to see the stream go by. In a world where there is no static being there would be no such thought as movement or change, and the very statement of Heraclitus involves his own static being to recognize the flux.

---

[1] Acts 17: 28.

But what is that static element in man? It is not
his body, for we are told that it undergoes a complete
change every seven years; it is not the content of the
mind, for that may be continually changing.   Then
it is the ego, the self, the I, which is the same all the
way back to one's earliest memory.   In the words of
Wm. James: "That something which at every moment
goes out and knowingly appropriates the *me* of the
past, and discards the *non-me* as foreign, is it not a
permanent abiding principle of spiritual activity identical with itself wherever found?"[1]

There is therefore a static element in the world
in the individual ego or human self that recognizes
change; but that same mind reasons that back of all
change must be that which changes not.   Back of all
form must be a static being of which the various forms
are but manifestations.   In the analyses of men this
being has not been found, but, as said above, the tendency is ever toward the ethereal or spirit.   Then, if we
assume that all material being is but form, and that
ultimate being is spirit, then we may conclude that all
things are the manifestation of the one ultimate being
—God.

Another essential thought for the human mind is
unity.   All education, all investigation, is a process or
attempted process toward classification or unification.
If there is not oneness underlying all things, on what
grounds can we claim likeness and unlikeness, simi-
larity and difference?   And without classification how
can there be knowledge?

Our word "universe" is but a reflection of our
assumption that at last all is one.   What is that element
common to all that makes for unity?   It can not be in
the form, for therein is the dissimilarity; therefore it
must be back of all form, or in the ultimate being,
God.   Hence, it is said of Him there is none beside
Him, and He is the same yesterday, to-day and forever.

---

[1] "Psychology," p. 202.

Another characteristic we give to the being of God is eternality. "Eternal" is a word which immediately suggests time, but time in endless duration.

"In beginning God" brings to our attention not only the idea God, but a point of time known either as time's beginning or the beginning of God's activity in bringing into existence this material universe. How shall we apply the word "eternal" to the past? Was there a time when God was not? Certainly not, else He must have had a beginning, and therefore a cause, which breaks down the theory of an uncaused cause. What was He doing all those ceaseless ages before creation?

In the first place, all that we have to account for is our own universe and God's relation to it. The Scriptures are given us from the point of view of the earth, since the narrative says: "In beginning God created the heaven and the earth." Why earth? Because the record is for inhabitants of the earth, not Mars, Jupiter or Saturn.

Now, time is a measure of duration, and duration is marked by change, and change is found in form or matter, not in the static or permanent being. Then, time is a term applicable only to this world of change and not to God. We may suppose that God knows our thoughts and their time limitation, but it does not follow that His thoughts have the same limitation.

As it is necessary for man to begin with an uncaused cause, so it is necessary for him to have a point known in time as the beginning. What better point could there be than the beginning of our own world or universe? If we allow that to be the point and accept the statement, "In beginning God," to be true, then it is not legitimate to ask what happened before that point, any more than it is logical, once we have accepted God as the uncaused cause, to ask who made God.

"Eternal" applied to futurity does not hold the same difficulty as when applied to the past, for we seem to

5

think we can conceive of endless duration in that direction. It is when we come to the question of foreknowledge that the problem arises again. That will be discussed later. But let it be remembered, if there be any difficulties in conceiving of God as eternal, there are difficulties, and graver ones, confronting any opposing theory. May it be repeated that where knowledge and reason fail, faith must fill the breach?

God in being must be not only spirit, ultimate and eternal, but He must be omnipotent as well. By omnipotence we mean all-powerful within the range of possibility. The range of possibility is circumscribed by reason. "But," says one, "is that not an unjust limitation of the power of God, and is it not bringing him down to the level of man's knowledge?" No, it is assuming that for man's thought a system must conform to his reason or else it were futile to attempt to think at all. If we admit, for instance, as a part of the omnipotence of God, the power to turn a grindstone both ways at the same time, or to make a round square, or a white blackboard, we may as well stop, for we have no thought with which to follow such a system. And if the tools we have are useless we may as well drop the task, for we have no others. "But," says another, "will that not eliminate the power to make water stand up in a wall, and, in fact, do away with the miraculous, since it is not within reason?" Not so, for we have seen water stand up in a wall against soil, wood or glass, and it is only a question of power to make it so act, but a round square is unthinkable. We have seen bodies live, and it is only a question of power to join life and the body, but two contrary motions of a body contemporaneous in time are beyond our comprehension. Then God may do all things within the bounds of reason.

If God be not able to do all things, then there are some things He can not do, certain powers He can not exert. This runs amuck immediately of our assumption that He is the first cause and therefore the cause of all things. If there are things He can not do, either they can not be done or some other person or power can do them. Then, who is that other person, or what is that other power? We can not have two lest we run into the blind alley of dualism, and, if but one, that one may as well be God.

God being the cause of all things, the ultimate being of all things, being spirit and eternal, it is natural to assume that all forms of being are His manifestations and therefore the emblems of His power. And when we think of this being as an intelligent personality, good, wise and just, what confidence it lends one to know that he is in the charge of such an all-wise power, and that one's destiny is in the keeping of such infinite justice. On the other hand, how dark the picture to think one is the product of blind forces driving him mercilessly on by the fickle law of chance to be cast at last upon the rocks of ruthless destruction.

The fifth and last characteristic of the being of God to be considered in this discussion is omniscience. A necessary corollary of the omnipotence of God is that of omniscience. For how could God be all-powerful without at the same time being able to know all things? It is well in the approach to this subject to keep in mind other characteristics of God's being, and to see how He is different in nature from man. God in being is *static;* that is, not *becoming* as are we. Just so His knowledge is not that which comes through a process of knowing; in other words, He has, besides a cognizance of things as we know them, an absolute knowledge, a knowledge not dependent upon the element time and the changing nature of things. Let us return to a former statement, that all things are a manifestation of God. If this be granted, then the omnipresence of God is easily accounted for; likewise we may see the relation of God to all things from the standpoint of knowledge. If God initiates His own action and all things flow from His activity, then, being cognizant of His own acts, He must necessarily know all things. But the question is raised, Can He know all the conse-

quences of His acts, and especially such as are brought
about by the freedom exercised by man? This brings
to attention immediately the most difficult question concerning God's knowledge, and that is the foreknowledge of God. We must, in dealing with this problem,
return to the question of time. Shall we conceive of
the existence of God as duration, or is His being outside of such limitation? To accept such limitation is
to admit that there is some being or force external to
Him which leaves Him dependent in some way upon
such force or being for existence, and this in turn
denies to Him the place of first cause and the source
of all things. But, being the cause of all things, He
is not limited in His being and existence by that which
He created. Since time is a form of thinking applicable only to changing phenomena, it can in no way be
a necessary limitation of God, hence could not limit His
knowledge. Then, God's knowledge is apart from time.
This is not to deny to Him the ability to know the way
in which man thinks; that is, a sequence of events in
time. While it is beyond the mind of man to comprehend how God can exist in what is, for man, time yet
to be, and how He can know that which for us has
not yet come to pass, nevertheless we must posit in God
certain qualities and abilities which are outside human
experience, else He would not be God at all, but just
a part of this finite system. Our task is to conceive
of God in such a manner as will make of Him an adequate cause, violating no necessary principle of reason,
yet placing Him beyond the power of reason to explain.
Again let it be repeated, any system will require reason
to be supplemented by faith.

Another problem may as well be given attention
here. Put in the form of question, it is: If God fore-
knows an event, must it then not necessarily occur?
Or, in other language, does not foreknowledge necessitate foreordination? It seems that the easiest way to
deal with this ancient problem of lapsarianism is to recognize that with God was the possibility of knowing

all the particulars of any system that might be inaugurated, else He would be but experimenting. But, knowing all the special parts of the system, which included in itself the free activities of human beings, would be knowledge based upon what those acts would be, rather than the acts depending upon the knowledge. Just as we know past acts by what they were, so God would know what we please to term future acts, in the same way. The knowledge is dependent upon the act, and not the act upon the knowledge. On this principle Calvinism divided into supralapsarianism and infralapsarianism.

In being we have considered God as spirit—the ultimate being and cause of all things. Being spirit and ultimate, He is eternal above and beyond the limitation of time. To be thus an adequate cause and sustainer of all, He must be omnipotent and omniscient. In this way we have assumed all that is necessary to make God adequate to bring into existence and sustain the material universe. It will be necessary next to determine what shall be the character of God in order to the right use of His power.

Why is it that the learned and dignified systems of thought that the various philosophers have produced from time to time have not received a greater following, have not laid hold upon the minds and hearts of the common people, while most any system of religion will count its followers in large numbers? The explanation is to be found, no doubt, in the fact that the philosopher's God, if indeed he finds room for one at all, is so lacking in personality that He is useful only as an answer to the demands of intelligence for a why of all things; but the man of the street wants a more practical God, one who may satisfy the affectionate and volitional side of life as well as the intelligent. In fact, he wants a living personality who not only made man, but is concerned with what man is and does.

What constitutes a personality is generally conceded to be self-consciousness and self-determination. If we turn to human consciousness, we realize how, of all the things we know, the one that stands out with distinction is the consciousness of self. I think, and I think that I think. The tongue tastes, but it does not taste the tasting; the eye sees, but does not see the seeing process; so the I or ego is the only thing able to turn in upon itself. How? We do not know. Now, what is not only possible, but actual, in human thought can surely obtain in divine intelligence. If God has knowledge at all, He must be able to know Himself, else His knowledge began with the beginning of His not-self or the material world, which is absurd.

If human minds may within certain limitations determine their own action, initiate their own thought and movement, on what ground shall we deny to that greater intelligence like power? If God is to be omnipotent, He must be able to determine His own acts and to carry into effect His own purposes. Consciously directing activity toward definite ends, initiated because of purposes held by a known self, God is a divine personality. He carries out His plan in the world by His constant power and presence. To such a God men appeal for help in times of trouble.

No matter what the scale of evaluation man may use, he is nevertheless measuring things in terms of good and bad. He so measures the acts of men, the seasons, the universe. And since man estimates the physical system as good or bad, naturally the same evaluating process must be applied to Him who is responsible for its being.

Then, first of all, God in character must be good. By the word ''good'' as applied to God is meant, not the absence of evil, but a positive, active good or righteousness. A power non-personal might be thought of as good in such a negative sense, but God, who is a living personality, is good in a positive way.

We have tested previously the meaning of good in asking the question, Good for what? And we found the answer to be, ''Good for life.'' Further, life was considered in the ascending order of physical, social and spiritual. Now, if God be good, then His work must be good, and so He pronounces it in the Genesis account of creation. But is the world good? Applying our test, it must answer the demands of good for life. If we take into account only physical life, then the system might not stand the test. If we take in, further, life as social, the system may yet fail to be satisfactory, and will not be pronounced good. But, taking life in its threefold meaning, the physical, the social and the spiritual, the system must be good or God can not be good. If God be not good, then we are ready to cast Him aside and the whole system that has in it such a being. Therefore, when we know that it is claimed by the Scriptures that God called the world good, and we further see so much depends upon our attitude at this point, let us beware lest we too hastily draw our conclusions. Being influenced by disappointments and failures in our own lives, our judgment may be clouded. Since the question of the character of the system in which man finds himself will be treated under the chapter devoted to man, no answer will be attempted here. Suffice it, then, to say that a being all-wise and all-powerful, with no selfish end and purposes to be furthered, can only be thought of as good if any good at all obtains in the world. For if the author of all things be evil and have all power and wisdom, it stands to reason He would do only evil.

Now, when we apply the characteristic "good" to God, and at the same time have in mind infinity and therefore perfection in any quality, we seek for a term which will describe His being as without evil—pure and righteous altogether. That term we find used frequently in the inspired Word; it is holiness. God is holy. He who knows evil, who sees the vulgar element in the imperfect, sinful, created beings, turns naturally to the perfect being—God—who is without these imperfections, and who is pure in thought, purpose and deed. While man may tolerate or condone the weaknesses of his fellows, yet he demands that his God be holy. As wisdom is the right discernment and understanding of all relations, so holiness is the choice and affirmation of the highest consideration. It is that characteristic of the divine personality which is manifest in the highest purposes, in the noblest ends, in the greatest good obtainable. It guarantees to man that all the acts of God are righteous, and that conformity to His will shall bring the greatest security. God thus becomes man's pattern for righteousness in this life.

Where freedom is and where actions are weighed by the scale of right and wrong, the question of justice arises. Because of freedom responsibility enters, and with responsibility comes the demand that we shall suffer for our misdeeds as well as enjoy the fruits of good conduct. We have found no other way of restraining the selfish than that seen in nature which causes man to suffer for the violation of law. Justice demands that each shall have all that is rightfully his. Absolute justice, requiring perfect wisdom for its dispensation, can not therefore be found among men, but we have a right to assume that a perfect being is capable of being absolutely just.

The first thing making for justice in God is perfect wisdom. The next is unselfishness. God has no need of anything; as Paul says: "Neither is he served by men's hands, as though he needed anything, seeing he himself giveth to all life, and breath, and all things."[1] Therefore God can not be moved aside by any selfish interest. Next is His universal fatherhood. Seeing God is Father to all His offspring, loving all His creatures, "shall not the Judge of all the earth do right?"[2]

On this side of the character of God many attacks are made. Some say if God is the author of things in this world, then He is not just, for on every hand there is injustice. Grant it. But to rid our minds

[1] Acts 17: 25.
[2] Gen. 18: 25.

of God would not rid the world of injustice nor lighten the burden of it. "Nature red in tooth and claw" is repeatedly quoted. Pictures are drawn of the innocent victims of pain and suffering; and the gloom of life is assembled in one panoramic view to attest to the injustice in the world. But set aside the notion of God, and how is it bettered? Then, attacks are made upon the idea of hell with the claim that a just being would not create a man and then make a hell in which to torment him after death.

Has any better law been found to substitute for this: "The wages of sin is death"? It is nature's inexorable rule. Surely the man who stands on the railroad track should be killed by the moving train, not the man who sits in his easy-chair at home. The man who plays with fire is the one to be burned. But when we come into the reign of human power we find that this law does not always obtain, and that the great injustices of the world are those for which man is responsible. It is unbecoming in any one to criticize any system, claiming it is unjust, when he can have at best only a partial knowledge of that system; much less if he has not appropriated what may be known of it. Hence the whole system of God should be taken into consideration—its purpose, its method, its end. If the purpose of God is the development of a righteous character, and that can be accomplished only through the free moral agency of man in a world where there is both the possibility to do good and to do evil, then this world is good for that end, and what justice lacks in this world may be provided for in the next. "So the last shall be first and the first last."[1] But to seek to administer justice with this life as the end of all things, is to face the impossible. Man is forced to posit God and posit Him as just. Then, there must be another existence for man in which to balance accounts, or else our sense of justice remains

[1] Matt. 20: 16.

unsatisfied, and this would further add to our unhappiness.

While man cries out for justice, and even demands it, yet he fears it. He demands justice in protecting himself from the acts of others, but fears it when applied to his own acts. Where law is inexorably enforced and justice prevails, as in the forces of nature, how helpless and defenceless man feels. He swallows by mistake a dose of poison. He may cry out again and again that it was a mistake, that he did not intend to take it, but nature's law goes heedlessly on. How different when we appeal to some of our fellow-men, for here we see justice tempered with mercy. And if this quality be found in man, how much more in God. We may expect, then, that God will be not only just, but merciful, and this opens the door for the operation of His great love. How can both justice and mercy be exercised? Was it not an act of mercy that the murderer was restored to his home and family to support and educate his children and thus contribute to their happiness? Yes, but how can the one murdered be restored to his home and family? How shall his children be cared for? Or, in other words, is justice had in such a case? It was with great heroism that our forefathers died at Bunker Hill and Brandywine, but is it not just that they who purchase a thing shall have the right to enjoy it? We are enjoying the fruits of being spared the awful calamity which would have befallen the world by a conquest of German hordes, but how about the noble youth who fell on the fields of France? The answer to our question seems to be that for this world justice and mercy can not both be exercised. It must be left to a wise, just and merciful God to dispense justice, and at the same time exercise mercy. Hence He called on us to leave it with Him. "Vengeance belongeth to me; I will recompense, saith the Lord."[1] The mystery of God's ability

---

[1] Rom. 12: 19.

to be just and at the same time be merciful is shown
forth in the atonement. "For God so loved the world,
that he gave his only begotten Son, that whosoever believeth on him should not perish, but have eternal
life."[1] It is the principle of the innocent suffering
for the guilty, the sinless for the sinful. Mercy is
extended, but not at the price of injustice to man.

Above all else, God is love. That which makes
Him a friend, a confidant, that which satisfies the
hungering human heart, is that He loves mankind.
What though He had power, it might be fatally used.
Though He were just, yet He might be sternly indifferent to our weaknesses. Though He had wisdom, He
might not care. But if He loves us, then His power,
wisdom and justice will be administered for our good.

In seeking to know divine love we must perforce,
as in other matters, study human love. Love is affection, desire of companionship and desire to further
the welfare of the one loved. Affection may be provoked by the sacrificial acts of another; it may arise
in the heart of the one rendering the unselfish service,
and, again, it may arise independently of either. The
first is illustrated by the love of children for parents
or guardian, of a patient for a nurse, etc. The second
case may be seen in a soldier's love for the flag. The
third case is seen in attachments formed by newly
made acquaintances.

The second element found in love is the desire for
companionship. This companionship may not be actual-
ized, but the desire is there. Third, there is the effort
to contribute to the welfare of the one loved. All
these may be found in divine love, and that unadulter-
ated with selfishness. God has affection for man. No
doubt it is the very nature of God to love. This is
supplemented by the fact that man is His offspring and
was created in His image. It may be assumed without
irreverence that God also desired the companionship

---

[1] John 3: 16.

of intelligent, righteous beings. This being true, He
will seek man's welfare in the system in which He has
placed Him. "God so loved the world"—herein is expressed His affection. "That he gave his only begotten
Son"—here is the supreme effort put forth for man's
welfare. "That whosoever believeth on him might not
perish, but have eternal life"—here is the association
and companionship with God in Christ.

The supreme and crowning characteristic of God is
love. This makes of Him a personal being that comes
in closest contact with every individual, and in terms
of the highest good.

CHAPTER III.

CREATION

BY way of foreword, attention is called to what seems to the writer a common fallacy in the thought of many concerning the difficult problem of creation, and that is the tendency to overlook the weaknesses that lie hidden in any theory of an automatic mechanism. In other words, the problem of how God operates the world is just as great as how He began it. If one can conceive of an unintelligent world running on by inherent forces, such a world might be posited as eternal and self-existent, and thus God could be ruled out entirely. Or, on the other hand, if the world is dependent upon God for its continuance, how can He operate and control that which is external to Himself? How God operates the world is called by many the "theory of interaction." In common language, what is the method of contact between God and the material universe? Hence, our problem is not only one of how the world came into existence, but how it is kept in existence. Though this may seem like "rushing in where angels fear to tread," yet, since the opponents are constructing theories which may destroy the faith of some, it is necessary to meet these with speculations which reason may approve.

The first meaning given to the English word "create" is to bring into existence for the first time. In a looser sense it may mean to form some new combination out of existing material. The English word "create" is used in translating the Hebrew word *bara*, and that word only. *Bara* is used in Gen. 1:1 in reference to the heavens and the earth; again in Gen. 1:21 in reference to the sea monsters; and lastly in Gen. 1:27 in reference to man. Now the question arises, Can the primary meaning of create—to bring into existence—be applied in each of these cases? When it is said, "God created the heavens and the earth," surely the meaning is clear that this language was used to indicate that God brought into existence a material universe where there had been no such existence. In the second instance there was in existence the material out of which the bodies of the monsters of the sea were formed, hence "create" must apply to another element, and that is animal life. In the third instance, that of man, there is material for body, and there is already existing animal life, but not human life, or that created in the image of God.

But the question must be raised, How account for vegetable life, which preceded animal life? The expression found in Gen. 1:11 is, "And God said, Let the earth cause to spring forth grass," etc. Here the word *bara* is not used, but the *hiphil*, or causative stem of the verb *dasha*, is used, and this may be sufficient to cover the needs of the fiat of God by which He brought into existence for the first time vegetable life. God said, "Let the earth *cause* to spring forth," etc., but how cause except God furnish the causative element or life germ?

Another difficulty meets us in Gen. 1:20, where it is said: "And God said, Let the waters swarm, swarm soul of life," etc. This accounts for the appearance for the first time of animal life in sea and on land. This verb meaning swarm is not in the causative stem, which would seem to annul the argument used above. But directly following the language of Gen. 1:20, in reference to the smaller life, is the use of *bara* in the account of the appearance of the larger life of the sea. This was on the same, or fifth, day. Now, what is being described as occurring on the same day might easily be classed together, though somewhat different language was employed. Since the waters were called upon to swarm and no cause named, we may find that cause in the language applied to similar life brought in on the same day. Whether the language will technically bear out the theory in each case, nevertheless we are safe in employing the interpretation that "create" means to bring into existence.

Among the theories that are presented to account for the presence of a material universe is the eternality of matter. It seems easier to some in accounting for matter to assume that it always existed, and that God has changed its form and operated it to suit His will. The reader's attention is directed here to what appears to the writer axiomatic; that is, that no two substances, essences or beings, ultimate or eternal, could ever affect one another. This, if accepted, disposes of any form of dualism. But why this axiom? Two beings, if ultimate, must be wholly unlike, and, if unlike, could in no way affect one another. How can two men converse except they have a common thought and a common speech? Can one crush another's spirit with a material weight?

If dualism be rejected, we must reject the eternality of either God or matter. Then we pass on to the theory of "something out of nothing." Where nothing was, something is. But this is abhorrent to the human mind; it calls not for faith, but for credulity. Deism regards the world as having been brought into being and thereafter as able to exist on its own account. Here we run into the theory of an automatic mechanism, as though the world was run by a big, hidden spring which needed only to be wound up, and it would then need no further attention. But when we go to look into things for the force, we find that things are the force, and therefore the force or energy is but the expression of something or some one behind the whole. One might as well try to discover pure apple by taking away juiciness, roundness, redness, sweetness and mellowness, as to seek for pure material by taking away the properties of matter. This has been well named "pin-cushion" philosophy, because qualities are thought to adhere to things.

Or if with Borden Bowne we say the world was produced by the divine will, have we avoided the difficulty of obtaining something out of nothing?[1] For the question comes, If God produced the world by His will, out of what did He make it? It seems to be an explanation that does not explain.

Another theory is that of emanation; that the world emanated from or out of God. If it emanated from God, then how? Or if out of God, then the world is a part of God, which makes Him to be divisible, having extension, and therefore material, which is no better than pantheism.

If in any theory of the world's creation by God's will, by emanation, by fiat, in which the world becomes a material entity apart and separate from God, how will He control it? This, as noted above, is as serious a problem as that of creation.

Next is the theory of pure idealism; that is, that there is no real material universe. It is all a seeming. But this is to belie our own minds and reject their plain and oft-repeated testimony. If we reject the evidence of our minds on this subject, with what claim shall we accept their testimony on other subjects? For instance, the idealist believes his mind to be thinking logically when coming to the conclusions of idealism.

That which remains to us, then, is that God, being the ultimate cause of all things, being Himself intelligent energy or mind, manifests Himself; and that the form of His manifestation we call the universe. We begin with something, an ultimate energy or being called God; we end in a form of being not ultimate, but changeable, which we call matter. What, then, is the relation of God and matter? God is the world-ground—reality; matter is the phenomenon, the form

---

[1] "Theism," p. 226.

of being. In God is the static, the unchangeable; in matter is change. God furnishes the permanent element, matter the flux. And what is the manifestation of God the first moment is the manifestation of God each subsequent moment of time. Phenomena are real to our senses. We believe our minds and accept as fact the reality of this physical world, but reality only in form. We accept as real one moment the solid body called ice; in a few moments the same is real as water, and still a few moments more, after the application of heat, it becomes real as vapor, although it has become invisible. While these forms are real for the physical senses, yet their shifting, changing being convinces us that they are not that ultimate reality which alone is changeless. Back of the liquid are hydrogen and oxygen. Back of these elements we are told is the molecule, then the atom, and so on, but where is the ultimate reality, and what is it? It is spirit, or God. God energizing according to His will produces that form of energy which is made visible and knowable, but no one knows—meaning direct knowledge—God, the ultimate reality. To have such knowledge one must be equal to God.

When in the beginning God created the heavens and the earth, He manifested Himself by His eternal power or energy, and the form of that power or energy as it came to the knowledge of man is called heaven and earth.

Having treated briefly the word "create" and its use, and having considered some of the theories of creation, including the problem of interaction, we turn now to the Biblical account.

"In the beginning God created the heavens and the earth" (Gen. 1:1). Since there follows a more detailed account, it is the natural interpretation to take this statement as accounting for the bringing into existence of all material being. Corresponding to man's construction of a building, this would mean the assembling of the building material without regard to its subsequent arrangement.

6

But why the statement "heaven and earth"? It must be that the account is given with especial reference to the earth, and given to people of the earth. That is to conclude that it is not a general scientific account in the field of astronomy, but a description applicable particularly to a viewpoint of the earth and the earth's inhabitants. This interpretation, if correct, is important because it contains the viewpoint from which further interpretations are made.

Gen. 2:2 begins: "And the earth was waste and void." Why the earth, and not Saturn, Jupiter, or some other planet? For the reason cited above, that the account is given from the viewpoint of the earth. The earth was waste and void, showing that though the material was in existence it had not been brought out of chaos into an orderly form.

"Darkness was upon the face of the deep [abyss]." Since darkness is the absence of light, the question arises, If all matter had been brought into existence, including, of course, the sun, how could there be an absence of light? Light is defined by physicists to be that sensation produced by wave motions of ether interpreted by the mind as light. Let us keep in mind that the narrative is from the viewpoint of the earth and earth's inhabitants.

First, light is a mental interpretation, as are sound, smell, etc. There must be an eye to see and there must be a mind behind the eye to interpret. One explanation that may be offered is that since light is caused by wave motions of ether and by such as are recorded by the eye, might it not be possible to have such wave motions or lack of wave motions of ether as could not be recorded by the human eye? If so, then for the human eye there would be no light, hence God would simply be describing a time and condition which from the viewpoint of man was complete darkness. Again, the density of vapors about the earth in this chaotic period may have been so great as to be opaque, and hence leave the earth enshrouded in dark-

ness. Now, if we can imagine man looking upon the
earth in that earliest period, he would have seen nothing—all was darkness and chaos. Then, with the coming to his eye of the wave motions of ether which his
eye could record, he began to see, though the source
of light was not yet visible, being obscured by the
gaseous vapors and mists.

Next in order is the placing of the firmament, or
shroud of atmosphere. This is further evidence of the
previous chaotic condition that surrounded the globe.
But in the development process of condensation many
of the gases became stable in their relation to the
earth, and much of the water became liquid in form,
while yet a large portion remained as vapor. Thus was
formed the dome of heaven, and the waters were divided; some rested on the earth as liquid and others
were carried above as vapor or cloud.

Following in order there is an upheaval of the
land and a receding of the waters forming the seas.
Then by divine fiat God orders the earth to cause grass
to spring forth, and the vegetable kingdom is introduced. Since there are light, heat and land, together
with moisture, all that is needed is present for the
sustenance of vegetable life.

This life was made stable in that everything was
to reproduce after its kind. If it had been made otherwise, or so one plant might at random produce another,
the world never could have furnished a fitting abode
for animal life. One generation of palatable grass
might thus have produced some poisonous weed which
would have exterminated succeeding animal life. This
would have been fatal to the plan of God.

On the fourth day God said, "Let there be lights
in the firmament." These had been created in the beginning, as stated in Gen. 1:1, but now appear as lumi-
nous for the earth for the first time. They are, by
their appointment, designated "signs for seasons and
for days and years." They furnish the calendar for
the earth and the earth's inhabitants.

Now that the atmosphere has cleared, as shown by the appearance of the sun, moon and stars, the stage is set for the introduction of animal life. So God brings into existence animal life in sea and on land. First, there is the small life of the sea, the air and the land; then the larger life of the sea, then the beasts of the earth or the largest animal life of the land. This follows the order of vegetable life, then herbivorous animal life, then lastly the larger herbivorous and the carnivorous animals. This, as can be readily seen, is the natural order. This order is necessary to the life of each.

The last to appear is man. Of his creation it is said: "God created man in his own image, in the image of God created he him; male and female created he them." The likeness of man's bodily structure to that of the animal forbids our thinking that the image is to be found in the body; the other alternative is that the image is to be found in his intellectual and spiritual nature. In this respect God brought into existence a new creature, and therefore the account has it that God created man.

Orders given were "to subdue the earth" and "to have dominion over the fish of the sea, and over the birds of the heaven, and over every living thing that moveth upon the earth." In order for man to do this he must be able to think and reason; he must have the power of intellectual progress, and this must be accompanied by moral and spiritual thought. But to have such intellectual power he must have means of expression, therefore speech. With reason must reside imagination and memory, or else there could be no advancement. All these man possesses, making him distinct from the animals, and by virtue of these gifts is he constituted in the likeness of his Creator.

By memory he stores up his past experiences; by imagination he lays hold of future possibilities; with reason does he solve the problems before him and systematize his observations; with moral and spiritual insight he reads purpose into activity, guides his actions toward his fellow-man and keeps before himself the high ideals that lead him on to life eternal. So man subdues the earth, outwits and rules the animal and builds for himself generation by generation more stately structures of civilization.

As to other than the Genesis account of creation, Professor Price says: "Almost all of the great nations of antiquity have preserved legends or traditions of the creation of the world, of the origin of man, of the fall and of the deluge. These traditions vary greatly in value. Some of them are not worthy of mention, while others are so startling in their resemblances to the accounts in Genesis as to demand careful consideration. Of all the traditions found to-day in the documents of the old nations, those embodied in the cuneiform language of Babylonia-Assyria are by far the most interesting and important."[1]

The similarities between the latter and the Genesis account may be summed up under six heads. First, there was a time when the earth was waste and void; second, light dispels darkness; third, the dry land appears; fourth, sun, moon and stars are set in the heavens; fifth, animals and creeping things are created; sixth, mankind is created. The outstanding difference in the accounts is that the Genesis account is monotheistic, attributing all to one God, while the Babylonian is polytheistic, giving as cause many gods.

But how are the likenesses to be explained? There are four theories: First, the Genesis account is drawn from the traditions; second, the traditions are drawn from Genesis; third, the likeness is to be explained by like ways of thinking, so each people told a similar story; and, fourth, their likeness is due to a common inheritance; that is, that all have a common source. Of the fourth or last explanation, Professor Price says: "Early races of men, wherever they wandered, took

[1] "Monuments and Old Testament," p. 80.

with them those primeval traditions, and with the varying latitudes and climes their habits and modes of
life, have carried these, and present them to us to-day
in their different dresses. One ancient religion did not
borrow these universal traditions from another, but
each possessed primitively these traditions in their
original form. A careful examination of all these traditions shows that the Genesis record is the purest, the
least colored by extravagances, and the nearest to what
we must conceive to have been the original form of
these traditions.''[1] Aside from the trustworthiness of
the Genesis account, it is the opinion of this scholar
that Moses did not borrow his account from Babylon.
That the human race seems generally to hold some tradition of a creation story, and that the evidence seems
to point to a common source for that tradition, would
appear to be further proof that God gave to man such
an account. If God had given man information concerning creation in some pre-Mosaic time, it would not
invalidate the claim that He inspired Moses to write it
down in a book. For inspiration includes not only the
process of imparting new knowledge, but guidance in
the assembling of known material.

The conclusion is that the Genesis account of creation is the only clear-cut, intelligent, monotheistic
account of creation. It challenges man with the claim
that it came from God. It challenges the scientific
world as to fact.

This leads to the question so often raised, What
about the conflict between the Bible and science? Science comes from *scio*, meaning to know, and may be
defined as that realm of thought in which the unknown
is reduced to the known, and the known classified into
a system by means of observation and experimentation. Outside of knowledge are theories, hypotheses
and speculation. These belong to philosophy and theology. Not that either is confined to the unknown,

---

[1] "Monuments and Old Testament," p. 96.

but that their field of inquiry includes both the known and the unknown.

With this view of the limitations of science before us, let us proceed to see wherein there is conflict, if any, between the Bible and science. The Bible says: "In the beginning God created the heavens and the earth." What has science—not scientists—to say here? Nothing, for outside the revelation of God there is nothing known upon this subject of creation. Are there not theories concerning the beginning? Yes, but theories are not science. Then, since science has nothing to say, there can be no conflict, for it takes two to start a controversy. There can be no conflict with only one account.

Science has nothing in the realm of observation or knowledge to offer on the subject of the beginning of light or firmament, so there can be no conflict there.

Now let us turn to the science of geology or the study of the composition of the earth. In this science there are certain observations of changes and formation which have taken place in the historic periods, and from these, it seems, certain reasonable deductions can be drawn as to what occurred in prehistoric times. For instance, it may be observed that sand is deposited in places covered with water which in time becomes sandstone, thus indicating that certain areas were once under water. The presence of shells belonging to sea life may also indicate former sea or ocean beds. Inclining strata of rock may indicate upheavals at former times. These and many other phenomena become in a way stepping-stones to conclusions of what took place prior to man's appearance on the earth. Hence, here science will naturally be heard to the extent of reasonable conclusions drawn from well-established data as to what was probable, at least, before the time of observation. Admitting this element of inference as science, let us proceed with the next point.

God caused the waters to recede and the dry land to appear. Since geologists have found evidence almost universally of the previous submergence of land, they can have no question with the claim that the land appeared contemporaneous with the recession of waters.

Next, God caused the earth to spring forth grass, herb, etc., bringing into being the vegetable kingdom. This is agreeable to geologists, as they testify from the deposits that vegetable life preceded animal life. On the order of appearance there is no conflict. As to what was the cause of life, or how it began to be, science has nothing to say. For scientists have not observed this process or anything on which to base an inference, and, of course, there can be no conflict. "Science can assemble every element known to exist in the grain of wheat—proteins, nucleo-proteins, lecithins, phosphotides, carbo-hydrates, fats, colloids, the sulphur, phosphorus, iodine, chlorine and fluorine salts of iron, potassium, calcium, magnesium, manganese, sodium, silicon, including the extraordinary substances known as vitamines, but science can't make the combination sprout in the ground."[1] If science knows nothing of the beginning of life to-day, surely it knows nothing of how it originally began, therefore science can have no conflict with the Bible on this subject.

Next the smaller animal life appeared in the sea and on the land. This, too, geologists corroborate from the study of fossils. Then follow the larger animals in turn, and this likewise finds corroboration in the testimony of fossilology. Last of all came man. Even here it is impossible to start a controversy as to the order of appearance. Then, where is the controversy? There is none between science and the Bible. There may be between some scientists and the Bible, but it is over some of their speculations and theories, and not over what is really scientific. We need always to distinguish between science and scientists.

Since we are unable to find any conflict between science and the Bible, we will consider a conflict between

---

[1] "God—or Gorilla," McCann, p. 99.

some scientists and the Mosaic account of the beginning and continuance of life. In Gen. 1:12 it is said: "And the earth brought forth grass, herbs yielding seed after their kind, and trees bearing fruit, wherein is the seed thereof after their kind." Again, Gen. 1:25: "And God made the beasts of the earth after their kind, and the cattle after their kind, and everything that creepeth upon the ground after its kind." Here the statement is explicit; there is no chance for quibbling. The statement is not that God created life or gave animal life its beginning from which it might evolve into higher and higher forms, but the language indicates that God gave a beginning to different forms or species of life and caused them to continue as such.

About the middle of the nineteenth century the French naturalist Lamarck contended for the transmutation of species by natural forces. In 1859 Darwin published his "Origin of Species," and from that time on the theory of evolution, whose main element is the transmutation of species by natural forces, has been very popular among a large number of scientists. To-day many evolutionists say Darwinism is discarded. If Darwinism is cast aside and evolution retained, then what was discarded and what was left? Darwin's method of evolution, or means by which one species evolved from a lower, was natural selection. Grant that the Darwinian method is proved insufficient to explain, we still have the fundamental element, and that is the transmutation of species, which is still in conflict with the Genesis account. What is the method proposed to take the place of the discarded Darwinian process? Scientists seem to be silent at this point.

First, as to whether evolution is fact or theory, hear the words of Darwin himself, the father of evolution; he says, as quoted by McCann in "God—or Gorilla," page 102: "When we descend to details we can prove that not one species has changed." No transmutation of species is provided for in that language, hence no evolution. For, if the scientists mean only development within the species, such as the work of Burbank, then there is no issue and no conflict. Earnest Haeckel, one of the staunchest advocates of Darwinism in the past, says: "Most modern investigators of science have come to the conclusion that the doctrine of evolution, and particularly Darwinism, is an error, and can not be maintained."[1] This, Haeckel did not say in order to support the Bible statement, since he referred to God as "a gaseous vertebrate."

Science being the realm of the known, and its methods being observation and experimentation, let us go afield to see which is the more nearly scientific, evolution or the Bible. We find among the plants a fertilization of like kind and a reproduction of like kind. It is common knowledge with the agriculturist that wheat and oats may be grown adjacent to each other and there is no mixing. Likewise pumpkins may be grown between the rows of corn without producing something which is half pumpkin and half corn. We notice that among birds and beasts male and female of like kind mate to produce their offspring. And, what is peculiarly noticeable, where two varieties more or less akin are crossed, as, for instance, the horse and the ass, the offspring is hybrid. That which gives stability, then, to horticulture, grain-growing and stock-raising is this very principle, that everything produces after its kind. Even the work of Burbank would be impossible without this law; moreover, all life would be thrown into chaos.

Then, from the common observations of life the Bible statement is scientific. Let us add to our testimony the words of a scientist. Lionel S. Beale, physiologist, microscopist, and professor of anatomy in King's College, London, says: "The idea of any relation between the non-living, by a gradual advance from lifeless matter to the lowest forms of life, and so onwards to the higher and more complex, has not the

[1] "Theistic Evolution," Fairhurst, p. 69.

slightest evidence from any facts of any section of living nature of which anything is known."[1] This authority takes in the whole wide range of the known —scientifically known—and yet finds no evidence for the theory of evolution.

Evolutionists are undaunted by the absence of testimony from the realm of observed fact, and resort to what they please to term testimony from embryology, comparative anatomy and paleontology. Since they are so insistent on establishing this pet theory of evolution at any cost, let us venture on in the chase after the phantom—the so-called proof of the theory of the transmutation of species.

In brief, embryology is the study and classification of facts concerning the formation and development of organisms. That observation used by scientists in support of the evolutionary theory is the likeness that the embryo of one species bears to another. If alike, then one came from the other, or, at least, both had a common source. Scientists pretend to see in the human embryo all the stages of development to be found in the human race, and therefore conclude that man descended from the beast. Erich Wasmann ("The Problem of Evolution," p. 61) says in answer to the fish-gill and human-ear argument: "The so-called bronchial arches and clefts are merely curves and folds of the pharynx, which are quite unimportant in themselves, and eventually develop into something bearing no resemblance to real bronchial arches or clefts. They are, in fact, pharyngeal arches and clefts. In the case of fish, to whose existence gills are essential, a similar arrangement develops into real gills, and so with regard to fish alone it is correct to speak of real bronchial arches and clefts as existing in the embryo."

Carl Vogt is quoted also by McCann as saying: "It has been laid down as a fundamental law of biogenesis that the development of the individual and the devel-

---

[1] "Theistic Evolution," Fairhurst, p. 71.

opment of the race must exactly correspond. This law which I long held as well founded is absolutely and radically false. Attentive study of embryology shows us, in fact, that embryos have their own conditions suitable to themselves, very different from those of adults. The development of the individual of all organic beings, without exception, is the normal result of all the various influences which operate upon such beings.''[1]

If scientists reject the so-called testimony of embryology, we, of course, can not accept it as science. Comparative anatomy is that science which treats of the modifications of structure in different groups of organisms, especially as bearing upon the structural relation of the higher organisms to that of lower types. According to the Standard's definition, we see the ground upon which the evolutionist strikes for his evidence; it is the likeness in structure between higher and lower forms of life. We have a vertebral column, limbs, stomach, heart, eyes, ears, nose, etc.; so have many of the animals; therefore, being like them, we descended from them. That seems easy. But try to imagine, if you will, the kind of a world, including the kinds of plants and animals, God should have created, and, last of all, think what man must have been, if all likeness had been avoided by our Creator in order that His word should not be denied and He Himself excluded from the process. Every species of plant would necessarily have been constructed differently from every other. Each kind would use different mineral matter for food. Every species of animal would have had to be different, also using different kinds of food and breathing different kinds of air. And then man would have to be fenced off from all this life, for he would have had nothing in common with it. How foolish! On the other hand, God used enough of likeness to make an economical world, and

---

[1] God—or Gorilla," McCann, p. 112.

yet variety enough to give individuality and difference enough to reach the end of His holy purpose in the creation of man in His likeness.

It used to be argued by evolutionists that because the infusion of blood without evil results was a proof of kinship, and the blood of man could be infused into the ape with but little reaction, it consequently followed that man descended from the ape. But, since the blood of the sheep, goat and horse can be used to inoculate man, it should follow, then, that man descended from one or all of these. This, of course, proves too much even for the evolutionist. Mr. McCann cites as facts by reputable authority that human milk most resembles, of all animal milk, that of the donkey. Does it follow, therefore, that we are close akin to the donkey? If we speak scientifically of man and other apes, then why not of man and other donkeys?

There is further to be considered the evidence, as claimed, from paleontology. The word means literally a study of ancient being or life. It is a study of the earlier forms of life as found in fossils. Since men have been unable to point out in historic times a single case of the origin of species or the transmutation of species, the attempt is made to find the missing links among the fossilized life of other ages.

Dr. Ethridge, of the British Museum, one of England's most famous experts in fossilology, says: "In all this great museum there is not a particle of evidence of transmutation of species. Nine-tenths of the talk of evolutionists is sheer nonsense, not founded on observation and wholly unsupported by fact. This museum is full of proofs to the utter falsity of their views."[1] Such a statement by so eminent an authority is not encouraging, to say the least, to one just starting into the field of fossilology for proof to support the theory of evolution. But we will be patient and hear the evolutionists further by considering some of their claims.

[1] Quoted by Fairhurst in "Theistic Evolution," p. 71.

Among all the fossil remains of earlier life upon which evolutionists center their hopes for evidence of the "missing link" between man and animals is what is technically named *Pithecanthropus erectus* or *Trinil* ape-man. "In September, 1891, Dubois, a Dutch physician, discovered a tooth on the island of Java, about forty-five feet below the surface of the earth; one month later he found the roof of a skull about three feet from where he found the tooth, and in August, 1892, he found a thigh bone forty-five feet farther away, and, later on, another tooth. A year or two later the world's famous zoologists met at Leyden, and, among other things, examined these remains. Ten of these leading scientists concluded that they were nothing but the bones of an ape, seven held that they were those of a man, and seven concluded that they were really the missing link connecting man and the ape."[1] Dubois himself said of this specimen: "He is the ancestor of man." At a more recent convention of anthropologists in Vienna, Virchow said: "The attempt to find the transition from animal to man has ended in total failure. The middle link has not been found and will not be found. Man is not descended from the ape. It has been proved beyond a doubt that during the last five thousand years there has been no noticeable change in mankind."[2]

But as to the specimen formed by a piece of skull, femur and two teeth, Professor Osborn says ("Men of the Old Stone Age," p. 77): "We may form our own opinion, however, from a fuller understanding of the specimens themselves, always keeping in mind that *it is a question* [writer's italics] whether the femur and the skull belong to the same individual or even to the same race." If Professor Osborn, who seems even eager to establish the evolutionary theory, can not be sure that these bones belong together, and, if they do, scientists are still divided as to whether the individ-

[1] "Theistic Evolution," Fairhurst, p. 74.
[2] *Ibid*, p. 75.

ual was man or ape, it may well become the rest of us to doubt the assured results of such testimony. We should rather cling to that which is apparent in life all about us—the stability of the forms of life in well-established and continued groups or species. Is the conflict then between the Bible and that which is not fact? The Bible may conflict with what is merely the fancy of an overanxious mind eager to find something to bolster up an unsupported and tottering theory.

Another example of the products of the anthropologist's fancy is the so-called Piltdown man. About 1909 to 1911 Mr. Dawson collected a few fragments of bone, found by laborers near Piltdown Common, Fletching (Sussex)—a piece of parietal bone, a fragment of the frontal region of a skull, a piece of jaw-bone and a tooth—out of which the scientists constructed the Piltdown man, naming it Eoanthropus, or Dawn-man. This so-called restoration modeled by J. H. McGregor is displayed by Professor Osborn ("Men of the Old Stone Age," p. 145), and is given an antiquity of 100,000 to 300,000 years." Elliott Smith concluded that members of the Piltdown race might well have been the direct ancestors of the existing species of man (*homo sapiens*), thus affording a direct link with undiscovered Tertiary apes."[1] Thus is constructed, out of three or four fragments of bone that one could easily hold in his hand, not only one individual, but a race, and that race made to be the missing link between man and the next lower order of animal life. No, this is more than is claimed; this hypothetical creature serves only as the link between man and another missing link—the undiscovered Tertiary apes.

But let us hear the testimony of other scientists on the fragments of bone used to construct this mythical being called the Piltdown man. George Grant MacCurdy, of the Archæological Department of Yale University (*Science*, Feb. 18, 1916), said: "Regarding the

---

[1] "Men of the Old Stone Age," Osborn, p. 142.

Piltdown specimens, we have at last reached a position that is tenable. The cranium is human, as was recognized by all in the beginning. On the other hand, the mandible and the canine tooth are those of a fossil chimpanzee. This means that in the place of Eoanthropus Dawsoni [the Piltdown missing link], we have two individuals belonging to different genera." No wonder, then, if to the restored cranium of a man there was attached the jawbone of a chimpanzee, Mr. Osborn would say of this monstrosity: "The ape-like structure of the jaw does not prevent the expression of a considerable degree of intelligence in the face."[1] If this man had been permitted to have his own jaw, he would have given evidence of yet greater intelligence.

We might go on to consider the Neanderthal man, the Heidelberg man, and various other reconstructed specimens, but space forbids. If their methods seem so questionable in some instances, how can we trust their testimony in others? Further, so long as scientists are hopelessly at variance over these specimens, the material can not be introduced as *fact* to support any proposition. Suffice it, then, to close the consideration of the evidence from fossils with the words of Erich Wasmann: "The whole hypothetical pedigree of man is not supported by a single fossil genus or a single fossil species."[2]

Upon such flimsy and uncertain evidence as this, from a group of men divided among themselves, shall we throw away our Bible and cast aside the testimony of our own minds as to what is going on about us every day and everywhere, to follow after this vague phantom? And whither? To a world of skepticism, materialism, where law, merciless law, reigns and God is not; where man appears as the blade of grass to bud, blossom and die. A tree is judged by its fruit. Evolution as claimed by some may be theistic, but it binds God to a method man conceives to have been the

---

[1] "Men of the Old Stone Age," p. 145.
[2] "God—or Gorilla," McCann, p. 41.

one used, while the only message we have from the Creator contradicts the claim. Since the Genesis account does come in conflict with the theory of evolution, the evolutionist seeks to explain away the Genesis account. It is myth, poem or a pedagogical method given by or through Moses. If myth or poem, who knows how much of the remainder of the Bible is myth or poem? If a pedagogical method of Moses, it was a poor one, since the very opposite of what he sought to convey has been taken from his language. A good pedagogical method is one that conveys the true idea, not a false one. Then, if myth be granted, in stalks the whole gruesome theory of destructive criticism, for there is no safe middle ground. That means that all is reduced to a cold, materialistic system. That the fruits of the teaching of evolution are skepticism, materialism and atheism, is fast being recognized. The work of W. J. Bryan and others is stirring the public consciousness to the realization of the serious menace the doctrine is becoming to our youth.

That there is no conflict between science and the Bible must be apparent to any one who informs himself as to what is scientific. That there is conflict between the Bible and those scientists who hold to the theory of evolution is granted. If, in spite of all the evidence, one shall see fit to discard the Bible and hold on to an unsupported theory, and that, too, which is more and more being discredited by scientists themselves, then he makes his choice, and must abide by it. God makes no provision for coercing man to believe. To Dives, Abraham said: "If they hear not Moses and the prophets, neither will they be persuaded, if one rise from the dead."[1]

We find in Genesis the only clear, intelligent account of creation. In so far as the other accounts existing in the literature of nations are to be considered, they add weight to that of Genesis.

---

[1] Luke 16: 31.

7

We find, in comparison with the various metaphysical theories propounded in the philosophies of men, the Bible account will stand the test of being the most reasonable as to how, as to why, and for what purpose the world was created. It is linked up with the greatest system of religion known to man. It fits this religion, yet the theory of creation was given to man centuries before the Christian religion was revealed in Christ.

In so far as this story of creation contains matter bearing upon science, it antedates science, much of it, by millenniums, and yet has not been superseded by the most modern discoveries.

History as unfolded by man in the study of ancient documents, so far as it touches the issue, corroborates Genesis. Archæology tends to confirm it. Geology, as shown above, finds no conflict, but, on the other hand, adds testimony to its truthfulness.

What more can one ask? Granting the existence of a God who is all-wise, all-powerful, righteous, just and good, it must be concluded that He could have created the world, and that He could also have made known to man how He did it, if He so desired. Being righteous, just and good, He would, if He could, therefore He did, make known to man the desired information. If He did make the matter known to man, then where shall we find the account if not in the Bible?

One other problem connected with the account of creation remains to be considered, and that is the creation day.

First, let us think of duration. Was it a day of twenty-four hours, or an indefinite period of time? The Hebrew word *yom* is used to mean the time from sunrise to sunset, also twenty-four hours. It is used especially in the plural to indicate time in an indefinite sense. In the use of the word "week" we find the symbolic sense, as when Jacob fulfilled the week of service for Rachel, which was seven years. Then in 2 Pet. 3:8 it is said that "one day is with the Lord as

a thousand years, and a thousand years as one day.''
Since, to begin with, there was no light, and it could
not be said that the earth was then turning regularly
on its axis every twenty-four hours, how could day be
forced to mean the one particular thing and not be
used in one of its other meanings? It therefore seems
more reasonable to think of its use in Genesis 1 to
mean an indefinite period of time.

Next it is said, "And it was evening and it was
morning day one," and so it is stated from verse to
verse under different numbers. Why evening and
morning? The word for evening comes from the Hebrew root meaning to be black. In the beginning we
meet the darkness of chaos, then follows the appearance of light. Hence, to describe the outstanding phenomena of this period it would be the evening (chaotic
darkness) and the morning (light). Then in each succeeding period or day there is the lack of order followed by further order. Since the earth's development was marked by such periods, it might figuratively
be said that period by period or day by day, chaos, or
lack of order, is followed by some form of order. So
it was evening (blackness) first, then morning (light).

When man appeared the world had already entered
into its regular order, and from that moment time as
used by man could be measured. The signs of meas-
urement were the relation to the earth of the sun, moon
and stars. May they also be to us as to the Psalmist,
that which declares the glory of God—an evidence of
His handiwork.

CHAPTER IV.

MAN AND THE FALL

TO any one at all acquainted with the contents of the Bible, it is apparent that the books are written, not from the viewpoint of science, history or government, but from that of religion. Hence the early narrative of Genesis passes quickly over the creation of the world in general to that of man. While man is mentioned in the first chapter of Genesis along with other creation, his beginning is taken up again in the second chapter and described in detail. This, then, is not a second or duplicate account, but another and fuller description of what is but briefly mentioned in the first chapter.

As introductory to our study of man, let us first undertake to determine what constitutes man. On the physical side he may be said to be that form of life having a relatively large brain and brain-case in proportion to the face, an erect posture in locomotion, and the great toe not opposable. On the mental or psychical side the Standard Dictionary quotes Minart as saying: "He is distinguished from the mere animal by (1) abstraction, (2) intellectual perception, (3) self-consciousness, (4) reflection (5) intellectual (rational) memory, (6) judgment, (7) intellectual synthesis and induction, (8) ratiocination, (9) intellectual intuition, (10) higher (or intellectual) emotions or sentiments, (11) rational language, and (12) a true power of will. To this might be added moral judgment, conscience and religion.

While there is a vast difference in the physical make-up of man from that of the nearest animal, there is a vaster difference in the psychical or mental nature. When we use the word "man" we mean not only a being who maintains an erect position in walking—a bear may be trained to do that—but one who thinks abstractly, reasons, has moral judgment, a conscience and religion. These powers may be in a low state of development, but they must be present in order to constitute a man. Then for anthropologists to call the Piltdown specimen, or any other, a man is to grant him these necessary characteristics of a man. But to assume he is man and at the same time not man is ridiculous.

In all the writings of evolutionists the argument is given over almost wholly, if not entirely, to accounting for the body of man in the evolving process, and none to the appearance of his intelligence. Some evolutionists frankly admit that evolution will not account for the mind of man. If it were granted as claimed by the materialist that mind is but a functioning of the brain, the task would be made simpler, but the phenomena of mind's influence over the body forever annihilate that position. If, then, the mind is something apart from the body and connected with the body—using it as a means of expression—how account for the human mind which is to go into the body that has been evolved from that of an animal? We have a dual problem—that of the evolution of body and the evolution of mind.

Now, the Bible story states that God made man dust from the earth and breathed into his nostrils the breath of life, and he became a living soul. This stands the test so far as the composition of the body is concerned. It has the same materials that are found in the earth. Having assembled the body, God put into it that principle known as life. This likewise fits our experience because man can assemble, as stated before, the material that makes up a grain of wheat, but he can not put into it life. Since life is not material substance as shown by scientists, then what else can it be other than the breath of the Almighty?

It is said of man he became a living soul. Here starts self-consciousness—the first creature able to think and to say "I am." Not only a body, not only life, not only intelligence, but an intelligence of that higher class of organization which is known as an individual spiritual entity—a self.

As further evidence that here is begun a new species, it is said of man "there was not found a help meet for him." Why not, if he were but infinitesimally withdrawn, in the evolving process, from his sister apes? But the quotation is from God's word, not man's. So God took from the side of man and made woman. This is a further direct contradiction of the claims of evolutionists. There is no compromise, the statement being clear as to the creation, not only of the male, but of the formation, from the only existing individual of the species, another to become his mate. Adam said, "Bone of my bone," etc.

Thus was the race of man started. It has continued unto our own time, so far as anything is known, by the same law of God—each producing after his kind— as was given to all other life.

The first pair were placed in the garden of Eden. The site of the garden is generally placed by commentators at the head of the Persian Gulf along the Tigris-Euphrates Rivers. Ethnologists place the beginning of man somewhere near this region of the world. Even now there is an expedition penetrating the interior of Asia looking for evidence of the earliest home of man.

Man was given orders to keep and dress the trees of the garden. He was privileged to eat of all the trees of the garden—including the tree of life—except the tree of knowledge of good and evil. "For in the day thou eatest thereof thou shalt surely die."

After the creation of man there were in existence, so far as the Scriptures inform us, three orders of spiritual beings: First, God, including the Godhead— God the Father, Christ the Son, and the Holy Spirit; second, angels, and, third, man. "For thou hast made

him but little lower than God [Elohim in Hebrew].''
God is the uncreated spiritual being, angels created
spiritual beings, and man a created spiritual being
living in a physical body. While in a physical body,
naturally his activity would be in a physical world.

Whether or not angels were created with the
knowledge of good and evil we are not directly informed, but, since some of them rebelled without a
tempter and fell from their high estate, it might be
inferred that they were. Since there seems to be no
redemption for these beings who originated their own
acts of rebellion in defiance of God, it seemed good to
God to create an order of beings in whom was the absence of the knowledge of good and evil, that, though
they should come into the realm of sin through a
tempter, they might be led out by a Saviour.

Then, the first pair were not the normal beings we
know as men to-day, for they were non-moral, not
knowing good and evil. But will this not open up
the case to the evolutionist's claim of a ''missing link''?
This being was potentially a man morally, and was
a man in all other respects. God simply by His power
began with an adult man in all respects except that of
morality; in that realm he was as a child.

Since God foreknew what man would do, the stage
was set for that procedure from the beginning; that
is, the world was created to suit the purpose of God
in dealing with man as he was to become, a trans-
gressor, to be put under the law of death. Therefore
it is useless to speculate on what man would have done
or may have become had he not transgressed. He did
transgress and God knew he would, and inaugurated
the system accordingly and in conformity to the plan
suited to this action on the part of man.

Whether or not man's body prior to his transgression in the garden was perishable, we do not know.
But that he ate of the fruits is stated, and that he had
access to the tree of life is a matter of record. The
fruit of this tree had the power to continue life

(Gen. 3:22). Then, so long as he had access to this tree he would live.

Though man was non-moral, not able to know the consequences morally of his act, yet he was able to do or not do what God told him. Just as a child can understand what is commanded and do or not do it without knowing the nature of the act morally, so was this first pair.

Having taken, through the solicitation of the tempter, the forbidden fruit, their eyes were opened. Here let it be noticed that the Scriptures nowhere refer to this act as a fall. But, because of man's constant use of the word, it may be some erroneous ideas have crept in and have been propagated. For instance, it is sometimes advocated we are in a process to restore man to that estate from which he fell. If we are correct in claiming it to be a state of non-moral being, then who wants to regain it? Surely we do not want to give up our moral consciousness, for it is proclaimed to be godlike even by God Himself (Gen. 3:22). But did not God create man to be as Adam was? If so, then He didn't know what man would do, and is therefore experimenting, and neither God nor man knows the outcome.

Now, what is man's nature after the transgression? His body becomes subject to death, as is evidenced by his expulsion from the garden and from access to the tree of life. His spiritual being passes into the moral realm, and, since the "wages of sin is death," he becomes, to the extent of his own individual sin, subject to the law of death in the spiritual realm.

How man changed from a non-moral to a moral being may be an enigma, but it is going on about us all the time as children come to the age of accountability. What the tree of knowledge of good and evil had to do with the change, we can not know, except that upon certain conditions God's fiat brought other things to pass. Since all knowledge has this element of relativity in it, and all causes evade our search, we may well be content with what the Lord has pleased to give to us on this difficult subject.

Following the transgression we begin with normal man as we know him to-day, and his nature has been the same from that day to this. He has changed his clothes, his customs and his business, but he has not changed the laws of thought, the fundamental principles of his psychical being. A law of conduct that would do then would, under similar circumstances, do now. Man, from the time of his exit from the garden under God's edict of dismissal, has had those characteristics which were named above as distinguishing him from animal life. Man, in the garden, was an adult being physically; mentally he seemed to have a complete consciousness except his range of thought did not include moral concepts. After his expulsion he was as we know him to-day, complete in all his thought, including morality and religion.

The three states of spirituality were now opened to man; he was first in a state of innocence, then in a state of sin, from which he might emerge into the state of virtue. To ask for a restoration to the state before the transgression is but to ask for the state of innocence. What is of more value is to pass by, if possible; if not, to overcome sin through Christ. This, we take it, was the purpose of God in inaugurating the system, to develop a virtuous or righteous man. Then, what of the fall? Was it a fall upward? No, a passing from innocence to a state of sin and guilt is not upward, but downward. Yet, if it be necessary to pass through this state to virtue, it is onward, though downward. The contention is that virtue is higher than innocence and much more to be desired. But virtue is to be had only at the price of potentiality to sin. Where there is no choice or freedom there can be no virtue, and one can not choose except there be at least two alternatives from which to make the choice.

Adam, then, was given the same experience as a child has to-day, though he began as an adult; that of pass-

ing from innocence to a state of responsibility. And
this experience was passed on to the race with its accompanying law of death, which, of course, abbreviates
man's existence in this world. This earth was not
intended to be the final home of man, but a sort of
incubator in which to bring forth a new and higher
form of life. It is important that we keep in mind
the purpose of God—the development of righteous or
virtuous beings—and hence the preparatory use to be
made of this life.

When man and woman partook of the forbidden
fruit their eyes were opened and they knew that they
were naked. It was after the coming of this consciousness that children were born to them, and, so far as
we know, there was no provision prior to this time
for a propagation of the species, man (*genus homo*).
Now they were able to interpret their acts in terms
of right and wrong. God condemned the woman, because of her part in the transgression, to child-bearing,
a further confirmation of the absence of any plan to
multiply the human race. Man's part brought the
responsibility to till the soil, to battle with the useless
vegetation that would dispute his claims to possession.
The serpent—some beast not at that time abhorrent to
man—was condemned to crawl in the dust, and eternal
enmity was put between his posterity and that of the
woman. Such was man as he turned his back upon
the familiar scenes of the garden and began the long
march of generations up the toilsome, but withal necessary, ascent of the steeps of progress toward the
higher planes of virtue and righteousness.

But did not God frown upon this act and give to
each his portion of condemnation because of the sin of
transgression? If so, how could this act be considered
as necessary to reach the end which is claimed to be
also the purpose of God? It must be concluded that
God creates man and brings him into a state of innocence, but forces man to accept the responsibility of

going further, while we must, of course, admit that indirectly God is responsible for all things, including evil. But since man entered the realm of morality by his own choice he became directly responsible and should bear the consequences. But Adam's act was a representative act, and continues to be the choice of humanity, since, if we were able to give our children some drug which would prevent their becoming morally responsible beings, though not interfering with their physical development, we would refuse to use it, saying, "We want them to have the opportunity of becoming virtuous, regardless of the danger of their going the other way."

Only a perfect being in the moral realm could be perfect morally, but man, being a created, dependent being, must of necessity be imperfect. As water can not rise above its level, so this imperfect being can not pull himself up morally by his own bootstraps. God, foreknowing that man by his own choice would enter into this state of moral being, and, through his disobedience and imperfection, into sin and death, held as His eternal purpose [1] the gift of Christ His Son to be man's Saviour. In the first chapter we considered man's need of revelation in order that he might have a pattern for right, and history seems to prove man's inability to advance without outside help. Furthermore, man needs a Redeemer to remove the law of death. What man could not provide for himself God has supplied, and thus the system is made complete for man's advancement.

Let us next give attention to some puzzling questions regarding the first man. One question asked by some is, "Why did not God create man so he could not fall? Why let him have access to the tree whose fruits became his downfall?" Without this step man was non-moral. There are plenty of creatures all about us that are non-moral, and if this were the end of

---

[1] Eph. 3 : 11.

the purpose of God He should have stopped with them. So far as intelligence alone is concerned, God could give of His own intelligence to these creatures under what we call instinct, such marvelously complex activity as to dumbfound man, but that would be no glory to the creature and certainly not glory of the highest order to God.

Why, then, did not God create man already virtuous? It is an impossibility, just as making a round square, or turning an object both ways at the same time. Virtue is the fruit of righteous acts performed by a free agent, hence can not be created.

Why did not God kill the devil, or at least exclude him from the presence of man? Again we must say if it be made impossible for man to fall it is at the same time made impossible for him to rise. When sin is eliminated by decree, the possibility of virtue must also be excluded.

This brings us to the outstanding characteristic of man, that of his religious nature, and the one that has to do with those matters of greatest value. This is the function of mind or soul called free will. Here is found the keystone to the arch of human nature. This is the true plummet-line for any system of theology or religious philosophy. In other words, if a system does not provide for the free will of man, in the judgment of the writer that system will not stand. To give ground here is fatal. It is to throw away one's compass and go adrift on the sea of uncertainty.

To relinquish this position of free will is first of all to leave us purposeless. If there be no free will, then the purpose could not be to develop righteous character. This noble end discarded, what have we? Has God created a world just to "watch the wheels go round"? On the other hand, if we accede to the claim that man is but a part of an inevitable fatality driving on to he knows not what, then how can we justify God? It is not enough to posit a God; He must be righteous, just and good, not an unfeeling monster.

Involving this question of free will and the nature of man following his transgression or fall, is that of predestination or foreordination. It is claimed that in the fall man's nature was changed or became depraved so completely that man of himself could do nothing good, and that in order to his regeneration God must somehow so operate on his heart as to make it possible for him to do good. Further, since it was observed that not all men were turned to God, giving evidence of regeneration, and that the Scriptures spoke of those who were lost or would be, it was concluded that God chose some from the foundation of the world to be saved and some to be lost. This was eventually carried far enough to include infants among the condemned. This extreme position naturally became a most abhorrent one, but, nevertheless, was the logical conclusion from the premises used. The fallacy lies in the nature assumed for man. Man, in partaking of the forbidden fruit, entered into moral responsibility instead of losing it. God placed upon him certain obligations not before imposed. God gave to man a form of religious worship and held him responsible for his reaction to it, as in the case of Cain. If there is any one thing we realize most in a civilized community, it is responsibility—responsibility to self, to man and to God.

Whether in the fatalism of philosophy, the determination of psychology, or the predestination of theology, the absence of free will is the doctrine of gloom, despair and pessimism. Tell the mother that God has predestined her newborn babe to eternal death; tell the humble laborer fate has decreed his subordinate position of toil, that he must walk while the wealthy ride; tell the suffering and downtrodden of earth that what is, of necessity must be—and you stir the sense of injustice in man to the point of rebellion. It may be good theory, but it is a failure in practice. It was surely born as an "idol of the den."

The doctrine of free will is the foundation of government. Every law upon our statute-books assumes its truth. Every trial conducted in our courts has for its basic tenets this fundamental principle. Every system of ethics propounded by man has consciously or unconsciously held to this doctrine, for the very use of the words "right" and "wrong" must assume individual responsibility, and therefore free will. All business is conducted under the recognition of its presence. We drive cattle, hogs and sheep; we attract men. We haul wheat, oats and corn to market; we persuade men. And when the process of driving is undertaken and carried beyond a certain point with men we have wars. Blood is shed again and again to keep fresh in the consciousness of man that he is a creature made in the image of God free and unfettered.

Should we grant that man has evolved through a slow, but steady, process from the lower animals, what effect would it have on this question of free will? First, if man evolved from lower forms by resident forces, we are in the vice of a materialistic system of fatalism. This seeming freedom I possess is but the product of my physiological make-up, and my acts may be attributed to the same power. Such is the case with each individual, and we can not know which man is right in his system of thought, for we can not know which has the proper physiological combination in his body.

Then, again, we can not know that we are the end of the system, but may be just a species in the long procession which in turn may give way to higher forms which in turn become extinct. Hence we can not claim continuity of being in another world. This would make our religion a hoax and deception.

Even if God be made the cause of our evolving from a lower life, we can not know His full system; since we have rejected part of His word, we have no reason to rely on any other part. That is, if we reject Moses and the prophets, it can not be expected that we would believe though one should rise from the dead.

Moses told us how we came into being as a race—by special creation.

If we would be safe in our contention for free will, it seems necessary to hold to the distinct nature of man given to him by God in a special act. That man was the climax of creation as made known in Genesis. Therefore for this life no higher form may be expected, and we may rely on the promises of God that through the transgression of Adam all shall die, yet through the resurrection of Christ all shall come forth from the dead: "They that have done good to the resurrection of life; and they that have done evil unto the resurrection of judgment."[1]

---

[1] John 5: 29.

CHAPTER V.

SIN AND LAW

BY him who overdraws on his imagination in picturing the felicitous state of the first pair in the garden, their exit can correspondingly be painted in very dark and gloomy terms. Adam and Eve, with downcast countenance, go stealthily out past the beautiful shrubbery, unmindful now of the beauty and fragrance all about them as they think only of their guilt and the displeasure of God, whose stern command to depart is ringing in their ears. They are going, not to a home whose bright and glowing warmth will speak a welcome, but to a cold, feelingless world that shall contest with them every effort they put forth to make themselves happy and comfortable. They will build but to see the forces of nature destroy. The burning heat of summer and the cold, desolate winds of winter will cause many a hope to wither and die. They shall bring forth children, nurse and nurture them, binding them to their hearts with the strong cords of love, only to see the merciless hand of death tear them from their bosoms and feed their bodies to the worms. Then one looks up through the falling tears and says: "Is this the work of a kind, loving God?"

On the other hand, let us keep in mind that God said: "The man is become as one of us, to know good and evil." If, then, in this new state there is more of likeness to God, the case is not wholly bad. While man must turn his back upon the beauties and joys of the garden, yet he passes out into a world fuller of meaning. As a child develops through the years and comes to see the higher meaning in acts as they are weighed in the scales of good and evil, so man could now pass upon his own life in the terms of a higher relationship to God. A different meaning could now be given to life as he compared it with death. He was like a boy coming to a mature age; he could choose for himself and have the consolation of directing his own activities and having them weighed in terms of his own motive.

The world outside the garden was not without its beauty and grandeur. The lofty mountains beckoned to man and challenged him to ascend their slopes. The rivers and seas murmured to him as he passed and invited him to lave in their cool depths. While he must work he had the incentive—life—to sweeten his toil. He had the means all about him with which to solve his problems. The joys accompanying fresh discoveries awaited him at every turn, and so vast are the hidden wonders and beauties of God's great universe that after many ages have passed man feels he has only begun to fathom the mysteries about him.

What if difficulties met him at every turn, they but challenged his courage and determination, and victory became all the sweeter by the greater effort necessary to conquest. This gave him not only labor for the hand, but for the mind. In searching for the solution of this and that problem which confronted him, he pushed up higher and higher in the realms of thought. Education is just that—man's attempt to solve the mysteries about him and subordinate the world to his own service. With God to direct in the moral and religious fields of thought man was able to order his life by choice in conformity to nature and nature's God. This is happiness. Adam could be happy, and, so far as the Bible record gives us information, we know of but a few things to mar the earthly joy of this first couple.

Then, did Adam "fall up," as is sometimes charged against this theory? No, he passed, as did Bunyan's pilgrims, through the valley of death, but ever onward

8

toward the Celestial City. Though he descended by transgression, he went forward to greater possibilities. Though he left the state of innocence, he passed into one of potential virtue. There is no way that leads to virtue except by the way of the possibility to sin. Is sin then necessary to salvation? Not in the opinion of the writer. That is, individual sin is not necessary. If we bring our children up in the "nurture and admonition of the Lord," when they come to the age of accountability they will be ready to enter, without personal sin on their part, the kingdom of Christ, and spend their whole life in His service.

But in bringing clearly to view the transition of the first man from a state of non-morality to a state of morality, we would in nowise minimize the awfulness of sin. There is no pictue too dark to portray its hideousness. When we think of crime in all its various forms—the horrible fruits of the liquor traffic, the white-slave traffic, graft in politics, profiteering in business, "fornication, uncleanness, lasciviousness, idolatry, sorcery, enmities, strife, jealousies, wraths, factions, divisions, parties, envyings, drunkenness, revellings and such like"[1]—we are justified in decrying sin in the most severe terms. It may well stir all the horror of our souls and rouse us to the bitterest enmity in opposition to its efforts to overthrow the precious ideals of an enlightened civilization. No, the monster of evil is not to be underestimated, and the works of the devil are not to be tolerated. There is no compromise, no armistice, no cessation of battle in the contest that is on for the possession of the human soul.

Sin is defined by the Scriptures as lawlessness or the transgression of law. Paul says further, "Where there is no law there is no transgression,"[2] allowing us to conclude that without law there is no sin. Yet he says that they who are without law are a law unto

---

[1] Gal. 5 : 19.
[2] Rom. 4 : 15; Rom. 2 : 14.

themselves. Sin, then, is lawlessness, disregard of authority, opposition to order and system.

But what is law? Who shall presume to lay down rules of conduct for another? Who has a right arbitrarily to limit the actions of any one? The anarchist claims the ideal system is the elimination of all law. How shall his claims be refuted? Certainly not with consistency by him who defies the laws of God.

Law is a term applied to uniform activity, whether seen in the operation of nature, government or religion. Civil law is thought of as being on the statute-books of the state, while more properly it is the uniform activity of the citizens of the state; just as the laws of gravity are not, strictly speaking, in the text-books on physics, but are to be found in the uniform activity of material bodies. In like manner, as Newton discovered those great uniform relations of matter and reduced them to law which then was incorporated in books, so society from time to time discovers more of the true relations of man to man, and, by the authority invested in legislative bodies, has them placed in our statutes.

Law may be divided into two classes—natural and statutory. By natural law is meant that which is seen in nature, and, so far as man is concerned, is unchangeable. First there is the law of the material realm. Here laws are discovered and classified under the sciences of chemistry, physics, geology, astronomy, etc. In his search for law in material being man discovers more and more the unity and uniformity of matter. For instance, in the study of gravitation it is found that every particle of matter is related to every other particle of matter in a uniform way, thus making a homogeneous whole. This fact, it will be remembered, was used as an argument for the unity of a being back of all things; that is, God. Without this relation which exists in matter it could have no organized form, and therefore no being at all. Then, law, which is uniformity of activity, is necessary to the very existence of matter.

As an illustration we might assume that if matter could and would defy and transgress its law then it would cease to exist. For just as small particles of matter stick together is it possible to have a ball of mud, a planet, or a universe.

Second, there is the law of life. When we pass from the inanimate to the animate we find the same rigidity of demand for uniform activity, the same uncompromising attitude toward regularity and system. There is not the remotest possibility of a plant functioning in the process of growth without the ingredients of light, water, etc., that are necessary to its development. Likewise, with animal life, it must have the unobstructed operation of the law which governs it or it ceases to be. The laws of respiration, circulation, digestion and assimilation must be adhered to inviolably or the damage done to life becomes irreparable.

What is true for material and life is likewise true of mentality. We must observe faithfully the physiological laws that make for the development of mind, or mind ceases to be. The study of genetics—the science of producing strong offspring—is doing much to bring society's attention to the laws in this field of nature. Then, again, there are the laws of thought, which are just as important. What would it mean to deny that two and two make four, or to assert that a body is in two opposite motions at the same time? It would be anarchy in the thought realm which would annihilate the value of thought. We would have in the place of organized intelligence nothing but the wild ravings and hallucinations of the madman.

But more apparent, perhaps, is the uniform working of mind seen in what we please to term instinct. Mind here—for instinct is intelligence—works with almost exact precision and uniformity. Every cell constructed by the bee seems to be exactly like every other cell. The nests of birds are so uniform as to enable the ornithologist—yes, even the uncritical person—to determine, without seeing the builder, the kind of bird that constructed it. The habits of animals are so well known to man as to enable him to deal with each individual without having first to make a study of that particular specimen. It is this fixity of law or uniformity, regardless of the minor differences, that makes the world habitable for man and possible for him to maintain his sanity. Were all things different each morning we arose, we would cease to know anything, not even ourselves.

The other division we made of law, other than the natural, was statutory. Statutory law is that which is enacted and made obligatory in the realm of human freedom. These laws may have to do with material, life or mind, but they are given only to responsible human beings and for the purpose of governing their actions. A stock law, for instance, is given to men to govern their actions in the handling of stock. Cows, horses and hogs are not expected to obey them. Land laws are to govern man's handling of land, but the land is not expected to hearken or obey.

Statutory laws are derived from two sources: those from man and those from God. In turn, those made by man will be classed as civil and ethical. Under civil laws will be classed, in this treatment, those that have to do with property, education and life.

Man, being forced to earn his living by the sweat of his face, must use the means about him given by God for that purpose. As the world becomes year by year more densely populated he finds it necessary mutually to restrict himself in the use of property. Were each man allowed to roam at will and use indiscriminately the property of earth, such confusion would result as to make it impossible for the human race to live at all. 'Every man to his work'' comes to be the slogan for a well-organized and efficient group. If a man must labor to live, he must protect himself so as to obtain the fruits of his labor. The religious fanatic who quotes ''The earth is the Lord's and the fulness thereof,'' and, by his claim of being one of the Lord's

children, goes promiscuously into the other man's corn-
field, violates this fundamental law.

Man, upon the rise of exigencies of each new situation, undertakes to discover what is the uniform action
that will make for the conservation of society; and,
having discovered it, he enacts it into law. In the realm
of human freedom we can not have enforcement of law
except by the will of intelligence, either human or divine. Since human intelligence is imperfect, we can
have only imperfect discovery of true law, and then
imperfect enforcement of that which is made statutory. Herein does the law of man differ from natural
law and the statutory laws of God.

Under property laws would be classed all laws having to do with man's relation to the material world
—laws of industry, business, commerce, agriculture, etc.
The problem for man in his legislative function is to
discover the uniform activity that will make for the
greatest prosperity of the largest number, and will, if
possible, secure to each man the possibility of providing
for himself and his dependents the necessities, together
with some of the comforts, of life. For instance, when
the population of a section was small and scattering,
stock could be allowed to run on the common and such
fields as were cultivated would be fenced. But as the
section increased in population it was necessary to keep
stock in enclosures, as there was no longer a common.
When but a few men were running vehicles on the
street they might be allowed to go without restraint,
but when the traffic becomes dense strict rules are necessary. Hence the more people there are to use the material of the world the more need of uniform activity
in its use.

As with property, so with the development of the
mind. Man by nature is gregarious. He finds it convenient, profitable and conducive to happiness to live
in groups. To live in groups means to use the same
shelter, the same sources of food and clothing, and the
same water supply. Hence he is forced into an order

or system of life. This uniformity, expressed or implied, is the law. As children grow up it is necessary that they become acquainted with the laws to the end that each individual may properly fit into the group. As society becomes more complex this process of training the young grows until it becomes a school. Good and efficient citizenship calls for education. So, again, we see society is protecting itself by laying down in expressed terms, as laws, what men discover to be the uniform activity necessary to the existence of society. An ignorant savage may roam the vast wilds of the forest, contending with the beasts, and survive, but the same savage placed in the midst of a modern, civilized nation would be practically helpless in providing for himself.

Education, viewed from this angle, might be said to be that discovery made to or by the individual of the laws of relationship between himself, the world, his fellow-man and God. This is, of course, based upon the assumption that there is a true system of uniform action which, when put into operation, makes for the best interests of man. Man does not really make the law, as suggested before, but discovers it. *Education is that discovery*.

The third item covered by civil law is life. As human society advances we find the problem of balancing the rights of the group with the rights of the individual to be the outstanding one. We are leaving behind us the time when the life and property were lost in the interests of the group. Neither are we ready to swing to the opposite extreme of individualism. With the emergence into recognition of the value of the individual have come more efforts to protect him in his property, education, and especially in his physical life. The basis of all is the physical life of the individual. As examples of man's concern about the physical life of the individual are the laws of health and hygiene, laws protecting life in industry, laws for the care of dependents, deficients, etc. This question of the protection of physical life, while a little tardy in receiving due recognition, is coming more and more into prominence because, after all, the thing of greatest value is life, and that to each of us is individual life. We shall welcome discovery of law in the field of genetics—how to be well born; in the field of health and hygiene—how to continue strong; in the field of surgery and medicine —how to assist nature to meet accident and disease.

Other statutory laws of man are classed as ethical. These are they which have to do with the moral conduct of men. Such, for instance, are marriage and divorce laws, laws concerning dress, language and other forms of moral conduct. These actions may in nowise affect the matter of obtaining food and other things necessary to the comfort of the body; they may not affect the education, nor in any way detract from the health of the body, but they do affect man's moral sense of decency, propriety and right conduct. Are these laws, then, but the arbitrary action of the group instigated by the caprice of some fanatical reformers, or are they also fundamental to the life and existence of society? If the latter, then these, too, must be discovered by man and put into force for his own good. The writer has previously laid claim to the latter of these alternatives, that law is a rule of action or a uniform activity, and that there is fundamentally such uniform activity possible as will make for man's best interests or life in the highest sense. Since man is a moral being he has interests in the moral realm. He is forced to the attempt to discover what are the true laws in this department of life.

The writer will admit that ethics may be considered apart from religion, and that an act may be thought of as right or wrong without any relationship to God included in the idea. Yet, as contended in a previous chapter, the claim is made that there can be no just and complete system of ethics formulated in which there is given no consideration of another life, and to admit this element brings in the subject of religion. Therefore, while some religions may seem to be unethical or non-ethical, and some systems of ethics are non-religious, the normal condition demands an interlocking of these two. True ethics must find its basis in religion, and the true religion must include the purest ethics. In this characteristic of morality does man realize most his likeness to his Creator, and in his moral activity does he feel most his relationship to God. This being true, we must go to religion for justification of some moral laws, and only in the realm of religion may some, if not all, of the true laws of ethics be discovered.

Man is a dual being—physical and spiritual—but this duality is not to be presumed to be inharmonious. What is good for him morally in a normal condition is good for him physically, and *vice versa*. Hence, many moral laws seem to lap over into the civil realm in that they make for the physical welfare of man. But there are laws, such as those forbidding nudity, profanity, vulgarity, etc., which do not bear upon the physical well-being. Superficial attempts have been made to justify these on the ground of the needs of this present life, but how feeble the attempt, and how puerile the argument! The only sane and safe conclusion is that they must have a religious background, and then the same rule of the existence of a fundamental law of activity which will make for the highest well-being of man can be maintained.

This leads up to the second division of statutory laws, those which come from God. These laws, having to do with the relationship of man to his Maker in terms of his highest well-being in this life and the life to come, take us into the realm of religion.

As previously claimed, so here repeated, man unaided can not discover the laws pertaining to another life. Man's intelligence supplemented by instinct enables him to cope with the forces of nature in his struggle to live here. But how shall he meet the conditions of the life beyond except God, the only one

who knows, makes known to him those conditions?
Jesus said: "I came that they may have life, and may
have it more abundantly."[1] Couple with this the question of Thomas: "How know we the way?" and the
answer of Jesus: "I am the way."[2] This reflects the
helplessness of man, also the helpfulness of Jehovah.

Man, being unable to discover the true laws governing his relation to God on which hangs his eternal
destiny, the great Lawgiver condescended, yea, more,
with loving solicitude made known to man the underlying principles of that relationship. More than that,
He came to earth in the person of Christ and set an
example, giving us an object-lesson of how to live.
Then, having Himself made possible our redemption
through His own precious blood, He gave us the conditions by which we can appropriate that sacrifice to our
own eternal welfare.

Law is a term applied to observed uniformity of
action, whether in nature or the realm of human freedom. Law for man is really discovered, not made.

Uniformity of activity is necessary to the existence
of matter, life or mind. There can be no such concept
regarding these which includes violation of law and
continued existence. Obedience to law is the price of
existence.

In the sphere of human freedom there is not apparent the same rigidity, yet man's experience teaches him
that even here obedience is the highest virtue. Think
how much depends upon discipline in an army. How
jealously a nation guards its authority and how vio-
lently it deals with traitors and spies. Uprisings and
rebellions are peremptorily dealt with. No authority
can tolerate disobedience. "In unity there is strength,"
and "A house divided against itself will fall," are proverbs setting forth this truth of the necessity of law of
the uniformity of action.

---

[1] John 10: 10.
[2] John 14: 5, 6.

So runs this principle on through the whole gamut of human experience, whether physical, mental or moral. The conclusion is that in conformity to law there is being, existence or life; in disobedience to law there is non-being, non-existence, or death. The Scriptures say: ''For the wages of sin is death, but the free gift of God is eternal life in Christ Jesus our Lord.''[1]

Since law is a uniform activity that makes for life and well-being, not in this world only, but in that to come; and since God is, by our hypothesis, the source of all activity, then God is the author of all law, that discoverable in nature, morals and religion.

Now, sin, as quoted above, is lawlessness or the transgression of law. In this transgression there are two elements to be considered; first, the attitude toward the lawmaker, and, second, the result of the act of disobedience. Sin is heinous in its attitude toward God. It disregards His wisdom, assuming sufficient wisdom in the creature; it denies His righteousness, setting up self-righteousness instead; it ignores His authority, displacing it with anarchy. His holiness, goodness and love are spurned in willful and malicious enmity. How can the holy One tolerate such action? Every organization must have a head, and that head must be respected. How much more should the Creator and Sustainer of all life be venerated and His will scrupulously obeyed.

Shall the Lord of all the earth be trodden underfoot of man? Shall His name be mixed with the vilest epithets of the tongue and His acts of mercy be classed with the vile practices of demons? The Lord of heaven must be high and lifted up. His holiness must be exalted and His glory receive the loftiest praise of His creatures. ''Let all the earth keep silence before him.''[2]

''Lift up your heads, O ye gates;
And be ye lifted up, ye everlasting doors:
And the King of glory will come in.

---
[1] Rom. 6: 23.
[2] Hab. 2: 20.

> Who is the King of glory?
> Jehovah strong and mighty,
> Jehovah mighty in battle.
> Lift up your heads, O ye gates;
> Yea, lift them up, ye everlasting doors:
> And the King of glory will come in.
> Who is this King of glory?
> Jehovah of hosts,
> He is the King of glory." [1]

Sin is first a choosing of low, vulgar and corrupt ways. It is missing the mark of the high ideal, the worth while in thought and life. It is an acceptance of mammon rather than God.

As God is the very essence of good, holiness, mercy, love, etc., He embodies in Himself all the best and holiest ideals. To reject these ideals is to reject God and all His manifestation.

This act of choice by man is the all-important element in connection with sin. What has the individual put before himself as the most worth while? What is his purpose, his motive in life? "Choose you this day whom ye will serve." [2] "Know ye not that to whom ye present yourselves as servants unto obedience, his servants ye are whom ye obey, whether of sin unto death, or of obedience unto righteousness?" [3]

This selection of a master is the selection of a course in life; it is taking one road or the other which is marked at the entrance; it is the acceptance or rejection of God as ruler in one's life. The term "sin" is applicable to the acts of morally responsible beings, and therefore has to do primarily with the motive of the act, the purpose of the heart or the choice made by the individual. Sin is, therefore, heinous because of the sinner's rejection of God, who is the embodiment of all that is good.

---

[1] Ps. 24: 7-10.
[2] Josh. 24: 15.
[3] Rom. 6: 16.

We have concluded in the foregoing discussion that there is true law or a fundamental uniformity of action underlying and necessary to all existence. In the material realm this is the law of the being of matter. In putting one force against another man may break up a certain form of matter which results in other forms, as, for instance, applying fire to combustible material. But this process is limited and can not go so far as to break up the universe. If man could so far transgress or suspend the law of gravitation, destruction of matter would follow. What man does to inanimate matter where life, mind and morals are not involved is of no consequence in that it is not defiance of God or opposition to His purpose. But when either of these are involved it becomes a matter of importance.

Life is the precious jewel. "What shall a man give in exchange for his life?"[1] Life, then, is that by which we evaluate all things. Now, to interfere with the law of life by impeding its operation is sin. Just as we can see if material were to disobey the law of its being it would cease to exist, just so violation of the law of physical life results in death. Then, it is sin not only because of the false and defiant attitude toward God, but because it destroys existence as well. To destroy existence is opposition to the whole system.

As with life, so with mind, violation of its laws means destruction. It has been discovered by biologists that certain conditions make for the birth of a normal mind in the child, while other conditions tend to prevent normal mentality. Sin, then, is the transgression of the laws that make it possible for a child to be potentially intelligent. Our homes for the feeble-minded are to a great extent monuments to the sins of men, and to the laxity of society.

Now, the existence of government depends likewise upon the observance of law—observance of those uni-

---

[1] Matt. 16: 26.

form activities without which no organization can exist. Why did the Colonial Confederation cease to be? Because it could not or did not enforce its laws. Governments define transgression of their laws as crime and assess penalties for disobedience. One's citizenship depends upon obedience.

Men have found by experience that society depends not alone on life and property for its continuance, but upon morals as well. In order, then, to the maintenance of government, there must be included a standard of ethics. These laws must likewise be obeyed. But what can be the incentive for moral action? That it is merely the fiat of society is not enough. Why should society encroach upon individual freedom?

Passing over to religion and the laws of God, we find this proper incentive. Since the purpose of God is to develop righteous character in man, He has so ordered the system that every part fits into every other part. Hence the material fits life, life fits mind, and mind fits morals or righteousness. Material is good for life, life is a support for mind. Mind is moral, and therefore capable of being righteous.

Then, why should one obey a moral or religious law? It leads to virtue and righteousness or godlikeness. Good morals in turn make good society; good society maintains good government, and so on down the scale. A virtuous or righteous life, therefore, furnishes an incentive and key to the whole situation.

But why should one be virtuous? Because it brings the highest form of life, and therefore the state of true happiness. It prolongs life to its greatest longevity here and projects itself by the mercy of God into that pure state of felicity beyond this world which is made possible by the elimination of all that detracts from life. "And he shall wipe away every tear from their eyes, and death shall be no more; neither shall there be mourning, nor crying, nor pain any more; the first things are passed away."[1]

---

[1] Rev. 21: 4.

But if, on the other hand, one chooses evil, if it be his preference to defy God and violate the laws of life, if he enjoys more the association of the wicked and vile of earth, then there is nothing for him but to reap from the seed he has sown. "But for the fearful, and unbelieving, and abominable, and murderers, and fornicators, and sorcerers, and idolaters, and all liars, their part shall be in the lake that burneth with fire and brimstone; which is the second death."[1]

The purpose in this chapter has been to show the nature of law, its relation to being and life, and to show that all true law is but the fundamental activity by which all things are sustained and carried on, whether of the material universe, life, government, morality or religion. That law is not the arbitrary fiat of either God or man, hence to disregard and disobey puts one in opposition to life and existence itself. A sinner—that is, a willful sinner—is an outlaw, an anarchist with regard to the system whose law he transgresses. He is an enemy to existence and life so far as his act of disobedience reaches. No wonder, then, that the prophet of old cried out to Saul: "Behold, to obey is better than sacrifice, to hearken than the fat of rams."[2]

God dare not, yea, He can not, tolerate disobedience. God can have no part with sin. He loves the sinner, but hates the sin. Sin is the transgression of law, a defiance of His authority, and an effort to break up His plan and thwart His purpose.

Man knows that if he goes contrary to the laws of nature he must suffer the consequences; he knows that the probability is if he transgresses the law of man he will be punished; but how does he know just what God will do?

"For if the word spoken through angels proved stedfast, and every transgression and disobedience received a just recompense of reward; how shall we es-

---

[1] Rev. 21: 8.
[2] 1 Sam. 15: 22.

cape if we neglect so great a salvation?"[1]   Nadab and
Abihu offered strange fire, thus disobeying the law, and
were slain.   God rejected Saul from being king and
allowed him to be slain in battle because of his disobedience.   He spared not David, who was a man after
His own heart, but brought punishment on him for his
sin.   Uzzah, who, with good intentions, touched the
ark, was stricken down as an example of the violation of
law.   "For if God spared not angels when they had
sinned, but cast them down to hell and committed them
to pits of darkness, to be reserved unto judgment,
and spared not the ancient world, but preserved Noah
with seven others, a preacher of righteousness, when he
brought a flood upon the world of the ungodly; and
turning the cities of Sodom and Gomorrah into ashes,
condemned them with an overthrow, having made them
an example unto those that should live ungodly," etc.[2]

Surely by this testimony we may know how God
will deal with the sinner.   But is the wrath of God
against sin implacable?   Yes, but not against the sinner.   "For God so loved the world, that he gave his
only begotten Son, that whosoever believeth on him
should not perish, but have eternal life."[3]   "And if
any man sin, we have an advocate with the Father, Jesus
Christ the righteous."[4]

Though man may choose the right, yet, being imperfect, he finds himself in fault.   For this emergency a
blood covering for sin has been provided in Christ.

For him who chooses to do evil, let it be repeated,
there is nothing left for him but to take the consequences of his evil-doings—if not in this world, then
in the one to be.   Dives had his good things here and
Lazarus his evil things.   In the other life, "there are
last who shall be first, and there are first who shall
be last."[5]

---

[1] Heb. 2: 2.
[2] 2 Pet. 2: 4.
[3] John 3: 16.
[4] 1 John 2: 1.
[5] Luke 13: 30.

CHAPTER VI.

RELIGION

IN a study of the purpose of God, as reflected in the Old Testament, there is involved the process of arriving at the meaning of things. Therefore it has seemed necessary, before entering into a study of the Old Testament narrative itself, to detour somewhat by way of looking into the reasons for revelation and inspiration; the reasons for the existence of God, the nature of man and the fall, and the nature of sin. For the same reason it will be profitable to examine the nature of religion. Then with the conclusions obtained from these discussions we shall be better equipped for the study of the main theme before us.

Having accepted the claim that the Bible is a book dealing primarily with the religious side of man's life, it becomes the more necessary that we understand what is meant by religion. While religion is a familiar word, we must not assume that its meaning is, therefore, clear to all.

While a definition belongs, properly, at the close of a discussion of any subject, yet it seems proper at the outset in the consideration of religion to state some of its essential characteristics by which it may be identified, and then give a fuller definition later on.

Any thoughts of God as to His being and relation to man are always consigned to religion. Acts of worship, praise and sacrifice given to God are also listed as religious. The theme of immortality or the question of another life is likewise termed religious in its nature. Hence we may conclude that man's consideration of

God, His nature and being, his acts of worship, praise
and sacrifice rendered to Him, and his thoughts and
beliefs concerning another life, may be classed as that
department of man's activity known as religion.

Let us first look into the question of how man
came to be religious. Is religion something imposed
upon man from without? Is religion something to be
taken up or left alone, as membership in fraternal
orders? Is it merely custom inherited from previous
generations? To undertake to find a solution for these
and other problems, we enter upon a study of the origin
and nature of religion. To have right conceptions here
may help us to take a more intelligent attitude toward
religion.

Much here depends on the theory to which one holds
of the origin of the human race. If one accepts that
theory of evolution—monophyletic—which holds that all
life came from one original parent form, then, as man
emerged from the lower animal life but gradually, it
will be concluded that, in like manner evolving, he
gradually came to be religious. This is the theory put
forth by authors of psychology of religion in the United States. This seems consistent, for how could man
become religious otherwise than by building his religion out of his own ignorance and superstition, when it
is held that his parents were not religious, and he had
no communication from God? For one who believes
that evolution does account for the body of man, but
can not account for his mind, there seems to be here, as
in other phases of the nature of man's mind, a hopeless tangle. Man has his body as the offspring of an
animal ancestor, but whence obtained he his mind?
If given as a direct creation of God, what did He
do with the mind that should have been inherited with
the body? If God, by special act, created the mind,
then why not the body to go with it?

Upon the basis of evolution what is the origin of
religion? J. H. Leuba says ("A Psychological Study
of Religion"): "Until recently the accepted view was

that set forth in 1877 by Edward B. Tylor in "Primitive Culture." Tylor seeks to demonstrate that out of naive thinking about the visions of dreams and trances, and from comparisons of life and death, and of health with sickness, arose a belief in the existence of spirits as the powers animating nature." Further on he says: "An increasingly large number of competent writers would now place earlier than the Tylorian animism, or, at least, side by side with it, another fundamental and universal belief, arising from commoner and simpler experiences than visions; namely, a belief in the existence of an omnipresent, non-personal power or powers."

The theory of Tylor was that the primitive man dreamed, and from his dreams drew the idea of a double, or that there were two of him. This gave the idea of spirit. He proceeded to the idea, of course, that others had spirits, and then on to rocks and trees until all were animated by spirits. The next step upward in this theory is that after a time man developed the notion that these spirits were not bound to any particular thing, but might depart and go into something else. This was called Spiritism. Next, if an object containing a favorable spirit was carried by an individual, it would ward off evil, accident or hurt of any kind. This was Fetishism. So the process went on through Totemism, magic, etc., to religion, and from polytheism to monotheism in religion. Now Professor Leuba complicates the matter by saying: "For that conception of nature which most probably preceded the Tylorian animism, or, at least, existed side by side with it, I would suggest the name dynamism."[1] Just as the evolutionists seemed to have an explanation of how man began to believe in spirits, here comes the claim that prior to animism is the belief in an omnipresent, non-personal power, and we are forced to ask, Where did this come from?

---

[1] "Belief in God and Immortality," Lenba.

Now, all of this theory *supposes* not only that man came from the lower animal life, but that he emerged little by little from this savage-animal ancestor through each stratum of society, from the lowest to the highest, and that, too, without any supernatural aid from above. Hence, what we have to-day as religion is the ignorance and superstition of our savage ancestry glossed over with the polish of civilization. No wonder that only 8.8 per cent. of psychologists, classed by Professor Leuba as eminent, believe in immortality. Considering the assumption that we derived our religion by such a process, the wonder is that a single one of them believes in either God or immortality.

But what are the facts concerning this claim? Here, too, we find men who pose as scientists building upon the sand of an unestablished hypothesis. First of all, this evolutionary theory is founded upon the biological theory of evolution. If man did not come from the animals below him, then all this contention as to the origin of religion loses its force—the whole structure totters and falls. To the falsity of the claim of evolution in the biological realm, the reader's attention has already been called.

By taking the lowest ideas of the savage mind concerning religion and the next higher, and the next higher, and so on, and arranging these in order, the psychologist puts in the assumption that they are in this order related as cause and effect, each producing the next higher, or at least the higher coming out of the lower. But these are not so found chronologically—each following the other. And if they were it would not absolutely prove each caused the other. It would be the fallacious reasoning called *post hoc, ergo propter hoc*—after this, therefore because of this.

There is not a case cited by anthropologists of one form of religion evolving into another. Not a single case of a polytheistic religion becoming monotheistic. So with this explanation of modern psychologists we have theory, not fact. Until we find a people who have come through these stages of development from the savage ideas unto the religious ideas of a civilized nation, how can we know that any such process ever occurred?

Let us consider, for instance, the mountaineers of the Appalachians. These people are the descendants of the same colonial pioneers as are other people of the United States. Then, why do we not find them progressing as are people of other sections? Why may they not have even progressed faster and farther? Simply this, that becoming isolated in their mountain fastnesses they lost contact with other influences and went down, just as we find animals degenerating when the guiding hand of man is removed.

But this theory of evolutionary progress demands an upward movement without any guiding hand. A savage ancestor believing in all sorts of hobgoblins and ghosts is succeeded by a civilized offspring "sitting clothed, and in his right mind." That is, he thinks he is in his right mind, but back of it all is this ignorance and superstition. It may be a little less false to believe in one God than to believe in twenty. It may be a little less foolish to utter an audible prayer with good diction than to turn a prayer-wheel. It may seem more intelligent to carry a Bible than a fetish. But, after all, if the fundamental element is false, the whole system ought to be discarded.

The opposing theory, based upon the Bible, is that man came by special act of God into an existence which is denominated the image and likeness of God. After Adam partook of the tree of knowledge of good and evil, God said, "The man has become as one of us to know good and evil." Thus man begins in the first individual as man with the nature of man. Among other characteristics of his nature was the ability to think in terms of God, his relation to God and also to contemplate the possibility of another existence.

As each human being comes into the world he is potentially musical by nature; that is, the mind as it develops will be able to think in musical terms, and, if normal, will be able to produce music, or, at least, appreciate to some extent the production of music by others. Each normal human being born into the world is potentially mathematical. He does not know, without study, the multiplication table, but he is able to learn to count. So in the realm of language, physics, astronomy, and so on, the human infant is distinguished as capable of entering these fields of thought. Not so with the animal mind. The canary may sing, but she has written no oratorios. The parrot can speak, but she has no use for a grammar.

Now, as man by nature is born to thought in these mental spheres, so is he by nature born to be religious. The child is born without any innate ideas, but he is born with the ability to have those ideas when his environment furnishes the provocation. J. B. Pratt says ("Religious Consciousness," p. 74) : "Thus the inborn nature of the individual determines what might be called the form of his religious life. The matter is chiefly the contribution of society."

That religion is a fundamental characteristic of the human mind is further supported by the fact that no human being has been found who was without a religion. In "Principles of Religious Development" (p. 73), Professor Galloway says: "The fact that men everywhere and always have developed religion—for there is no evidence that any tribe or race has existed without—points to the truth that religion must have its roots in human nature. No accident of environment or tenacity of tradition can account for what is constant and persistent; that which is universal in experience must be a genuine expression of man's inner life." But what constitutes this "human nature," this "inner life" of man? Was it brought into being by the false interpretation of dreams and the superstitious act of a savage in which he was trying to ward off the evil influences of some spirit, created by his own abortive imagination?

We must ever keep before our attention the fact that there are two things under consideration, the content of mind, and the nature of mind. While mind receives the material, out of which it constructs its content, from the outside, the nature of the mind itself is not determined nor altered by that which is external to it. The newborn babe is formed before it comes into contact with the outside world in which it is to function. After birth the mind emerges into activity from within, and does not depend for its existence or nature upon the outside world; but mind, in its own time, takes the air waves and ether waves that have been striking ear and eye from the first moment of individual life and begins to translate them into sound and light. The waves are the raw material out of which the mind on its own initiative constructs ideas, but they do not make the mind itself, nor alter its nature. A child born with mental defects with regard to these senses would never hear nor see, though sound and light waves came to ear and eyes as in any other person. Just so religious environment will never make a dog-mind think God. The family horse that went regularly to church, and, from his position at the hitch-rack, heard much of the singing, praying and preaching, had no thoughts of God or a life hereafter, because this outside influence was unable to make him religious.

The nature of the human mind comes by heredity under the law that like produces like, or everything produces after its kind. Then, for the nature of man, we must go to the first man. The answer is as previously given, that God created man in His own image.

Further, it is claimed by many scientists to-day that there is no transference of acquired characteristics in heredity. The musician's child is not born with the ability to perform on the instrument. He is born potentially a musician, but must learn to play, while the puppy is born not only without the ability to play, but without the ability to learn to play. The human infant, potentially a musician, learns to play,

and fills his mind with ideas of music made of material
which comes from without. The canine infant, by nature not a musician, can not be taught to play.

Grant, according to the theory of evolution, that
there was a time when in the animal ancestry of man
the individual who was not musical, mathematical,
moral or religious, happened on to some mathematical
notion in his contact with environment. How, then,
since science denies the transference of acquired characteristics, could the offspring of this individual get the
same mathematical notion? The next generation would
be left to stumble on to it just as was the preceding.
That is the case with animal life to-day; no matter
how much a dog or a horse learns, his offspring must
begin where he began, hence they have no method
for the conservation of knowledge. Man bridges this
gap, not by biological inheritance, but by social inheritance, made possible by the powers of memory and
speech.

"But," says one, "is not the nature of animals
changed by domestication? Do not the horse and the
dog become more susceptible to training after generations of association with man?" Yes, but they are
yet dogs and horses, even as some people, taken out of
a savage state, become civilized by education, but they
are still human beings. Why does not man use the
wolf for a watch about the house? He is stronger
than the dog. Why not grow the quail in a domestic
state instead of the pigeon, when it is, by many, pre-
ferred as a food? Why not train the whale to draw our
ships and thus economize on fuel? Why not train the
eagle to carry messages? The answer is evident to all.
It is not the nature of these animals and birds so to
be trained. Then, we are back to the point of fixity
again, that of nature. We can modify or develop
anything as far as the bounds of its nature will per-
mit, and no further. But evolution demands that training and modification go on beyond the bounds of the
nature, even to the altering of the nature itself, until it

becomes a new and different thing; and that, too, without any hand to train or guide except the blind forces of nature in the environment. Here the theistic evolutionist would probably interpose to claim that the guiding hand is that of God. All we know here is that God said He did not do it that way, and if we are not to believe what He says, then how are we to know that He had anything to do with the process at all?

The theory of evolution assumes that an animal precursor of man, who was neither musical, mathematical, moral nor religious, became all of these through a slow, but continuous, process of change caused by his reaction to his environment. It is just as reasonable to suppose that in the continued process man may develop a sense of the fourth dimension, there now being three—length, breadth and thickness. We may also look for another physical sense, like unto sight, hearing, etc., by which we will be able to detect the presence of spirits, and that we may develop a physical organ for the transference of such sensation. In fact, we may, in the course of some thousands or millions of years, change our natures completely so that what seems to us now to be true may then fade into dream or fantasy. That is but to cast ourselves into the maelstrom of confusion wherein identity, stability and reliability are not to be found. We become but the chance links in an infinite chain of change. We are but the stepping-stones for some other beings unlike us, and indifferent to the part we play in the fatalistic process.

If, on the other hand, we hold that man came into being as man, and will continue as man so long as time shall last, with the same nature from the beginning, and capable of development within the bounds of that nature, we have a secure foundation on which to build. We have the comfort of knowing that in dealing with each new infant we have a human being fresh from the hand of God. It may be somewhat marred by inheritance, but capable of being raised to the heights of a virtuous man or woman.

Some psychologists have claimed that man's instinct of fear became the starting-point for his religion. In trying to protect himself, he began to invoke the spirits, which he imagined inhabited moving objects or forces about him. But fear has never made such a timid animal as the hare religious. Others have put forth the idea of dependence as man's source of religion. We just as well concede to man the ability to think religious concepts to begin with as to concede him the mental power to ideate dependence. How did man become able to think dependence? Again, there are those who attribute the rise of religion to volition, such as curiosity to know the cause of things, or the desire to live on after death. What was said in answer to the idea of dependence applies with equal force here. While granting these volitional powers of the mind, we just as well grant the religious characteristic of mind. Therefore, given a human mind to start with, we need only furnish it the material and it will construct things musical, mathematical, moral and religious. Given an animal mind to start with, and out of all the material furnished it will be unable to construct anything which is musical, mathematical, etc. Neither can a human mind, without material from the outside, construct a mathematical or a religious system. Given a flour-mill, and we can, by putting wheat into it, obtain flour; but pour all the wheat you will into a gasoline refinery, and you get no flour because it is not the nature of a refinery to manufacture flour. Neither will the wheat put into it change the nature of the refinery and make of it a flour-mill.

Next, let us consider how man comes to have a particular religion. Some oppose religion because men have so many different kinds of religion. That man is religious by nature does not determine the kind of religion he will hold to be genuine. That man is, by nature, musical, does not determine whether he will make the crude sounds of the savage's tom-tom or whether he will execute some work of Beethoven on a baby grand; whether he will be able to count no higher than three, or whether he will be versed in calculus. Being by nature astrononomical will not determine whether he will believe the world to be round or flat. Even though he erroneously says the world is flat, by that very statement he classifies himself as an astronomical being. Just so, the man who says there is no God places himself in the list of religious beings, because no non-religious beings, such as horses and cows, ever have any idea of God at all.

Let us repeat here the quotation from Prof. J. B. Pratt: "Thus the inborn nature of the individual determines what might be called the *form* of his religious life. The *matter* is chiefly the contribution of society."[1] The nature of man determines that he is religious; the kind of religion he has is chiefly the contribution of society; Adam and Eve were, as distinct from all other life about them, religious beings, but the kind of religion they had came from their teacher, God. The Arab, by nature, is religious, but he receives Mohammedanism from his teacher. A man in the United States is, by nature, religious, but he receives Christianity from his teachers. Hence, Jesus said: "Go ye therefore and make disciples of all the nations."[2] His method was to teach the true religion to those who were teachable—the nations; that is, people, not animals.

No doubt civilized man is the only one that defines religion, and, observing his own manifestation and classifying it, he regards that as religious that has to do with God, man's acts in relation to God, such as worship, praise and sacrifice, and thoughts of immortality. Then, a belief in God, with acts of worship and sacrifice which secure to the worshiper the blessing of God in this life and a life of blessedness to come, constitutes religion. Civilized man observes the life of the lower stata of humanity, and, while he finds these main ideas

---

[1] "Religious Consciousness."
[2] Matt. 29: 19.

corrupted, he, nevertheless, finds them all represented in some form. Hence, such definitions as the following: "Religion is the serious and social attitude of individuals or communities toward the power or powers which they conceive as having control over their interests and destinies." [1]

How does religion fit the human mind, and what need does it supply? First, the human mind, though acting always as a unit, functions in what we please to term a threefold way, that of intelligence, emotion and volition. For the intelligence, religion offers the belief in God; for the emotions, it offers praise, adoration, worship, etc.; for the volition, desire, ambition, hope.

As to the needs of the human mind, Christianity, the true religion, brings an answer to the human mind that satisfies its query as to the source of all things, the end or destiny of all things, therefore the purpose of all things. It satisfies man's emotional nature in that it gives him a being who is worthy of his highest praise —worship, adoration and service. And, lastly, it satisfies his volitional nature in that it sets up the highest mark possible for his attainment. This service philosophy has been unable to render, no matter how much food for thought the various systems have presented. This contribution has not been made by music, poetry and other forms of art, regardless of how they have stirred the emotional nature. And all the systems of ethics, fraternal organizations and governments have not been able to set up such standards of activity to bring forth the best that is in man, as has religion. This being true, then let us do honor to that activity of thought and life which displaces the darkness of "the cold and barren peaks of two eternities," with the glorious light radiating from the countenance of a loving and merciful God; and which stirs the human heart to the profoundest gratitude in contemplation of

---

[1] "Religious Consciousness," Pratt, p. 2.

a crucified Saviour, and which follows one to the tomb to say: "Let not your heart be troubled: believe in God, believe also in me. In my Father's house are many mansions; if it were not so, I would have told you; for I go to prepare a place for you. And if I go and prepare a place for you, I come again, and will receive you unto myself; that where I am, *there* ye may be also."[1]

[1] John 14: 1-3.

CHAPTER VII.

THE PATRIARCHAL ERA

THE English word "Adam" is a transliteration of the Hebrew word, which is the same as the root, meaning to be red or ruddy. The Hebrew word for ground (*adhama*) is derived from the same source, and was most probably used because the soil was of a reddish color. The word "Adam" has two uses, that of man or mankind, and also that of a proper name for this first individual of the human species.

Adam and Eve, when expelled from Eden, which is generally thought to have been near the head of the Persian Gulf, no doubt passed into the near region of Mesopotamia, or some part of the Tigris-Euphrates Valley. What they did in obedience to the law of necessity that was laid upon them to labor is passed over, since the narrative deals with the religious side, and such matter as may be germane to the question in hand. Now, for the first time, the command of God to multiply and replenish the earth is complied with, in that there are children born to this first couple.

The firstborn was Cain, and then there was born his brother Abel. Cain was an agriculturist, tilling the soil, while Abel was a keeper of flocks and herds—a shepherd.

Nothing is said of God giving to Adam and his family any religious law, but since we find thus early in the narrative an account of their bringing offerings to Jehovah, we may well presume that they were given instructions as to how God would accept their worship. Further, since they were brought into their present state through the disobedience of God's law, it follows that He would give them other law for their guidance in this new relation. Again, this position is morally required, since God could not be justified in punishing man for disobedience of a law of which he was totally ignorant, and concerning which he had no means of obtaining information.

This religious law, according to the events in the narrative, must have included the demand that a life be sacrificed in the offering made to Jehovah. This accords with a principle enunciated later, that "without the shedding of blood there is no remission of sin."[1] Now, to Mother Eve it was said her seed should bruise the head of the serpent. This, taken as referring to Christ, holds before us a life sacrificed as the means of bruising the serpent, or Satan. That is, in Christ man shall be freed from the works of the devil. Thus God began by the method of type and shadow to work out the "eternal purpose which he purposed in Christ Jesus our Lord." "By faith, Abel offered unto God a more excellent sacrifice than Cain."[2] By taking a firstling of the flock, as we presume God had directed, and slaying it, the blood of this innocent victim became a covering for sin. While "it is impossible that the blood of bulls and goats should take away sin,"[3] yet these can be used as types of that which is efficacious, even the blood of Christ. Hence, until the fullness of time, when Christ should come to offer Himself a sacrifice for the sins of the world, it was necessary to have a substitute, and that substitute must have characteristics that picture the real offering. The three main elements to be noticed are life, youth and purity. The herbivorous animal, such as the calf or the lamb, had life, was taken while young, and was a type of sinlessness or innocence. The life must be the life of a being subject to pain and suffering in order that the

---

[1] Heb. 9 : 22.
[2] Eph. 3 : 11.
[3] Heb. 11 : 4.

element of sacrifice be present, hence vegetable life was excluded.

The Hebrew word translated atonement is *kaphar,* meaning to cover. When man presented the blood of an innocent animal as a sacrifice to Jehovah, that blood became a covering for sin, hiding, in a figurative sense, the worshiper's sin. God, being holy, can have nothing in common with sin, therefore, when a sinful man would approach Him it must be under a covering for sin. Hence it is that Jesus said, "Whatsoever ye ask in my *name,* that will I do."[1]

The sociological interpretation of sacrifice is illustrated in the following statement: "The Semites were originally nomadic, and this accounts for the conspicuous place which animals hold throughout their religion. The main lines of sacrificial worship were fixed before any part of the Semitic stock had learned agriculture and adopted cereal food as its ordinary diet."[2] Hence, according to Professor Ames and others of this school of thought, the form of sacrifice was determined by the food habits of the people, and not by the direction of God. Then, if there is any prefiguring of Christ to be seen in the animal sacrifice, it was merely accidental, and not prearranged by Jehovah. But the trouble is, all that we know of this ancient people, who were the ancestors of the Semites, is found in the Genesis account, and it tells us that Cain was an agriculturist, tilling the soil, yet, though he offered the products of the field as a sacrifice unto Jehovah, they were rejected.

We notice that upon the rejection of his offering Cain does not plead ignorance, but becomes angry. This wrath, reinforced by jealousy and hatred, leads him to commit murder, just as is common to human nature; the righteous act of one stands as a condemnation of the evil act of another, and if it does not help to lead to repentance, then it drives to jealousy and

---

[1] John 14: 13.
[2] "Psychology of Religious Experience," E. S. Ames, p. 48.

hatred. Cain, failing to repent, took the latter course. His crime of murder was followed by the lie that he knew not the whereabouts of Abel, and by the implied assertion which has ever characterized the selfish and sinful, "I am not my brother's keeper."

Upon receiving the curse of God he exclaimed that God had driven him out, and that from God he would be hidden; and that, becoming a fugitive and a wanderer, he would be in danger of being killed by any one finding him. But Jehovah appointed a sign for Cain to prevent his being slain. What the nature of this sign was we have no means of knowing, but the writer hazards the interpretation that this was the mark of humanity. When men hunt the wild beasts of the forest there is always the ready recognition of the human being, whether a Bushman of South Africa, the Weedas of Ceylon, or the Negritos of the Philippines. The hunter never mistakes them for gorillas, apes or chimpanzees. Now, it would naturally follow that Cain and his descendants, when cut off from contact with the teachings of God and their civilizing influence, would degenerate. Would they degenerate to the level of the beast and be subject to the same treatment? No; for the power of the Almighty fixed both boundary lines of the species, the low point of degeneration as well as the maximum of development. If man came from a beast, why can not he degenerate and go back to the beast? The mark of humanity placed upon him by God forbids. Hence, any one finding Cain would not kill him.

"Cain went out from the presence of Jehovah and dwelt in the land of Nod." This word "nod" means, in Hebrew, flight or wandering. We are then to see in Cain's dwelling a condition rather than a place. It was departure from God and His influence. It was a condition of sin and disobedience. Many near us to-day are thus dwelling in the land of Nod.

"And Cain knew his wife." It is said that after the birth of Seth, the third son, Adam lived eight hun-

10

dred years, and he begat sons and daughters. In whatever theory one may hold as to the beginning of the human race there would have to be intermarriage in the first family, so it is reasonable to suppose that Cain took a kinswoman, either a sister or a niece, for a wife. This was practiced as late as the time of Abraham, since Sarah, his wife, was a half-sister; yes, even as late as Cleopatra, in Egypt, 10 B. C., and among the Incas, of South America, in the seventeenth century.

It is said of Enoch that he walked with God; and he was not, for God took him. Thus early God gave a sample of His power over death by this special act of the translation of Enoch, and coupled it with a righteous life, further to convince man of the operation of His law that the wages of sin is death, but the gift of God is eternal life.

In Genesis, sixth chapter, it is said that as men began to multiply on the face of the earth, the sons of God saw the daughters of men that they were fair, and they took unto them wives of all they chose. The result of this intermarriage was increased wickedness upon the earth, so much so that the whole earth was in danger of becoming corrupt. It was no slight form of evil, since it is recorded that every imagination of the thoughts of man's heart was only evil continually.

In the departure of Cain into the land of wandering, the line of connection between man and God was taken up in Seth, and followed through his descendants. Thus the human race became split into two factions, or divisions, a righteous line following after God and a wicked and degenerate line in the family of Cain. Now, followers of God are thought of as sons of God, while those who follow the selfish purposes of men will be classed as sons of men. Then it is, in the writer's opinion, that the line of Seth began to intermarry with the line of Cain, and, as we commonly observe to-day, the evil draws down the good instead of the good lifting up the evil. "But why," some may ask, "was God so concerned about the line of Seth becoming wicked, when there seems to be no especial worry over the line of Cain, which was already wicked?" As to God's concern about individuals, there could be no difference. He would desire the salvation of a man in the line of Cain as much as that of one in the line of Seth, but, as to the continuity of a line, that was a different matter. That some men would sin, God could not prevent, but must tolerate, since man is a free agent; but to allow the whole race to become corrupt would abrogate His whole plan, for He promised the first woman that her seed should bruise the head of the serpent. To fulfill this promise a line of righteous seed must be preserved. When Cain went into sin he could not longer be used. Abel was murdered, and therefore eliminated. Then Seth became heir to the spiritual inheritance, and the line was preserved through his lineage—Enosh, Kenan, Mahalaleel, Jared, Enoch, Methuselah, Lamech and Noah.

"There appears to have been a growing corruption of mankind, more rapid, no doubt, in the family of Cain than in any other race, but still spreading far and wide. The line of the Sethites, traced in Chapter V., alone appears to have kept itself pure—in the midst of gathering darkness of the world around. They alone were the salt of the earth; and if that salt should lose its savor, all would be worthless and vile. When, therefore, some of the sons of God went out from their own little home circle to make mixed marriages with the general heathenized races around them, the elements of corruption were brought from the world into the church, the church itself became corrupted, and the single family of Noah appears to have been kept pure from that corruption. The salt had lost its savor. At all events, too little was kept to purify and save the world. It could but save the souls of the few righteous that were therein."[1]

---

[1] "The Bible Commentary"—Gen. 6: 2.

Co-ordinate with the activity of free moral agents is a separating process. As some choose the good and others choose the evil, there comes to be a division of mankind. In the effort to live, the righteous have frequently been forced to war with the wicked. The righteous have likewise called upon God for help in times of peril, being assured that God was on the side of righteousness.

Over and above these lesser divisions made by man, with the help of God, there are three outstanding separations made by Jehovah. The first partition made of humanity was by the flood or water; the second is being made through the gospel of Christ, or partition by blood; and the third great division will be made in the last day when the righteous are separated from the wicked, or partition is made by fire. The purifying elements used, then, are water, blood and fire.

In taking up the first process of separation or purification—the flood—we should keep in mind the purpose of God, that of preserving a righteous seed through whom He could send His Son into the world.

It was evidently not just to destroy the wicked, or else the occasion for such a destruction was present from the time Cain slew Abel. It was only when the righteous line was in danger of elimination that Jehovah instituted this method. It was not so much a method of destruction as one of salvation; not so much a process to kill off the wicked as one to save the righteous.

The ark, as constructed by Noah, with a length of three hundred cubits, breadth of fifty cubits, and height of thirty cubits, compares favorably with the dimensions of modern vessels, although it was not built to be propelled, but to float. It is said by German commentators that Peter Jansen built a vessel in 1609 of the same proportions as the ark, but using smaller dimensions; viz., length, one hundred and twenty feet, breadth, twenty feet, and height or depth, twelve feet. "It was found convenient for stowage, containing one-third more freight than ordinary vessels of the same tonnage, though it was unsuited for making way quickly through the water."

There was one door to the ark, which was all that was needed for entrance, and, following the subsidence of the waters, for exit. As to the window or windows, some criticism has been offered. The Hebrew word means light or lights. God said, "And to a cubit shalt thou finish it upward," which seems to mean a cubit from the ceiling of the story. Since there were three stories, it would be natural to suppose that the series of lights were put in each story one cubit below the ceiling. Since they were for light and ventilation, and not for the purpose of viewing the scenery, they were certainly placed in the proper position.

When the waters subsided—another statement that seems to bear out the theory of a partial flood, else whither would the waters recede—the ark rested not upon Mt. Ararat, but upon the mountains of Ararat that are in that region. Following the landing, Noah offered sacrifice to God. This was possible because of the clean beasts, of which seven were taken into the ark to furnish food and material for sacrifice.

Jehovah told Noah He had set His bow in the cloud, and henceforth it should be the sign of a covenant that "the waters should no more become a flood to destroy all flesh."

The next problem of importance in tracing the purpose of God is the extent of the deluge. Was the flood universal in extent, or did it cover only a locality? In the study of this question, it is well to keep in mind that the narrative is related from the viewpoint of an eye-witness. As was claimed concerning the creation narrative, that the language implied a description from the viewpoint of the earth, and not from a neutral, astronomical one, just so here the deluge story is not given from the view of one external to the earth's surface, but from the viewpoint of one on some particular part of the same.

The reasons commonly advanced for the belief in a universal flood are: First, the use of the word "earth"; second, the Scripture statement, "And all the high mountains that were under the whole heaven were covered;"[1] third, that there seems to be a universal tradition of such a catastrophe; and, lastly, there are remains of sea life to be found upon the mountains.

The Hebrew word *arec*, translated in these passages "earth," also means land, country, ground or field. Now, if using a rule of language—that is, the substitution of another word with no damage done to the meaning— we use the word "land" instead of "earth," we find the meaning is preserved. Hence, we must conclude that the translation was a matter also of interpretation. For where translators find words of two or more meanings it becomes a matter of interpretation as to which word shall be selected.

But, grant that the writer had in mind land, and not earth, we have, at any rate, the language of the second argument, "the mountains under the whole heaven were covered." As previously mentioned, the narrative is, no doubt, given from the viewpoint of an eye-witness. Since most likely these people were dwelling in the plain of Mesopotamia, the description should be viewed from there; so when the waters accumulated from the rains and from the breaking up of the fountains of the great deep, the highest hills within the view, or, perhaps, knowledge, of the eye-witness, were covered. For such, then, it could be said all the high mountains under the whole heaven were covered, for he could see nothing but water. As to the exaggeration to be found in the figurative language— "under the whole heavens"—like passages are found; such as, "I begin to put the dread of thee and the fear of thee upon the peoples that are under the whole heaven" (Deut. 2:25). "All countries came into Egypt to Joseph to buy corn" (Gen. 41:57). "As

---

[1] "Gen. 7:19.

the Lord thy God liveth, there is no nation or kingdom, whither my lord hath not sent to seek thee,"
etc. (1 Kings 18:10). The hyperbole is apparent in
these passages, and there seems no reason why it could
not also be used in the one under consideration.

As to the universal tradition, if so it is, of a
deluge, it could only be answered by those holding
the other view that such a tradition must have been
disseminated from the region where the deluge occurred. As to the last argument, the remains of sea
life found on the mountains would have had to be
carried up in earlier periods of the earth's history
in the times when the crust of the earth was crumpling
up and the mountains were first formed.

Some of the difficulties attending the theory of the
universal flood need to be considered. How could God
be just and destroy by flood peoples in other parts of
the world who had no warning, much less invitation,
to enter an ark? Some one may answer He was justified in so doing because of the wickedness of the people.
Not so without warning, or else God is justified in con-
demning man without the gospel of Christ. Yet Christ
commanded His disciples to go into all the world and
preach, warning men of the judgment to come. On the
other hand, if we take it that the region affected was
that in which Noah built the ark and preached the doctrine of obedience to God and warned them of the deluge that was coming, inviting them to come to the ark
for safety, then God is justified, for the people had
their opportunity to escape upon the conditions that
were made known to them.

Again, there is the difficulty attending the universal theory concerning the amount of water and its
source. Now, the writer gives place to no one in the
matter of faith in the power of God and the acceptance
of miracles. But a study of the Scriptures leads to
the conclusion that God often used natural means in
working out His purpose. He did not perform miracles
simply for display, which would lower His work to the

level of the magician, who performs just to excite wonder. He worked miracles for certain definite ends and purposes, sometimes using natural law, sometimes suspending it.

Ingersoll, in his satirical attack upon the Mosaic account and the theory of the universal flood, said it must rain, in forty days, enough to cover the highest mountain, an average of eight hundred feet per day. The question is, Shall we accept the theory that requires such an extraordinary display of miraculous power on the part of God, or accept a theory that calls for miracle, but upon a smaller scale, and that, too, which will satisfy all the demands of the narrative?

Not only did it rain forty days and nights, but the account says the fountains of the great deep were broken up. The natural meaning must be that water came in from below or from the surface of the earth as well as from above. This must mean, then, that water came from rivers, seas, oceans or subterranean sources. But this, it seems, would be meaningless if the whole earth was to be inundated. The water, if flowing in from a river or sea, must just flow back again. But if there was a sinking of land in this region, we can readily see how the water might flow in from adjacent streams, seas or gulfs and add to the volume of water even more than did the rain.

Another physical difficulty commonly advanced against the universal theory is the size of the ark and the number of animals to be put into it. Granting, as it seems we must, the large number of species that geologists say preceded man upon the earth, and the difficulty is a real one as to how two of each of the land animals and birds were to be put into the ark. But here, as before, the theory that but a region was affected, allows room for the gathering in of such life as inhabited that portion of the earth.

Last to be considered, and one of the most serious difficulties to be faced by advocates of the universal theory, is that of accounting for the repopulation of

the earth with human beings from the progeny of Noah.
How account for the dispersion of the races of mankind in time, place and genealogy? Is there time for
such a degeneracy as must have necessarily taken place
with some? Is there time for such dispersion, as to
place of residence, to all the continents and to the
islands of the sea? From which branch of Noah's
family tree did each spring?

Naturally, we must recognize that there are difficulties in this field of inquiry for any theory. But, with
the viewpoint of a partial flood, we may couple the
theory that, in the disaffection of Cain and his consequent departure from God, there would follow a drift-
ing away of his descendants more and more to remoter
regions of the earth; some to become isolated in one
region and some in another. This may have been true
also from time to time of other disaffected elements
in the offspring of the righteous line. These being at
distances, great or small, from the scene of God's special activity, would not be the contaminating influence
for His righteous line, and, therefore, would not be
affected. These went on in their isolated conditions,
some crystallizing in one plane of social activity and
some in another. Some elements degenerated to the
lowest degrees of human existence, which would account
for the savage and barbarous tribes of our own time.

The classification of the peoples to be found in the
Old Testament as descending from the sons of Noah
corresponds in general with other ethnological tables
compiled by students of anthropology, but they do not
adequately provide for the yellow, brown, red and black
races. Then, how account for these if they can not be
traced to Noah's sons, except they be descendants of
antediluvians not destroyed by the flood?

From Javan, it seems, descended the Greeks, Romans, Celts, Slavs, Teutons, Galatians, Scythians, Cap-
padocians, etc. These became the peoples of north-
western and western Asia and Europe. From Ham
were descended the Egyptians, Ethiopians, Philistines

and Babylonians, Phœnicians, Hittites, Hivites, Girga-
shites and others of the Canaanites, peoples of Palestine,
Abyssinia, and northern Africa. From Shem sprang
the Hebrews, Elamites, Assyrians, Syrians, Moabites,
Ammonites, Edomites and Arabians, peoples of western
Asia. Of course, much of the classification of nations
is more or less uncertain, and there is not much room
here for dogmatism. But, if all the peoples are to be
traced to Noah, the time from the flood seems all too
brief in which to obtain the vast changes that must have
taken place.

Another problem that is worthy of attention, before
we pass from this section of the Old Testament narrative, is the great longevity attained by the Patriarchs.
From Adam to Noah the age of each is numbered by
hundreds of years, culminating in the extreme age of
Methuselah, nine hundred and sixty-nine. Since we
observe the life of man to-day to be about fourscore,
how could it be that man lived so long in another age?

The growth of an individual from infancy to adult-
hood is by the multiplication of the number of cells in
the body, while at the same time there is going on
the process of replenishing the worn-out cells with new
material. When the average man reaches about five feet
eight inches in height and attains a weight of about
one hundred and fifty-five pounds, he stops growing
in size or the multiplication of the number of cells
ceases. The other process, that of replenishment of
worn-out material, continues until the individual is
eighty to one hundred years of age, and then it
ceases.

Now, what or who determines the point at which it
may be said the individual is tall enough or heavy
enough? Certainly not the individual himself, for
"who can, by being anxious, add a single cubit to his
stature?" Certainly not the unintelligent cells that
are doing the work. Scientists, by experiment, have
found that the proper functioning of certain glands
in the body leads to the proper development of the size

of the body as well as to the normal development of the mind. Granting this, the problem is somewhat localized, but still evades us. Why do these glands have such an influence? Here, no doubt, the scientist would have to declare his inability to answer.

Then, if the individual has no power over his growth, and the cells of his body can not furnish the intelligence necessary to such a process, where is the answer to be had? It may be said it is just the operation of natural law. But, since law is not a force, much less an intelligent force, such an answer becomes an obscuration, not a solution, of the problem. Since all things are the manifestation of God, then each individual is formed from the beginning of the conjunction of two cells up to the full stature of a man by the intelligence of God as He energizes in the process of life. When it is His will that the individual cease growing in size the process stops. Why should man develop to such a size—that which we know as a normal man? It is the fiat of God.

Why the cells of the body should cease replenishing worn-out material about a certain age and the individual is said to have died from old age is the same sort of mystery. Why should not the cells work in rebuilding at the age of eighty just as vigorously as at forty? For the same reason that it is the fiat of God, and, therefore, when He ceases to function in that particular form of His energy the process ceases. The result is described by us in the words, "The person died of senility."

When the population of the earth was yet sparse, it seems to have been the purpose of God to retain individuals longer. Because of the low stage of advancement at that time man's experience was much more limited. The greater length of life would add to the process of replenishing the earth and give greater opportunity for individual development. Later on, as life became more complex, man might obtain in a much shorter time the same experience, therefore God shortened his life to about one hundred and twenty years. Then, again, as the population had further increased and life was yet more complex, man's life was reduced to threescore and ten. But to live the allotted seventy to-day enables one to develop character to as great an extent as no doubt it was possible to do in the days of Methuselah, even with his great stretch of existence. Recent reports indicate that the average length of life to-day is over fifty years, but it is not probable that the maximum will be changed any more. Our task now is so to conserve life by hygienic processes as to raise the average nearer the maximum, and so to use the years given us as to develop the image of God implanted in us.

Of the descendants of Cush it is said that Nimrod was a mighty hunter, and that he built Babel, Erech, Accad and Calneh in the land of Shinar. Further, it is said all were of one language and one speech. They used their unity in concentration upon the work of building a city and a tower. The tower was to reach unto heaven. The fact that this area had been flooded, with the consequent destruction of life, and that no doubt the traditions concerning this catastrophe were still well preserved, must have led to this human scheme for the preservation of life. It shows likewise a departure from the true line of the righteous with which Jehovah was keeping in contact, and a resort to the ingenuity of man as a substitute for the will of Jehovah. This has been a tendency common to the human race: a desire to set up some system of human philosophy, ethics or religion by which man hopes to escape the dangers and troubles that beset him in this world, and by which he hopes to climb to heaven or another existence beyond death.

God placed His stamp of approval upon the principle of unity when He said: "Behold, they are one people, and they have all one language; and this is what they begin to do: and now nothing will be withholden from them, which they purpose to do." But God confounded the speech of the Babelites so that their unity was broken by dissension, and they left off building the city and the tower. It follows, therefore, that there are two essential elements to the success of human organizations, especially in religion: that of unified effort and conformity to the will of God. What might not the church accomplish in the world to-day if Christians were of one language and one speech; that is, were one in their message? But this unity is not possible upon human platforms; for in the making of creeds and confessions of faith, the language of the church became confused and its membership scattered. Unity may be had upon the Bible, and the Bible alone. We must build the tower according to the blue-print of God. Because of difference of belief, and, therefore, of interest, do people split up into groups, each going "unto his own." These groups, in turn, seek isolation for the purpose of propagating their dogmas; thus are they separated, giving rise to new nations and governments. The coming to America of dissatisfied citizens of Europe and the British Isles in the main gave rise to the United States. In like manner may we conceive of the dispersion of tribes from the plains of Shinar, giving rise to the various peoples found later in adjacent regions.

As God was carrying out His purpose in the antediluvian period by keeping in direct contact with a righteous line, and through it preserving the faith, so in the postdiluvian period the genealogy of the righteous line is traced from Shem, one of the sons of Noah, through Arpachshad, Shelah, Eber, Peleg, Reu, Serug, Nahor, Terah and Abram. Since there was, no doubt, little within the history of this period bearing directly upon the working out of Jehovah's purpose, the narrative passes over it hurriedly and takes up in greater detail God's dealing with Abram.

CHAPTER VIII.

JEHOVAH'S COVENANT WITH ABRAM

IF hitherto the purpose of God is not plainly discernible, we have now reached a point in the narrative when Jehovah speaks more definitely; it is that of the call of Abram and the covenant made with him.

There is a Jewish tradition not well authenticated that Terah, Abram's father, was an idol-maker, but that Abram, who helped in this work of making and selling idols, did not believe in idol-worship, and used to expostulate with those who came to buy, insisting that men ought not to worship the product of their own hands. Whether or not there is any basis of fact for this tradition, it remains that the only just conclusion from Abram's being called of Jehovah is that his character in actuality and potentiality justified Jehovah in singling him out for the mighty task he had in store.

Terah had three sons—Abram, Nahor and Haran. Haran's children were Lot, Milcah and Iscah. Haran died before his father in the land of his nativity, Ur of the Chaldees. Nahor married Milcah, his niece, daughter of Haran. Abram's wife Sarai had no children, being barren. At the time Jehovah called Abram they all had their home in Ur of the Chaldees. The identity of Ur has commonly been made in recent times with Mugheir, a city which was anciently known as Uru, noted for its temple of moon-worship, and probably for its manufacturing interests. But since we can not be sure of its identity, we are left in ignorance as to the religious and social customs of the home of Abram, father of the Hebrew nation.

"Now Jehovah said unto Abram, Get thee out of thy country, and from thy kindred, and from thy father's house, unto the land that I will show thee: and I will make of thee a great nation, and I will bless thee, and make thy name great; and be thou a blessing: and I will bless them that bless thee, and him that curseth thee will I curse: and in thee shall all the families of the earth be blessed."[1] What Jehovah promised to Eve in the words, "Thy seed shall bruise the head of the serpent," is here being reiterated: "In thee shall all the families of the earth be blessed."

We notice first that in this call of Jehovah to Abram there is the demand to leave his land and his kindred. Again, we see the process of separation, not by destruction of environment, but by removal from it. Just as the principle of Genetics functions in the biological realm in the selection of good seed or good individuals among animals, and in their separation for reproduction, so it operates in the field of social and religious development. Abram, if he remained in Ur, would be handicapped by the old environment. It would mean attempts at reformation, rather than a regeneration. There are times when the old can not be sufficiently reformed, and there needs must be a beginning anew.

In half a century after the last American colony was settled the people threw off the yoke of allegiance to Great Britain and began immediately a new and untried form of government, which began to function from the beginning; but it took a century and a quarter for some of the nations of Europe to put aside their kings, and that only through the influence of a world war. Even to-day notice with what travail and pain these nations struggle to make permanent their reforms.

---

[1] Gen. 12: 1-3.

How much faster have the principles of Protestantism progressed in the isolation made possible by their being transplanted to American soil. The change from Catholicism to Anglicanism in England is but a slight step removed, while the progeny of the Puritans and Pilgrims who came to America is a radical change. The old often makes greater contribution to the world's need by giving birth to the new, rather than by making some changes in answer to the demands of reform. Many a man or woman adds to the world's progress by breaking with the old environment, by leaving the home of parents to give themselves unreservedly and unhindered to a new cause.

Among the heroes of earth who have turned their backs upon the old way, who have, no doubt, with sorrow seen the old home and kindred fade from view as their footsteps carried them farther and farther away, is the great patriarch Abram. It was not, and is not, an easy task, that of turning one's face toward the new and the untried. To chart one's course by principle, not by the footprints of others; to keep one's eyes on the goal of a high ideal, and not upon the stakes set up by the achievements of others—demands great fortitude. This is the work of the heroic, this is the call of the truly great. Such was the challenge of Jehovah to Abram.

As has been cited, God has preserved thus far a righteous line. His purpose was, as it seems, nothing more than to keep in touch with man as his teacher, that righteous seed might be preserved from generation to generation. Now the scene shifts, and Jehovah begins a more specific plan for the fulfillment of His promise. He says to Abram, "I will make of thee a great nation." Hitherto His plan was to work through a righteous line; now it is more specific, since He is to work through a particular nation or people. Now it is not a question of preserving intact an unbroken line of individuals, but the task of preserving in faithfulness a nation. Hence, later on, the second main item of the covenant is enunciated by Jehovah: "Unto thy seed will I give this land." For how could God preserve and maintain a nation without giving to them a permanent home in which they might be kept separated from the contaminating influences of other peoples?

The covenant is, in its principal items, threefold: Abram is to head a great nation, a numerous progeny; second, Jehovah is to give this nation a land, or country; third, through the seed of Abram are all the nations of the earth to be blessed.

If, then, we are to read the *purpose of God* as seen in the Old Testament, we should keep in mind God's covenant with Abram. First, on Abram's side, he is to receive, in terms of this world, the two blessings, that of a great progeny, and a country in which to dwell. On Jehovah's side He is to have a righteous nation, who shall furnish the earthly parentage for His Son. They shall cradle the great religion, even Christianity, which is to furnish a blessing for all the families of the earth, even a salvation through Christ, offered to all the world.

The Abrahamic covenant is, therefore, the key that unlocks the treasure-house of the Old Testament. It is the candelabra that lights us through its great cathedral halls. It is the twilight which bespeaks for us the rising of "the sun of righteousness with healing in its wings."[1]

In leaving Ur, Abram took with him Sarai, his wife; Terah, his father, and Lot, his brother Haran's son. The first lap of the journey was made in going northwestward from the lower valley of the Tigris-Euphrates to upper Mesopotamia, or a region known as Paddanaram, to a point called Haran. Here Terah died. Since afterward we find in this same region the family of Nahor, Abram's other brother, we may infer that, in the lifetime of Terah, Nahor journeyed thither to visit his aged father and the family of Abram. Perhaps he

---

[1] Mal. 4:2.

11

liked the country, and, as a consequence, took up his residence there.

Why temporary residence was taken up at Haran, we are not informed, but it was not the permanent home God had in mind for this infant nation. Hence, some time after Terah's death, Jehovah called again to Abram to move on. It is not enough to make a start in the right direction. Attainment comes by completion of the journey.

Abram now continues his journey with Sarai, his wife, and Lot, his brother's son, with all their servants and substance, into the land of Canaan. The first stop is made at Shechem, by the oak of Moreh. Next, he pitches his tent between Bethel and Ai. But Abram journeyed on toward the south, a region known by the Hebrew word *Negebh,* meaning "south country." It is here mentioned that "the Canaanite was then in the land." This term is used generically to include all the tribes of Canaan, such as the Canaanite proper, the Hivite, the Girgashite, the Jebusite, *et al.*

"And then was a famine in the land; and Abram went down into Egypt to sojourn there." The valley of the Nile, as is well known, being irrigated by the overflow of the river, was not subject to drouth as much as regions round it depending upon rainfall. Hence, when there was drouth in Canaan there would most generally be plenty in the valley of the Nile.

This land of plenty, lying so near to the home of God's people, was a constant menace to their spiritual welfare. Here they obtained plenty for the sustenance of themselves and their cattle. Here they accumulated slaves, and silver and gold; but here also they were in affliction, in persecution and in slavery; here they learned to worship false gods. In like manner the world of physical plenty lies near the church to-day; while there is much of this world's goods to be had, there are the dangers of death concealed among them. When one goes to the world to trade, how easy to feel the constraint of the ways of the world, how easy to comply with its terms in order to prosper.

While Abram figured that he was going to a land of plenty, yet he realized that he would come within the power of an unscrupulous king; for in those days it was no uncommon thing for a king to add to his harem, by whatever means necessary, such women as attracted his lustful eyes. The Bible narrative here depicts, as is peculiarly distinctive of this book, the weaknesses of men's characters as well as their commendable traits. Abram, foreseeing the danger, planned with Sarai the deception of passing her off as his sister. Thus Abram committed himself to deception, and subordinated the higher duty of maintaining his position of husband and protector to the desire to obtain physical substance and to protect his own life. But Jehovah graciously interferes, and Pharaoh is plagued to the extent that the truth is brought out; just how we are not told, but, perhaps, during the twelve months' purification that a princess must undergo before being taken as a wife, Sarai may have disclosed the truth of her relation to Abram. For this deception Pharaoh justly expels Abram from the land.

Abram now returned to Canaan, going first to the *Negebh*, or South Country, and then on to the region of Bethel and Ai. It is said of Abram that he was very rich in cattle, in silver and in gold. Lot, who made the journey to Egypt with Abram, was also rich in flocks and herds and tents.

Among the early settlers of any country, when all are in more or less meager circumstances, when there are but few stock to roam the range, when nature responds bountifully and room is plentiful, there is found the smallest degree of friction. But when the flocks and herds grow larger, while the "commons" grow smaller, and with increased population, the question of how to deal with one's neighbor becomes more important. Thus the increased wealth of

Abram and Lot brought friction. Relations of mutual love and kindredship that obtained when they were poor were now strained because of the wealth which they commanded.

Here we must place on the debit side of Abram's account a very commendable act. While he was the one chosen of God to fulfill His purpose, and Lot had prospered with the prosperity secured to Abram, yet he said to his nephew: "Let there be no strife between us. There is the whole land before you; take your choice. If you go to the left, then I will take the right. If you go to the right, then I will take the left." Lot, disclosing his selfish character, looked upon the valley of the Jordan, with all its fertility, and chose that which he judged would make for his commercial advantage. And Lot was right if his purpose was that of raising stock and making money. But had he figured on a place in which the environment would be good for rearing a family, he might have chosen differently. What is a good place for raising hogs is not necessarily a good place in which to rear boys. Serious as is the charge, it must, nevertheless, be admitted that too often there are parents who select a place to live for its advantages for stock-raising rather than for advantages for the rearing of children. Lot pitched his tent toward Sodom. The time came when Lot was glad to escape from Sodom with his life, though he left empty-handed.

Among other possessions secured by Abram in Egypt was a handmaid for Sarai named Hagar. Now, with Hebrew women, the ideal was to be, not only a wife, but a mother. Sarai was denied this latter privilege, being barren, hence she took the course that seemed to be a custom of those days, of giving Hagar to Abram for wife, that he might not be left without seed. Hagar bore a son to Abram, and he was named Ishmael, who, later, marrying an Egyptian princess, gave rise to a people who joined the Arabian nation, thus giving ground for the claim of Mohammedans to be descendants of Abram; likewise a reason for their acceptance of part of the Jewish faith.

While God had promised Abram that his descendants should be as the sand of the seashore for multitude, yet it was not His purpose that the lineage should come by the son of the handmaid. It may seem strange that God should choose a man whose wife was barren to head a great nation. But, stranger still, he waits until Sarai reaches the age when women cease bearing before coming to Abram with the promise of a son. We must remember that Jehovah said: "*I will make of you a great nation.*" How literally this is fulfilled when Jehovah gives to Abram a son born of a woman who was hitherto barren, and was now past that time of life. Hence, it was a matter real to Abram that God gave him a son.

When Ishmael was thirteen years of age and Abram ninety-nine, the covenant of circumcision was entered into with Jehovah. By this fleshly mark were all the males separated unto Jehovah on the eighth day after birth.

Lest we fall into the error of thinking that God had no communication with any other people than Abram and his lineage, it is well to remember the meeting of Abram with Melchizedek, a priest of the most high God. Other instances given later were the relation of God to the prophet Balaam and the coming of the seers from the east to worship the Lord. While Jehovah had a special mission for Abram, He was not confined in His dealings to this one people. Here we have mentioned first the custom of tithing. Abram gave tithes to Melchizedek.

From the birth of Isaac, and the entering in more fully of His promise to make of Abram a great nation, God changed his name to Abraham, meaning "father of a multitude." Sarai's name was changed to Sarah. The name "Isaac," meaning to laugh or to mock, was given to Sarah's child, because she laughed at the idea of her bearing a son. Sarah's skepticism was expressed at the time the Lord's messenger was making the promise to Abraham.

When Isaac reached the marriageable age, the problem of securing a suitable wife for him confronted Abraham. No doubt that Abraham, known in that country as a wealthy sheik, could have secured the daughter of some royal house among the nations of the land, but Abraham was looking to the religious side of life, and, therefore, sought a union with a people more nearly akin to him in religious faith. He sent his servants with proper presents to the land of Paddan-aram, to the family of his brother Nahor, and there they obtained Rebekah for a wife for Isaac.

To this union were born two sons, twins—Esau, the firstborn, and Jacob. Esau was a hairy man, and a hunter. He seems not to have been ambitious to prepare himself for the leadership which, by custom, fell to the firstborn; but rather absented himself for long periods of time from the business of his father and the cultural environment of the camp, and spent his time in the uncertainties of the chase. Jacob, on the other hand, appeared to be ready to accept any chance for advancement that might offer. While the means used by Jacob and his mother for securing the birthright are not commendable, yet through this shift was the more able man selected for the great mission that lay before this people. Jacob's character could be purified by the consuming fires of trial and tribulation, but, changing the figure, Esau offered no foundation on which to build.

Esau carelessly and thoughtlessly, so far as the religious future of his people was concerned, took to himself wives of the people round about. By a providential set of circumstances Jacob is sent to the same land and to the same people to whom Abraham's servant went to secure a wife for Isaac.

On the lonely road toward Paddan-aram, Jacob, fleeing from the wrath of an angry brother, lay down at night to sleep, with the earth for a couch and a stone for a pillow. Here Jacob dreamed. In the dream Jehovah appeared unto him above a ladder connecting earth and heaven, on which angels were ascending and descending. In His message to Jacob, Jehovah renewed the covenant made with Abram, and renewed with Isaac, that He would make his descendants a multitude, that He would give to him and his seed the land wherein he lay, and that his seed would bless all the families of the earth. Thus are the terms of the contract kept prominent, and each succeeding patriarch is required to obligate himself to its fulfillment.

Not always to the mighty, the great, as men count greatness, do the visions of higher and nobler achievements come, but rather to those whose heads are pillowed upon the stones of hardship, who through tribulation and sacrifice look up to God to receive the beckoning call to a holier service.

Soon Jacob falls in love with the beautiful Rachel, daughter of Laban, Rebekah's brother. Jacob enters into agreement with the mercenary Laban to labor seven years for Rachel. After his seven years of toil he met with the same treachery he had practiced upon his father years before. He found, when the wedding-veil was removed, that he had married the weak-eyed Leah. But Jacob, not to be denied the wife of his choice, labors on seven other years.

In the land of Paddan-aram there were born to Jacob, his wives and their handmaids, eleven sons and one daughter. By the ages of the children it may be supposed that the text indicates that Jacob was in this land about forty years; fourteen were spent in labor for Leah and Rachel, twenty as assistant, or hired man, and six tending cattle for a share. By the blessing of Jehovah, Jacob prospered, which brought on him the envy and malice of his brothers-in-law. This friction, together with the shifting, changing business methods of Laban, caused Jacob to become so dissatisfied that he took his family and all his belongings and started back for the land of his father.

Jacob left home as Jacob, meaning deceiver, or supplanter, having deceived his father and cheated his brother. To flee from a wrong is not to right it. Using the words of the poet, with antithesis of meaning, he who wrongs his neighbor wrongs three— himself, his neighbor and me. That is, a wrong is not only a wrong to man, it is a wrong to God. So Jacob, on his return, was struggling with himself over the problem of his relation to Esau. He first wrestled or contended with God, and then, in the humility of repentance, sent to Esau an expression of his repentance and desire for reconciliation. Because of his righting the wrong first with God and then with his brother, he emerged from Jacob the deceiver into Israel a prince, or contender with God.

Jacob, in preparing for the meeting with his brother Esau, arranged his line of march in such a way as to expose to danger first that which to him was of least value; first the flocks and herds, then the handmaids and their children, next Leah and her children, and lastly, and consequently most dear to him, were Rachel and Joseph. As with Jacob, so with every one, what is exposed to danger last is held to be most dear. When men endanger character for money, it is because they hold money to be more valuable than character, and *vice versa*.

Jacob takes up residence at Shechem, but when the insult to Dinah was avenged by Simeon and Levi, Jacob thought it necessary to move on toward the south. Jacob began again the worship unto Jehovah at Bethel, and ordered all idols to be put away. While the religion of Laban's family was, no doubt, akin to that of Jacob's, yet an element of idolatry was present as evidenced by the teraphim Rachel brought with her from her father's house. These were, of course, disposed of according to the order of Jacob at Bethel.

In their journey southward, they came to Ephrath, or Bethlehem, where Rachel died, having given birth to her second son, Benjamin. Israel was now the father

of twelve sons, two each by the handmaids, six by
Leah, and two by Rachel, while Leah bore to him one
daughter, Dinah. Of these, Joseph, the firstborn of
Rachel, his most beloved, came to be the special object
of his affection. For him he made a distinctive gar-
ment, and by him sent orders to the other sons as they
cared for the stock. Jehovah likewise gave him distinction by revealing to him in dreams signs of coming
events. This favoritism bred envy and hatred in the
minds of Joseph's brethren and led to his being sold
to an itinerant band of tradesmen who, in turn, sold
him to Potiphar, an officer in the army of the Egyptian
Pharaoh.

Men can not always choose their environment or
determine the circumstances that surround them, but
they can choose their reaction to the environment. Joseph could not prevent his becoming a slave, but he
could determine the kind of slave he would be. And,
since character is the thing most worth while, it is
better to be a good slave than a wicked master.

Joseph withstood the temptations of his master's wife, but she, in resentment, falsely charged
him to Potiphar, for which he was cast into prison.
Even here his conduct was such as to lead to promotion.
Through the chief butler, whose dream Joseph had
interpreted while he was in prison, he was brought
to the attention of Pharaoh. Pharaoh had two dreams
which his wise men were unable to interpret. Then it
was that the butler, now restored to his position,
thought of Joseph and his ability. Pharaoh, therefore,
had Joseph brought before him and made known to
him his dreams. Joseph disclaimed any power within
himself to interpret dreams, but told Pharaoh that God
would give him an answer.

The dreams, when interpreted, meant that in Egypt
there were to be seven years of plenty, followed by
seven years of famine, and that the years of famine
would consume the years of plenty. Whereupon Joseph
admonished Pharaoh to select a man for the purpose of

supervising the storing of grain in the years of plenty, that the people might have food in the years of famine.

Now, these events occurred, according to the monuments, under the Hyksos, or shepherd kings. These are generally conceded to have been foreigners upon the throne of Egypt, and, therefore, not averse to showing favor to another foreigner. Pharaoh, being impressed by the message and person of Joseph, chose him to carry out the plan indicated in the interpretation. That such an office of authority and trust existed in the Egyptian Government is evidenced by an inscription on an altar, excavated at Am, in the suburbs of Zoan, which reads: "Chief of the chancellors and royal seal bearings." Thus did Joseph come to a place of power in the kingdom second only to Pharaoh. Those making objection to the story of Joseph's rise to power from such an obscure station in life may have the privilege of trying to explain how other obscure personages obtained like positions of power in other countries, such as that of a housemaid coming to the throne of China, or undertake to meet the charges of the Dearborn Publishing Company, made through their publications, of the positions of power held in our own country by Jews.

Joseph then took up the task of building granaries and storing grain. The common Egyptian tax of one-tenth was doubled at this critical time, and from the surplus in the period of prosperity there was stored up the precious food that would mean life to the people in times of dire need. Thus the providential hand of God provided not only for the Egyptians, but for His own people who came later to buy grain.

As in the days of Abraham, so in the time of Jacob, when famine came to Palestine, Israel sent his sons to the storehouses of Egypt to buy grain, but kept Benjamin, his youngest son, at home. All these years the aged patriarch had mourned Joseph as dead, and hence he clung the closer to Rachel's other son.

How the scene has shifted! Joseph, the helpless youth, sold by his brothers into slavery for twenty pieces of silver, is now next in power to the Pharaoh. He who was once in their power now holds their very lives in his hand. Because of the shifting relations of life, how much more necessary it is "to do unto others as we would have others do unto us." Joseph tested his brethren by a process which tended to bring out the best that was in them. Accusing them of being spies, he held Simeon in trust for the fulfillment of their promise to bring Benjamin with them on their next visit. Israel's consent to take Benjamin was secured only on the personal security of Judah.

The sight of Benjamin, his own brother in the flesh, was, to Joseph, the latchstring that opened the door to all his pent-up emotions. He sought the secrecy of his chamber to hide his emotion. Continuing to conceal his identity, which his brethren, naturally, had not suspected, because they thought him dead, or in some obscure position as a slave, he had his divining-cup hidden in the sack of Benjamin. Thus, on pretense of believing him to have stolen it, he had him arraigned. What consternation there was among the brothers; while stoutly disclaiming the charge of theft, they invited search with such confidence as to say, "With whomsoever it be found, let him die, and we will be my lord's bondmen," when, behold, the cup was found in Benjamin's sack. Then it was that the noble trait of sacrifice was manifest in the appeal made by Judah to allow himself to be substituted for Benjamin. By this test did Joseph bring out in the character of his brothers, by the act of Simeon kept in bond, and that of Judah offering himself a substitute for Benjamin, a sacrificial spirit as having displaced the selfish one. Now, instead of harboring murder in their hearts, they were ready to give themselves a ransom one for another. As a suiting climax to this great drama of life, Joseph made his identity known, and magnanimously overlooked their vile act toward him, and interpreted it as the hand of God directing him into a position of great service.

Then did the sons of Israel depart for Canaan with the blessing of Joseph and the invitation of Pharaoh to come and dwell in the land of Egypt. With sacks filled with grain, with not one of their number missing, they reached their home to greet their aged father with the strange, but joyful, news that Joseph was not dead, but living, and that he wore the royal robes of a monarch. How deeply the heart of Jacob was stirred by this message can best be inferred from his own words: "It is enough; Joseph, my son, is yet alive; I will go and see him before I die." So, with the assurance of God that He would be with him, Jacob took all that he had and moved to Egypt.

While it is not the province of man to say what God could or could not have done in a given set of circumstances, except He make it known, yet where He has not spoken we may reason as to probabilities. Had Israel remained in the land of Canaan, multiplying in numbers to the extent of becoming a menace to the tribes already there, the chances would appear to have been against them in maintaining a residence in that country. But, within the shelter of such a kingdom as Egypt, and under the protection of a friendly ruler, they could live in peace and increase in number without molestation. Then, when sufficiently great in numbers, they could be organized into an army of conquest. While the ruler of Egypt was friendly, being a foreigner, the Egyptians themselves looked down upon the Hebrews, hence a social isolation resulted which helped to keep this people a distinct nation rather than to be absorbed and lost.

Joseph presented his father at the court of Pharaoh, and, while Jacob was the sheik of a shepherd tribe, he, nevertheless, realized his nearness to God in that he pronounced a blessing upon the king. In like manner, long centuries after, did a man of God stand before an earthly king, and, forgetting his own chains, he sought to free the king from the bonds that held him away from God.

Israel was given the land of Goshen, a portion of land in the lower Nile Valley. Here in this fertile region they kept their flocks and herds and increased in numbers and in property, sheltered and protected by the friendly hand of a powerful king. Here Jacob died and was embalmed, according to the Egyptian art of embalming. Perhaps one of the greatest funeral corteges recorded in all history is that which followed the embalmed remains of the patriarch Jacob to the tomb of his fathers, the cave of Machpelah, at Hebron, in the land of Canaan. When this cave is fully explored it will be a matter of great interest to know whether or not there is found an embalmed body that bears the marks of that ancient period.

Before the death of Jacob, Joseph brought his two sons, Manasseh and Ephraim, to his father to receive his blessing. Jacob wittingly changed hands as he blessed, then predicting the ascendancy of Ephraim, the younger. Again, there is choice by merit among the people of God. Jacob also called about him his own sons and gave them a forecast of their future. Of Judah he said: "The sceptre shall not depart from Judah, nor the ruler's staff from between his feet, until Shiloh come; and unto him shall the obedience of the peoples be." It is generally construed that Shiloh refers to Christ, therefore, in this language, God is making known the continuity, not only of a nation, but of a family in the ruling office. Such became true, from the beginning of the rule of David, who was of the tribe of Judah, in an unbroken line to the coming of the Lord.

CHAPTER IX.

EGYPT AND THE EXODUS

FOR many centuries the valley of the Nile, with its great pyramids, was a source of curiosity to the traveler and student. The curious markings on sarcophagi and obelisks, as well as upon the pyramids, were an enigma. Scholars long wondered whether these were but meaningless decorations made by a savage people, or whether they constituted a language.

In 1799, while the army of Napoleon was in Egypt, a French engineer was excavating near Rosetta, at the mouth of the Nile, and hit upon a strange stone. It was of black granite, three feet nine inches in height, two feet four and one-half inches in width, and eleven inches in thickness. On this stone was carved a three-fold inscription. At the top could be seen parts of fourteen lines of characters resembling those seen on obelisks, temples, etc. In the middle were thirty-two lines of another species of script, and at the bottom were fifty-four lines, twenty-eight of them complete in Greek uncial letters. The Greek could be easily read, and it told the story of the inscription. This monument was set up 195 B. C. in honor of Ptolemy Epiphanes by the priests of Egypt assembled at Memphis because he had canceled the back taxes due from the sacerdotal body. They further praised the monarch for his piety and just rule, his acts of generosity and his noble sentiments.

After the Greek was read it was immediately surmised that the other two parts of the inscription told the same story, and so began the long, weary effort through twenty years of fathoming this ancient message with its curious characters. Finally, Champollion, a Frenchman, acquainted with Coptic, and a student of Egyptian, discovered the long-lost combination to the language of the ancient civilization of the Nile.

With this key scholars began to read the history of this nation which had left such interesting monuments. While historical criticism was discrediting the Bible, saying it had no corroborating witnesses, declaring Herodotus to be the "father of history," with a date of about 600 B. C., this stone unearthed and read opened the pages of a new-old book, and gave evidence of a civilization in the valley of the Nile, extending back to 5000 B. C. Hence, the entrance of Israel into Egypt, instead of antedating history, was brought much nearer, comparatively, to modern times. While reference is made to the date 5000 B. C., it must be remembered that scholars are not agreed in their theories of Egyptian chronology. The Greek writer Manetho, a native priest (cir. 250 B. C.), has left a chronology of Egypt containing thirty-one dynasties, and this has become the main basis of the computations of modern scholars. This has been variously dated from 3180 to 5613 as the time of the first dynasty. Bible chronology is somewhat obscure, but it can not be justly criticized by a secular one that is not yet firmly established. The kettle should be careful in speaking about the pot.

When all this history of a people bearing such close relationship to the people of the Bible is read, naturally there will be an eagerness to learn if there is any corroborating testimony to the Bible account. George A. Barton, in his work, "Archæology and the Bible," has assembled a valuable collection of material on the subject, and references will be made to some of the items he sets forth.

First, as to names, he notes that Thothmes III., of Egypt, who made extensive conquests in Asia, 1478 to 1446 B. C., records the name of a city, captured in Palestine, as Ya-'-k-b'-ra, the Egyptian equivalent of

Jacob-el. Another name in the lists of Thothmes is by many scholars taken to be Joseph-el.

Another Egyptian monument contains the story of the two brothers. The matter of interest in this is that the wife of the elder brother tempts the younger in like manner, as did the wife of Potiphar tempt Joseph, which gives evidence that such an event was not without its historical basis in those days.

Since the regularity of the Nile to overflow its banks has led to some questioning concerning the long period (seven years) of drouth related in the Genesis account, it will be very interesting to note an Egyptian inscription bearing on this point. This inscription was found cut on a rock between the island of Elephantine and the First Cataract. It relates how King Zoser, of the third dynasty, who began to reign about 2980 B. C., nearly twenty-eight hundred years before the inscription was written, appealed to Khumn, the god of Elephantine, because of a famine. Part of the inscription reads: "I am very anxious on account of those who are in the palace. My heart is in great anxiety on account of misfortune, for in my time the Nile has not overflowed for a period of seven years. There is scarcely any produce of the field; herbage fails; eatables are wanting." In the same inscription there is mention of the building of storehouses. This from an Egyptian source is surely not biased in favor of the Mosaic record. Another inscription bears upon the preparation for famine. A part of it reads: "I collected corn as a friend of the harvest-god. I was watchful in time of sowing. And when a famine arose, lasting many years, I distributed corn to the city each year of famine." Professor Barton says: "Baba claims to have done for his city, El-Kab, what Joseph is said to have done for all Egypt. His statement affords striking evidence of the historical reality of famines in Egypt, and of such economic preparation for them."

It is said that when Joseph was called to appear before Pharaoh, he shaved himself. Now, the monuments show that it was the custom of Egyptians to cut both hair and beard except when mourning for relations. According to Wilkinson, when the Egyptian artists intended to convey the idea of a man of low condition, or a slovenly person, they represented him with a beard. This harmonizes, too, with the Biblical statement that "the Egyptians might not eat bread with the Hebrews."

Another striking coincidence is the entrance of Joseph into Egypt when a foreign king was on the throne. This invasion of foreigners at a time when the Egyptian nation was weak enabled the invading people to rule for several centuries, especially over lower Egypt. As to who these people were, scholars are not certain. They are thought to have been partly Semitic. Some names seem to indicate Syrian descent. The common worship of Set, by both Hyksos and Hittites, have led some to believe the invaders were Hittites. The fact that Hittites were found as far south as Hebron in the days of Abraham would lend confidence to this view. But, of whatever people these Hyksos kings, so named by Manetho, they, being foreigners, were friendly to other foreigners.

Now, in Exodus, it is said: "There arose a king who knew not Joseph." How pointedly may this refer to the time when the foreigners were expelled and the native kings were restored to the throne. How natural it would be for this people who were looked down upon by the Egyptians to become the object of their hatred. How they would begrudge them the fertile region they occupied, and fear their presence as an aid to any enemy who might seek to invade their domain. Besides, they were increasing in such numbers as to become themselves a menace to Egyptian peace.

Hence it was that this king who knew not Joseph began to inaugurate means by which to weaken these foreign tribes and retard, if not altogether stop, their growth. As one means they were enslaved to the Government and put to work on public buildings under

12

overseers who became their taskmasters. Furthermore, the midwives were instructed to make way with the male infants. The Israelites were used in making brick, which then was done by the sun-drying process. They used straw to make the mud more adhesive. This was at first furnished them, but as the task was made harder they were called upon to turn out as many brick as before, and at the same time gather their own straw. It is a significant fact that in the ruins of some of those ancient buildings there have been found brick without straw. How natural for men pressed with excessive burdens to have accepted opportunity to evade this added task. On this point we here quote the forceful language of Ira W. Price ("Monuments and the Old Testament," p. 117): "The strawless brick in these walls almost re-echo the rigor of Pharaoh's words when he said: 'Ye shall no more give the people straw' (Ex. 6:17), but demanded the former tale of bricks. About these old walls we can see and handle some of the handiwork of the Hebrew slaves. Could those old ruins but speak, what tales of hard taskmasters, of bloody lashings, of exhaustion and distress would they reveal to us!"

During this period of the iron rule of an Egyptian king there was born to Amram and Jochebed, of the tribe of Levi, a son. Since the midwives feared Jehovah more than Pharaoh, these male infants escaped, but the mother of Moses feared to keep him about the house, lest in some way the anger of the king might fall upon him. So she made for him a basket and hid him among the reeds at the edge of the river, and stationed Miriam, his sister, near as guard.

Again we have in the Egyptian monuments' striking confirmation of similar practices to those recorded in the Bible. Part of one inscription reads: "My lowly mother conceived me, in secret she brought me forth, she placed me in a basket of reeds, she closed my entrance with bitumen, she cast me upon the river, which did not overflow me."

As has been previously stated, it is the opinion of the writer that the providential hand of God was guiding in the affairs of Israel, and that it seems more reasonable that a handful of people could be grown into a multitude with less difficulty within the sheltering bounds of a powerful and friendly nation. Likewise is God's hand to be seen in the providential circumstances of the life of Moses. When the time came for the birth of the Israelitish nation, there would be needed a leader equipped, not only with natural ability, but with the most adequate training the time could afford.

The story is familiar to all: how the daughter of Pharaoh, going to the river to bathe, found the infant hidden by the Hebrew mother. And how her motherly instinct was stirred with pity, and she not only saved the child, but adopted him as her own son. This led to his being taken, later, into the royal household and given training "in all the wisdom of the Egyptians."

This point of the narrative was once a favorite one for the attack of the "Higher Critics." It was once their contention that the period of time at which Moses was pictured as performing his task was one in which there was not sufficient learning for Moses to have obtained such an education as he was supposed to have had. Here, as elsewhere, the "cocksureness" of the "critics" has been put to ridicule by the facts brought forth by the archæologist.

The Rosetta Stone unlocked the history of the Egyptian, and, in like manner, the Behistun Inscription, found by Rawlinson in the Zagros Mountains, became the key to the Babylonian-Assyrian cuneiform. By the translation of the Behistun Inscription, the language of the Babylonians and Assyrians gave to the world the history of these ancient peoples. Even in the age of Abraham there was an advanced civilization with a highly developed code of law, as is preserved to us in that of Hammurabi. The records of the Assyrian and

Babylonian kings show that these countries were constantly making invasions into what they called the "Westland," and held in subjection the Palestinian nations. To these, of course, they carried their learning even to the point of establishing a postal system, according to M. G. Kyle ("Deciding Voice of Monuments in Old Testament History"). This shows that learning was common. Moreover, Palestine was the meeting-place of the civilizations of the East and that of the Nile. Furthermore, the Tel-el-Amarna letters discovered in Egypt have conclusively shown that there was correspondence carried on between various nations, tribes and kings in the court language of the Babylonian-Assyrian cuneiform, a very difficult language to learn. Professor Sayce ("Monument Facts and Higher Critical Fancies," p. 40) says: "The Mosaic age, therefore, instead of being an illiterate one, was an age of high literary activity and education throughout the civilized East. Not only was there a widespread literary culture in both Egypt and Babylonia, which had its roots in a remote past, but this culture was shared by Mesopotamia and Asia Minor, and more especially by Syria and Palestine." Further, he says: "The civilized world was a world of books, and a knowledge of writing extended even to the classes of the population who were engaged in manual labor." And, again: "We have learned many things of late years from archæology, but its chiefest lesson has been that the age of Moses, and even the age of Abraham, was almost as literary an age as our own." Certainly, testimony could not be stronger, and we are not only led to believe that Moses could have received a reasonable amount of learning, but would be more surprised had he not become educated in such an environment of culture. The former position becoming untenable, there is left to the "critic" the only alternative, that of denying that Moses ever was in Egypt. Of course, men can not be prevented from denying even that their own bodies exist.

Jehovah has His future leader educated in the court school of Pharaoh. He sends him to Pharaoh to be trained, but not to obtain his interpretation of life. It is all right for young people to go to the world to obtain its training in science, literature, history and art, but it is a dangerous place to go for the ideals of life. The dominant note in the life of Moses was: "By faith, Moses, when he was grown up, refused to be called the son of Pharaoh's daughter; choosing rather to share ill treatment with the peopl: of God, than to enjoy the pleasures of sin for a season; accounting the reproach of Christ greater riches than the treasures of Egypt: for he looked unto the recompense of reward."[1] With this, the true goal of life, Moses combined the wisdom and training of the Egyptians to become one of the greatest figures of all history. Had he obtained also his ideals and purposes—his philosophy of life—from the Egyptian schools, the story would have been different. So, to-day, many a life is wrecked or misspent by obtaining, not only a training from the world, but an interpretation of life as well. Many a teacher of secular subjects, such as that of science, misjudges his task and begins to set up standards of life for the student rather than furnish him with the tools of research, which task is more properly his sphere of activity.

Vigorous in mind and body, at the age of forty, Moses seemed stirred with the ambition to free his people from the cruel bondage to the Egyptian taskmasters. So incensed was he at the injustice that he was provoked to the point of slaying an Egyptian. This would naturally lead, one would think, to gratitude on the part of his kinsmen and cause them to follow his leadership. But, to his surprise, upon making an attempt at settling a dispute between two of his own countrymen, they resented his interference, and were ready to turn him over to the authorities for killing the

---

[1] Heb. 11: 24-26.

Egyptian. The time was not yet ripe for the birth
of this great nation. Perhaps the people were yet too
much enamored of the fertile pastures in which they
grazed their flocks and herds, and of the abundance
of edibles later referred to as the "fleshpots of Egypt."
Perhaps, too, Moses, though trained in the learning of
the Egyptians, and physically fit, was not yet sufficiently tested in the school of hard knocks. He was
the pampered child of a royal princess, brought up
at the court of a king. What did he know about
necessity? Would he stand under the pressure of hardship? Would he keep faith when all about him went
wrong? Not in days of sunshine, ease and prosperity
are men tried, but in times of adversity, strife and
misfortune. Was Moses a fitting leader? Who could
know? So he is sent to another school for another
forty years. It seems hard, it is true, but when the
great strain of the vast tons of traffic come upon the
bridge, how fortunate it is that men took more time
to temper the steel. So it is with the great movements of mankind: when the destinies of nations hang
in the balance, what a blessing that a leader has been
so prepared as to be properly fortified when the time
of stress comes.

Moses fled to the land of Midian, married there a
daughter of the priest Jethro, and joined himself to
his father-in-law in the occupation of a shepherd. In
this humble life Moses spent forty years. No doubt,
during that long period, he began to resign himself to
a fate of obscurity; his ambition was waning, and his
hopes of a career of leadership were disappearing. But
at the time when the human call was at low ebb, there
came the call of God.

While tending his flocks in the desert near Mt.
Horeb, Moses turned aside to see why the fire in the
bush did not consume it. Accompanying this testimony
came the voice of Jehovah out of the midst of the
bush. The voice of the bush, when it is consumed, is
but the voice of nature, which one may assign to God

and another to material, but there can be no question concerning the voice that comes from the bush that is not consumed; it is the voice of God.

Here Jehovah made known to Moses the mission He had in store for him—that of leading the tribes of Israel out of Egypt and unto the land of Canaan. The confidence which Moses possessed at the age of forty had been tempered with the sober thought of forty years of meditation. Now he hesitates and counts the cost, when once he was ready to enter in unhesitatingly. When, therefore, Jehovah calls on him to go to the elders of Israel with the message that the God of their fathers had appeared unto him, he says: "But, behold, they will not believe me, nor hearken unto my voice; for they will say Jehovah hath not appeared unto thee."[1] Then it was that God gave to him the two items of miraculous testimony, the staff becoming a serpent, and the leprous hand. So we see God did not ask the people then, nor has He at any time since, called on man to believe anything for which He has not given sufficient proof. The Christian religion is not based upon credulity, but upon intelligent faith.

Moses further pleaded his incapacity by claiming his inability in public discourse. This objection Jehovah overcame by substituting Aaron for this part of the work. While Moses, the meekest of men, was no doubt giving an honest estimate of himself at this time, we may well credit him with a great amount of progress in this department of service as we meditate upon some of the great religious discourses he delivered to Israel in the closing days of his ministry. No patriarch surpasses him in the exaltation of God and exhortation of His people to faithful obedience.

When next Moses appears before his people it is with the credentials of God, and his first task, we can easily see, is to convince the elders of Israel of his com-

---

[1] Ex. 4: 1.

mission. This accomplished, he and Aaron turn to
Pharaoh. It is said that God hardened the heart of
Pharaoh. It is also stated that Pharaoh hardened his
own heart. From one viewpoint, the writer attributes
all things to God; from the other, it is the act of
man. As has often been said, the same force that
softens wax hardens clay. The same message that
softened the hearts of Israel and led them to obey,
hardened the heart of Pharaoh and led him to opposition.

While Pharaoh used violent means to prevent the
increase in number of this foreign people, yet he
found them very serviceable in forwarding his business
enterprises. Hence, it was necessary to cause their
presence to be a plague in order to force his consent.
How true to human nature is this reluctance to progress. We must suffer loss before we protect the man
by covering the machine; we build fire-escapes after
great holocausts; we tardily put lifeboats on ships
after tragical catastrophes. Too often we lock the barn
door after "old Dobbin" has been spirited away.

How far the miraculous entered into the feats of
Pharaoh's wise men we do not know. We do know
that magic and sleight-of-hand have reached a higher
degree of proficiency among the Oriental nations than
in our own. How far God used the natural forces to
work out His purpose we do not know. That such
events excluding the death of the firstborn were common occurrences in Egypt, is claimed by the critical
writer, H. Preserved Smith ("Old Testament History,"
p. 57). But that the plagues were timed according
to the words of Moses and Aaron were convincing proof
to Pharaoh that it was not just a "happen so."

When, at the death of the firstborn, the wail of
sorrow went up from the whole land, even from the
royal household, the adamantine heart of Pharaoh
was moved. The people gladly bade the foreigners
depart, and, with presents, hastened their journey.
But the god of greed had a tenacious hold upon the

heart of the king, and he soon repented of his act and hurriedly sent his army in pursuit of the fleeing Israelites.

When the last great plague, the death of the first-born, was called, the people of Israel were directed to slay a lamb and sprinkle the blood upon the doorposts, that the death angel might pass over that household. Where the blood was not found the firstborn would not be spared. Thus arose that sacrificial feast known as the Passover.

Moreover, that night they were to remain dressed, their loins girt about, their staffs in hand, ready for departure. They were to eat of the paschal lamb with unleavened bread, having their bread-troughs packed. They were not to wait for the dough to rise. The directions indicated haste. In like manner, men, when found in the Egypt of sin, are called upon to make haste in their exit therefrom, and not to tarry to make money, to secure success in business or in a profession, but first of all to get out of the realm of sin. And, as Israel must have the blood upon the doorposts, so are we now called upon to have "our hearts sprinkled from an evil conscience, and our bodies washed with pure water." [1]

It is said (Ex. 1:11) that the children of Israel built for Pharaoh the cities Pithom and Raamses. For some time it was known by an Egyptian papyrus that Raamses was built by Rameses II., and, in 1884 Dr. Naville discovered the ruins of Pithom. Further investigation showed that this city was built by the same ruler, thus identifying Rameses II. as the Pharaoh at whose court Moses was brought up. It seems clear that the Exodus took place while the nineteenth dynasty was still reigning. Now, the geography of that period is well preserved to us by the monuments, and Professor Sayce, an authority on this subject, says: "History fixes the exodus of Israel in the epoch of the nineteenth

---

[1] Heb. 10:22.

dynasty, and geography assigns it to the same date. To that period, and that period alone, does the geography of the Pentateuch apply.''[1] Further, he says: ''We may rest assured, 'criticism' notwithstanding, that Israel was once in Egypt, and that the narrative of its flight under the leadership of Moses is founded on sober fact.''[1]

Israel journeyed eastward from Succoth in the land of Goshen to Etham, thence southward to a point before Pi-hahiroth, between Migdol and the seas. It is said God led them not by the way of the land of the Philistines, lest coming to battle with this warlike people they should become discouraged and turn back. This, then, turned them southward instead of following round the seacoast, which was the nearer route. Another reason unexpressed might have been that at this time the Egyptians had a strong wall from the Red Sea to the Mediterranean, following about the line of the Suez Canal. Guarding this wall were strong fortresses. Hence, Jehovah steered the march of Israel to a point at which they would not be expected to attempt an exit. Still further, to the mind of the writer, is the purpose of God to bring the people to a point where their own efforts are futile, and it would be apparent to all, both Israelites and Egyptians, that it was the hand of Jehovah that delivered His people, typifying that greater deliverance spoken of in Tit. 3: 5, 6: ''Not by works done in righteousness, which we did ourselves, but according to his mercy he saved us, through the washing of regeneration and renewing of the Holy Spirit, which he poured out upon us richly, through Jesus Christ our Saviour.'' Hence it was that Moses commanded the people to stand still and see the salvation of the Lord. They were to stand still to see the way of salvation provided, but to march forward when the sea was opened. In like manner we stand still in the presence of the sacrifice of the Son

---

[1] "Monument Facts and Higher Critical Fancies," p. 96.

of God for our salvation, but when, to us, the way is opened, we are to march forward in obedience to the command of our Lord.

When the waters were parted by the wind and the miraculous power of God, Israel marched through. But what was salvation for Israel was death for the Egyptians. Just as the lens is convex to one, but concave to him who takes the opposite side, so the gospel, that saves the one who accepts, is condemnation to him who rejects.

One thing distinctly peculiar to Biblical history is its typification of other events to come. Moses was a type of Christ, Egypt a type of the world of sin, and the Exodus was a type of salvation in Christ. The children of Israel listened to the message of Moses and beheld his miraculous testimony. Tired of the burdens of Egypt, and enamored of the promised land, they, believing Moses, turned from their old life to follow him into a new country. The act of deliverance was completed when they were "baptized unto Moses in the cloud and the sea," and stepped out on the other shore no longer subjects or slaves of Pharaoh, but free men in the Lord. In these acts we have the picture of a man who, believing in Christ, turns away from the old life of sin and completes the act of translation into a new kingdom and relationship by being baptized into Christ to arise to walk in a newness of life.

With every connection to the old life broken, Israel takes up the journey toward Canaan. The first point mentioned is Marah, so called because of the bitter water. How this, too, typifies the bitter experiences that so often meet men soon after their entrance upon a new life. Here Moses is called upon to manifest his power of enduring faith, for which God had prepared him in the forty years of trial in the land of Midian. It is strange, but true, that men soon forget the sweets of life to make complaint about the bitter. So Israel, soon forgetting the wonderful deliverance from Pharaoh by Jehovah, begins to complain that

Moses has led them into the wilderness to perish. After the bitter waters came the murmur for food. In answer to their cry, God sends quail and the manna.

The law given concerning the manna was that a single day's ration was to be gathered at a time, except that on Friday, the sixth day, they were to gather a double portion, that no gathering be done on the Sabbath, or seventh day. By this method Jehovah teaches them daily dependence upon Him. This principle is reiterated by Jesus in the model prayer given to His disciples in the words "Give us day by day our daily bread." Some of the Israelites, lacking faith in Jehovah and thinking perhaps in terms of a modern slogan, "Safety first," gathered more than they needed for the day, and laid it by in store for another time. But they found to their dismay, when they went to use it, that the manna was spoiled. Many a fortune assembled without trust in God has been found to react on man in a faith that has been spoiled with the worms of materialism and greed. "Seek first the kingdom of God and his righteousness, and all these things will be added unto you."[1]

At Rephidim the Israelites met the warlike tribe of Amalek and were forced to fight in order to continue their journey. We must remember that the contract God made with Abram, Isaac and Jacob called for the making of a great nation, for a country in which they were to dwell, and that through their seed were all the nations to be blessed. Hence, the carrying out of this program was the only hope of salvation for all the nations of the earth, and Jehovah would thus be justified in helping Israel against any opposing nation. On this ground Jehovah gave Israel victory. While Joshua led the forces in the valley, Moses upon the mountain held up his hands toward God.

Moses met his father-in-law Jethro, and from him received the suggestion to put judges over thousands, judges over hundreds, over fifties, and over tens, reserving only the most important matters to come before

---

[1] Matt. 6: 33.

himself. This is perhaps the first appellate court system
of which there is any mention in history.

Continuing their journey, the tribes of Israel come
to Sinai. Here it is, some fifty days after their exit
from Egypt, Moses ascends the mount and receives
the law from the hand of God. This people have a
distinct form of government in that the purpose being
worked out through them is primarily religious and
their life and activity are directed by Jehovah. This
we call a theocracy.

CHAPTER X.

THE MOSAIC LAW

WHILE Israel camped before Sinai, God called Moses up into the mount and gave him the words of the covenant. As Moses delivered these unto the people, they answered with one voice and said: "All the words which Jehovah hath spoken will we do." Thus the covenant made with Abraham and renewed with Isaac and Jacob was here voluntarily entered into by all the people.

While Moses tarried in the mount to receive the full instructions from God, the people lapsed into idolatry. This was speedily punished, and the people renewed their promise of obedience.

Because the religious feature in the life of Israel is the one of outstanding importance, the ritual of worship naturally receives a place of prominence. The unification of this nation was not obtained by centralization in a center of civil importance such as the capital cities of nations to-day, but in a place known as the meeting-place of Jehovah with the people. Hence there were given instructions for the building of a tabernacle and its accompanying ritual. Because of this central feature we will first consider the tabernacle and then the law proper.

The tabernacle was a wooden structure forty-five feet long (using the estimate given by some scholars that a cubit is about eighteen inches), fifteen feet wide, and fifteen feet high. It had a court round about inclosed by a screen or drapery seven and one-half feet high. The court was one hundred and fifty feet long and seventy-five feet wide.

The tabernacle proper was divided into two compartments, the first the Holy Place, occupying two-thirds of the entire length, and the inner room, the Holy of Holies, being a cube fifteen feet each way. The tabernacle was made of boards and had four coverings, the first of fine twined linen, the second of goats' hair, the third of rams' skins dyed red, and the fourth and, outer covering was of sealskins.

There were two curtains to the tabernacle, one a screen for the opening and the other the veil that separated the Holy Place from the Holy of Holies. This latter corresponded to the inner veil of the temple that was rent in twain at the death of Christ.

By the instruction of Jehovah the tabernacle was to be set up always facing the east. It occupied a central position in the camp of Israel, the tribes pitching their tents three each, to the east, to the south, to the west, and to the north. The tribe of Levi, which had been taken by Jehovah in lieu of the firstborn, which belonged to Him by redemption, was divided into three parts for the care of the tabernacle; the Kohathites, having charge of the furniture, camped on the south; the Gershonites, having charge of the cloth parts, camped on the west, and the families of Mirari, having charge of the wooden parts, camped on the north. Moses, Aaron and Aaron's sons camped to the east of the tabernacle before the entrance into the court, the place appropriate for the leaders.

In the court nearest to the entrance stood the Altar of Whole Burnt-offering. It was to this altar that the people brought their animal and vegetable sacrifices, which, by the hand of the priest, they sacrificed to Jehovah. The animal sacrifices were classed as the whole burnt-offering, the sin-offering, the trespass-offering, and the peace-offering. The whole burnt-offering was so named because all the animal was burned except the skin, which was reserved to the priest. The other offerings required that only parts of the animal be burned, while other parts were to be reserved to the priest, and still others to the one offering the sacrifice. When the priest waved or heaved the breast or shoulder of the victim before the Lord, it was called a wave or heave offering.

Between the great altar and the tent of meeting was the Laver. This was filled with water. Here the priests were commanded to wash their hands and feet, and, at times, the whole body, before entering the tabernacle, or before they ministered at the altar in offering a sacrifice by fire unto Jehovah.

Within the Holy Place, and on the south side, stood the golden candlestick. This lamp was seven-fold in its branches, and the whole was one beaten work of pure gold. This was fed by the olive oil furnished by the gifts of the people, and the priests were to light the lamps each evening.[1]

On the north side of the Holy Place, opposite the candelabrum, stood the table of showbread, on which the priests were to put twelve fresh loaves each Sabbath, taking away that which was on the table for their own use.

Just before the veil at the west end of the Holy Place stood the Altar of Burnt Incense. Hereon were the priests instructed to burn sweet incense morning and evening.

Within the Holy of Holies was the Ark of the Covenant. This was a box made of acacia wood, overlaid with pure gold. It was covered by a mercy-seat of pure gold. At the ends of the mercy-seat were the two cherubim, made of beaten work of gold. The cherubim, facing each other, spread their wings, covering the mercy-seat.

Now let us turn to a consideration of the typology of this, no doubt the most unique institution in all the history of religious worship. It was not only a form

_____
[1] Ex. 30: 7, 8.

of worship of great significance to the worshipers who used it, but it foreshadowed in its make-up the great Christian system, of which it was but a forerunner. It then served the double purpose of furnishing the Israelites with the highest form of worship possible to them, and at the same time was, by the index finger of type and shadow, pointing to the great universal system of Christianity, which was to be the fulfillment of the covenant.

First, there is the threefold division of the institution—Court, Holy Place and Holy of Holies. Taking it, then, as a type of the whole extent of life religiously, the Court typifies the world, the Holy Place the church, and the Holy of Holies, heaven. A man at the age of responsibility is to pass through each of these relationships in his approach toward God, from the world to the church and through the church to heaven.

In this approach toward God the first object encountered is the Altar of Sacrifice, so it is that men must accept the sacrifice of Christ, as the animal was substituted for the Israelite, and, in turn, be ready to offer himself a living sacrifice. If there is one word in the Christian religion more significant than any other, it is sacrifice. The blood of the offering is the crimson thread that runs through the whole fabric of salvation from Abel's first lamb until the last man shall have accepted salvation through the blood of Christ. The antitype of the altar is Christ and His cross.

Next was the laver, the place provided for the priests to wash. Washing is a means of cleansing the body, and is used as a symbol of cleansing when applied to spiritual matters. As the priests, after making the sacrificial offering, were required to wash before entering the Holy Place, so men, after accepting the sacrificial offering of Christ, are required to wash in the waters of baptism before entering the church. "Let us draw near with a true heart in fulness of faith, hav-

13

ing our hearts sprinkled from an evil conscience; and having our bodies washed with pure water."[1]

As priests were anointed with a holy anointing oil, which was not to be poured upon man, nor to be counterfeited by him, in like manner are those who become obedient to Christ to be anointed with the gift of the Holy Spirit. This gift is not for the world, neither are His words to be counterfeited by men. "For no prophecy ever came by the will of man; but men spake from God, being moved by the Holy Spirit."[2]

The candlestick which lighted the Holy Place was a type of the Bible, which is the source of light for the church. The seven-fold division may be represented by the following seven-fold division of God's word: Law, Prophets, Psalms, Gospels, Acts, Letters, Revelation. The Gospels, giving the life of Him who is the center of all history, constitute the antitype of the central stem of the lamp.

The twelve loaves on the Table of Showbread undoubtedly had reference to the twelve tribes of Israel. The literal meaning of the term is "bread of faces, or presence," thus Israel, through her priests, was to be constantly before Jehovah. In the bowls, or flagons, was kept wine. Here were the two elements to be found on the Lord's table. As the twelve loaves represented the presence of Israel, and were to be eaten only by the priests, so the one loaf on the Lord's table is symbolical of the presence of Christ, and may be eaten only by His disciples.

The Altar of Incense, though an altar, had no offerings of blood made upon it. It was rather an altar of praise, adoration, prayer and thanksgiving. They who had access to this altar had first to make the bloody sacrifice on the Great Altar in the court. He who would have access to the Father in prayer by the name of Christ must first accept Jesus as his sacrificial offering. This altar was a type of prayer.

[1] Heb. 10: 22.
[2] 2 Pet. 1: 21.

Now, we find the Altar of Burnt-offering in the court, so must the sacrifice of the old man and the washing of baptism occur as acts preliminary to entrance into the church. In the Holy Place are the candlestick, the table of showbread and the altar of incense. Their corresponding antitypes, the Bible, the Lord's table and prayer, are found in the church.

In the Holy of Holies there was but the one article of furniture, the Ark of the Covenant. In this ark were kept the tables of stone, the pot of manna, and Aaron's rod that budded. This ark that kept the people in remembrance of their covenant with Jehovah also preserved the law, kept the memorial of their dependence upon Him, and contained the reminder that the tribe of Levi was officially chosen to minister before the Lord. The mercy-seat would remind them of the salvation of Jehovah, and the absence of natural light was made up for by the blazing glory of the presence of God as it rested upon the mercy-seat between the cherubim. So in heaven there will be no need of sun, moon or stars to light it, for the presence of God will give it light.

As said before, the tabernacle occupied a central position in the camp of Israel. When they took up their march the ark of the covenant was in the midst of the line, symbolizing the presence of Jehovah as the central thing and first in importance.

In the last verses of Exodus it is said that a pillar of cloud rested over the tabernacle by day and a pillar of fire by night, in all their journeyings. When the cloud lifted they journeyed, but when the cloud was not taken up they remained in camp. Thus Israel journeyed by the direction of Jehovah. The church of Christ is as well equipped in its journey by the words of the Holy Spirit, the word of God. Had the church journeyed as the cloud (the Bible) directed, we would not now have the awful sinful condition of division. Certainly, the only way out of a divided Christendom is for all eyes to be turned on the word of God. Laying aside all human directions in the way of creeds and confessions of faith, let us look, for our marching orders, to the last will and testament of Him who redeemed us.

Israel did not hold councils and vote upon the way to journey. Oh that the church of God would be just as loyal to His holy Word!

The law proper will be treated briefly under three heads: The Fundamental Law, the Religious Code and the Civil Code. This division[1] is not found in the law itself, but is convenient for study.

The Decalogue, or Ten Commandments, bears to the whole law about the same relation as does our Constitution to the laws of the United States. Here were grouped the main principles that are fundamental to the existence of true religion, of life and society. Therefore, these constitute the fundamental law.

The Decalogue naturally divides itself into two main divisions, that of duty to God and duty to man. The second division may be subdivided into two parts, that of one's duty to home and duty to society. Duties to God are specified in the first four Commandments, three of which are put in the negative form: Thou shalt have no other gods before me, thou shalt make no graven images, thou shalt not take the name of God in vain, and remember the sabbath day to keep it holy.

Duty to the home is given in the Fifth Commandment, "Honor thy father and thy mother." Duties involving the welfare of others are prescribed in the negative Commandments, Thou shalt not kill, thou shall not commit adultery, thou shalt not steal, thou shalt not bear false witness, and thou shalt not covet.

These were given in the abbreviated form by Christ in the statement, "Love the Lord thy God with all thy heart, and with all thy soul, and with all thy mind," and "Thou shalt love thy neighbor as thyself. On

---

[1] "Class Notes on Sacred History," J. W. McGarvey.

these two commandments the whole law hangeth, and the prophets.''

Fundamental to religion is faith in the one true and living God. As the universe must have the one being back of it in which it alone can have unity, so that one being must be recognized in man's faith in order to the true expression of his religious life. It would be no more contradictory to our system to hold a duality or multiplicity of points of center to a circle, than to hold to a duality or multiplicity of beings as ultimate and eternal.

Belief in the one God can be maintained only by abstaining from the making of images, for this leads to idolatry and polytheism. This belief can be had in its true form only through reverence, awe, adoration and love, and by acts of worship and the expression of gratitude in benevolence. Hence, the commandments not to take the name of God in vain, and to keep one day sacred unto worship and praise.

The first institution to be established was the home, and within its sacred walls are centered all the issues of life. That the proper conditions here make for the welfare of all other human institutions is apparent to all. The thing most essential to the maintenance of this fundamental element of society is obedience to parental authority. Without it the home is but little more than a name.

When we come to society in general, we find that the things most sacred, and therefore to be protected, are life, property and morals. In the remaining portion of the Decalogue, we have these provided for in mandates against theft, bearing false witness, adultery, murder and covetousness.

It is not the purpose here, and lack of space forbids, to undertake an exhaustive study, or even a brief treatise, of all the law, but to give a summary of the most salient features of the Mosaic code. Standing out prominently in the worship and life of Israel was the priesthood. As previously mentioned, God, having

redeemed the firstborn, took in their stead, in order to
have them separately grouped, the tribe of Levi. This
tribe was, therefore, set apart to the Lord and sanc-
tified to His service. Within the tribe of Levi the
family of Aaron was chosen to the priesthood proper,
thereby setting up a distinction between the Aaronic
priesthood and the Levitical priesthood. Of the family
of Aaron, Aaron himself became the high priest, and
was to be succeeded in office by his eldest living son.
All other members of the family of Aaron were priests.
These were consecrated to their office by special cere-
mony, and were clad in special vestments. They who
entered upon the duties of the sanctuary were to be
physically without blemish.

The priests had for their duties the offering of the
sacrifices, the lighting of the candlestick, the burning
of incense, and the care of the table of showbread.
In brief, their task was the ministration of the worship of Jehovah. The duties of the Levitical priesthood
seemed to have been that of waiting upon the Aaronic
priesthood, performing the menial tasks in the care of
the tabernacle and its furnishings.

The Levites were supported by a tithe from the
other tribes, and they, in turn, gave a tithe. The
priests, as already noted, had certain parts of the animal sacrifices reserved unto them, and were permitted
to eat the bread that was removed each Sabbath from
the table of showbread. That the ministry of to-day
should give themselves wholly to religious work, and be
supported by the church, seems to be the meaning of the
Scripture in the words, ''Even so did the Lord ordain
that they that proclaim the gospel should live of the
gospel.''[1]

The worshipers were restricted in their animal sacrifices to those of cattle, sheep and goats; of the birds,
doves and pigeons. There were the whole burnt-offer-

---

[1] 1 Cor. 9: 14.

ing, the trespass-offering, the sin-offering and the peace-offering. Of fruits or grain there was the meal-offering.

The burnt-offering was perhaps an expression of the worship of the whole people, and was made at regular intervals, while the other offerings were more individual in their nature, and were made in atonement for some specific sin or transgression, or as an expression of the individual's worship and praise.

Of great importance in the religious life of Israel were the sacred feasts and holy days. On the fourteenth of Nisan (latter part of March or first part of April) began the feast of the Passover. This lasted one week, and contained two holy days, days in which the people were to do no labor. The principal thing in this feast was the eating of the paschal lamb with bitter herbs and unleavened bread. It commemorated the passing over of the death angel and the deliverance from Egypt.

Fifty days after the Passover was held the Feast of Weeks, or the Feast of the Firstfruits, called now by the Greek name "Pentecost." It was celebrated by offering the firstfruits, and contained one holy day. It is usually regarded as commemorating the giving of the law, as it is thought to have been about fifty days from the time the Israelites crossed the Red Sea until they reached Sinai.

The next in order was the Feast of Trumpets, held on the first day of the seventh month. The feast was celebrated by added sacrifices and the blowing of trumpets. It probably commemorated the "New Year's Day" of the civil year. This feast contained one holy day.

On the tenth day of the seventh month fell the Day of Atonement, another holy day. On this day only of all the year the high priest, wearing the vestment peculiar to his office, went into the Most Holy Place to make an offering before Jehovah for his sins and the sins of the whole people. Besides the offering of the blood of a bullock, there were taken two goats, upon

which hands were laid in token of the transmission of
the sins of the people to the victims—one to be sent
away into the wilderness, the other to be slain. These
were typical of Christ's bearing away the sins of the
world. As Aaron, the high priest, and his successors in
office entered in once each year into the Holy of Holies,
having made an offering for himself and all the people,
so Christ, our great High Priest, entered into the most
holy place, even heaven, once and for all having
offered Himself a sacrifice for the sins of every man.

The last major feast was that of Tabernacles, which
included two holy days. This feast was begun on the
fifteenth day of the seventh month, and continued one
week. At the coming together for this feast, the people
dwelt in booths. Thus, in after years, the people commemorated the itinerant life of their fathers in the
wilderness. At the three major feasts of Passover, Pentecost and Tabernacles, all the males were required to
appear before Jehovah.

There were certain vows recognized as sacred to
Jehovah, and upon which He granted certain blessings.
The most prominent was the one known as the Nazarite
vow. The conditions of this vow were: Total absti-
nence from wine and strong drink, letting the hair
grow, and no contact with a dead body. Upon the
keeping of this vow there seems to have been given
special powers, such as the extraordinary strength of
Samson and the prophetic ability of Samuel. The
one making the vow might be freed from it by a
certain ceremonial process.

Idolatry and human sacrifice were to be severely
dealt with. The one who should "give of his seed
to Molech" was condemned to death. Those who
turned to play the harlot after wizards, and those
having familiar spirits, were to be cut off from Jehovah's people. There was to be no compromise with
idolatry, human sacrifice or witchcraft.

Certain animals, birds and fish were specified unto
Israel as clean, which they might use as food, and from

which they were to make their offerings. Those animals
were clean which split the hoof and chewed the cud.
This law had a sanitary significance as well as a
religious one. They were further prohibited from eating the fats of certain animals such as were used in
making sacrifices, and to abstain wholly from the eating
of blood. Since the blood was accounted the life, this,
no doubt, was one reason for the latter prohibition.

Among the ethical precepts is that of demand for a
love of truth. "Thou shalt not take up a false report:
put not thy hand with the wicked to be an unrighteous
witness."[1] The laws teach inflexible justice. "Neither
shalt thou speak in a cause to turn aside after a multitude to wrest justice: neither shalt thou favor a poor
man in his cause."[2]

Kindness to strangers is demanded. "A sojourner
shalt thou not oppress: for ye know the heart of a
sojourner, seeing ye were sojourners in the land of
Egypt."[3] Kindness to enemies was also enjoined in
the law. "Thou shalt not hate thy brother in thy
heart: thou shalt surely rebuke thy neighbor, and not
bear sin because of him. Thou shalt not take vengeance, nor bear any grudge against the children of
thy people; but thou shalt love thy neighbor as
thyself."[4]

In treatment of the deaf and blind, it was commanded: "Thou shalt not curse the deaf, nor put a
stumbling-block before the blind; but thou shalt fear
thy God: I am Jehovah."[5] In the language, "Thou
shalt rise up before the hoary head and honor the face
of the old man,"[6] respect for the aged was demanded.
Concerning honesty and integrity in business was the
law covering weights and measures: "Ye shall do no
unrighteousness in judgment, in measures of length, of

---

[1] Ex. 23: 1.
[2] Ex. 23: 2, 3.
[3] Ex. 23: 9.
[4] Lev. 19: 17, 18.
[5] Lev. 19: 4.
[6] Lev. 19: 14.

weight, or of quantity. Just balances, just weights, a just ephah, and a just hire shall ye have."[1] There was no legitimate place in Israel for the profiteer.

Because Israel was a chosen vessel through whom God was to bring His Son into the world, the nation must be kept distinct in government. Hence the civil, as well as the religious, affairs must be directed by Jehovah. Now that the kingdom of Christ is here, it is a matter of appealing unto individuals to accept Christ regardless of what kind of government they may be under. The society of Israel was strictly of this world, no matter what its heavenly type and significance, while Jesus said, "My kingdom is not of this world."

Of the civil statutes, perhaps the one of greatest importance is that relating to marriage. Concerning the first pair, God said: "Therefore shall a man leave his father and his mother, and shall cleave unto his wife: and they shall be one flesh."[2] Jesus makes reference to this statement in the following quotation: "Have ye not read, that he who made them from the beginning made them male and female, and said, For this cause shall a man leave his father and mother, and shall cleave to his wife, and they two shall be one flesh? So that they are no more two, but one flesh. What therefore God hath joined together, let not man put asunder." This language is clear and explicit, showing that God initiated marriage in the monogamic form, and that His will was that it continue so. This is the construction put on it by Christ Himself. The fact that the people of God practiced polygamy is not proof that it was acceptable to God, much less commanded by Him. He tolerated it as He did slavery and the use of strong drink, until the system of Christianity might be inaugurated and work its overthrow.

There were strict laws governing sexual relations, with severe penalties. There were prohibitions against

---

[1] Lev. 19: 35, 36.
[2] Gen. 2: 24.

incest, adultery, bestiality and sodomy. See Leviticus, chapters 18 to 21. The fact that the death penalty was assessed against so many illegal sexual relations goes to show how much importance God attached to purity in the relations between men and women.

The general law of inheritance was that the property should go to the sons, the eldest receiving double portion, because it was through the males, and especially the firstborn, that the stability of family, tribe and nation was to be preserved. Because of the great loss of men in the families of Manasseh, son of Joseph, a special decree was made giving the daughters the inheritance.[1] The inheritance of the firstborn seems to have been by special decree, bestowed upon the descendants of Joseph, contrary to the law,[2] in that Ephraim and Manasseh shared equally with the other tribes in the division of the land of Canaan.

Provision was made to protect the poor by the prohibition of usury, the law protecting essential property against pledges, the laws for the prompt payment of hire, etc. Men were not to reap the corners of their fields, leaving this part for the poor to glean as did Ruth in the field of Boaz. Every seventh year the land was to lie fallow, and the poor were allowed to glean from that which grew voluntarily.

Since the ownership of property, especially that of land, seems ever to have been the basic element in the stability and continuity of families, tribes and nations, another law was given which furthered this end. Incidentally, it was a law of inheritance, and one protecting the poor. Every fiftieth year was to be a jubilee year. In this year the land was to lie fallow, and every man's possession was to be returned to him. There might, through the greedy processes of others, be a centralization of the ownership of large tracts of lands in the hands of a few, but, on the jubilee year, there was a redistribution. There was also the law of

---

[1] Num. 27: 1f.
[2] Deut. 21: 15f.

redemption. "And the land shall not be sold in perpetuity; for the land is mine; for ye are strangers and sojourners with me."[1]

As previously stated, slavery was tolerated, but governed by strict laws, which guaranteed to the bondsmen certain rights. There was secured to the Hebrew servant the right to go out free the seventh year, or, if he chose, he might become the permanent property of his master. Servants might be freed because of inhumane punishment. By law there was to be no return of fugitive slaves.

As to crime, the law was quite severe, specifying about seventeen different acts that carried the death penalty. They were: Murder, murder by a vicious animal, kidnapping, idolatry, blasphemy, false prophesying, witchcraft, adultery, rape of a betrothed or married woman, whoredom, incest, sodomy, bestiality, smiting or cursing a parent, stubborn rebellion against parents, rebellion against the judges, and swearing away a man's life. While this may seem a large number of capital crimes, yet J. W. McGarvey cites ("Class Notes on Sacred History," p. 121) the fact that as late as 1743 there were in Great Britain one hundred and forty crimes punishable by death.

For manslaughter there was a form of trial. If a man inadvertently slew another, or if with purpose of heart he killed him, he might flee to the nearest refuge city, of which there were six—three each on either side of the Jordan. There the matter was looked into, and if it was found that the man was not guilty of murder he was to remain within the walls of the city until the death of the high priest. If he was guilty, he was turned over to the avenger of blood, who slew him. If the man confined within the walls of the city wandered therefrom, and was found by the avenger of blood, the latter might slay him.

---

[1] Lev. 25 : 23.

There were laws covering theft, maiming a man or animal, against breach of trust, removing landmarks and sundry other matters. There were military exemptions granted to those who had some matter of importance pending, such as an unfinished house, a new vineyard, from which they had not yet obtained a crop, or betrothal to marriage. The fainthearted were also excused.

This code has been the basis of much of the legislation of modern nations, and while, in many of its details, it was fitted unto its day and time, it contains all the basic elements of present-day legislative systems. Under its administration a great nation came into prominence known for its wealth, its wisdom and its power, a nation admired or feared by all the others round about it. By this law was the nation preserved that gave in its lineage the Saviour of mankind to the world, and through Him the offer of salvation to all the nations of the earth.

CHAPTER XI.

WILDERNESS MARCH

AFTER receiving the law, and the construction of the tabernacle, Israel set forward on the journey from Sinai toward Canaan. The order of march given by the instructions of Jehovah was as follows: Judah, with whom the sceptre was to be, bore the colors and marched in front, followed by Issachar and Zebulun; next came Gershon and Merari, bearing the tabernacle; these were followed by Reuben, Simeon and Gad; then the Kohathites set forward bearing the Ark of the Covenant and the other furniture of the tabernacle; then followed Ephraim, Manasseh and Benjamin; and last of all came Dan, Asher and Naphtali.

As they journeyed Moses met Hobab, his brother-in-law, and said to him: "We are journeying unto the place of which Jehovah said, I will give it to you; come thou with us and we will do thee good; for Jehovah hath spoken good concerning Israel."[1] Hobab replied: "I will not go; but I will depart unto mine own land and to my kindred." But Moses further urged: "Leave us not, I pray thee; forasmuch as thou knowest how we are to encamp in the wilderness, and thou shalt be to us instead of eyes. And it shall be, if thou go with us, yea, it shall be, that what good soever Jehovah shall do unto us, the same will we do unto thee."

What a great call Hobab refused. It was the call to help carry out the plan of God—a call to service.

---

[1] Num. 10: 29f.

Hobab, as do many others, went back to his own land and kinsmen and fell into obscurity, while the name of Moses has become immortal. Hobab had the opportunity to help guide Israel through a land with which he was familiar, and then to have a share in the land that flowed with milk and honey. So men are being called to-day to help steer others through the world under the leadership of Christ, and then join in the blessings of the heavenly Canaan.

It is said that Miriam and Aaron spoke against Moses because of the Cushite woman whom he had married. Since Zipporah, the daughter of Jethro, was of the Midianites, it is thought by some scholars that Moses' first wife was dead, and he had married again, this time taking to wife a descendant of Ham. Whatever the facts as to the wife of Moses, it was evidently but an occasion for Miriam and Aaron to give expression to their growing jealousy of the power of Moses. For this complaint against God's leader, Miriam was stricken with leprosy, and, of course, must be quarantined. This necessitated a delay in their journey. In like manner the petty jealousies of Christians, criticism of preachers' wives, and other insignificant matters, are allowed to bring the leprosy of sin upon some, and through their sin a delay in the onward march of the kingdom of Christ. The covetousness of power, with its malicious accompaniments, is a source of great evil to the church.

Following the complaint of Miriam and Aaron, the tribe continued their march and came to the wilderness of Paran. Here Jehovah commanded Moses to send men, one man from each tribe, to spy out the land of Canaan. The men were selected and charged to go throughout the land to judge of its fertility and see how many people dwelled therein, their mode of life and military equipment. This they did, spending forty days on their mission.

Upon their return to camp, ten of the twelve made a favorable report as to the desirability of the country, but they reported adversely as to the possibility of its conquest, saying that the people lived in walled cities, and were mighty of stature. "We were in our own sight as grasshoppers, and so we were in their sight." But Caleb and Joshua urged the people to go up at once, saying, "We are well able to overcome it."

Now, Jehovah needed no information as to the land He had selected for His people, but it was a test for the tribes. Were they ready to go in and take it? They were in their own sight as grasshoppers, might, in one sense, be a proper state of humility, but, in their computation, they left out Jehovah. Surely they had already viewed sufficiently the power of God to deliver them, but here again their faith wavered; and how many lives are thus halted in the upward march to better things because they leave God out in their calculations. God was ready to give them the land, but not without their faithful co-operation, and so, when later they undertook to enter, having at the first rejected Jehovah, He then rejected them because of their lack of faith, and failure was the result of their attempt. Of the number here tested, as to their readiness to take the land, only two—Caleb and Joshua—were among the company who made a conquest of the land. In like manner, when one generation of people is not ready to enter upon a forward movement, progress must wait until a new generation is raised up and trained for the task. Forty years were they condemned to wander in the wilderness —one year for each day they were spying out the land. How precious, therefore, the *days of choice,* for they determine the *years of life.* One day of wrong choosing often makes a year of bad living, while the right choice is followed by a good life.

Again there was dissension in the camp over the question of authority; the other tribes became jealous of the tribe of Levi, because Moses and Aaron, being of that tribe, were directing the march. Rebellion against authority is the worst enemy to any institution, so Jehovah called on them to put up a rod in the tabernacle, one for each tribe, and the one that budded would designate His choice. This they did, and it was found that Aaron's rod had budded; therefore it was to be a matter settled from that time on that the tribe of Levi was the one in authority. This rod was put in the ark of the covenant along with the tables of the law and the pot of manna, that there might be a continual testimony as to the place of Levi among the tribes.

In the midst of the incidents of the journey described is given an account (Numbers 19) of the preparation of the water of purification, or what is elsewhere referred to as clean water. The priest was to take a red heifer without spot or blemish, on which had not come a yoke, and burn her body in a clean (ceremonially) place with cedar wood, hyssop and scarlet. The ashes were to be mixed with running water to constitute the water of purification. Therefore, clean water that was by law sprinkled on vessels and persons for a ceremonial cleansing was not pure water; it must contain the ashes of a heifer slain by a priest and burned in a clean place.

The narrative passes briefly over the death and burial of Miriam, which occurred at Kadesh, and follows with the record of another complaint made by the people against Moses and Aaron. This time it is the complaint about the lack of water, and, as before, the people hark back in their murmurings to the plenty of Egypt from whence they were led, but never mention the taskmaster and his lash. Just so people in the church, when facing some duty, allow their minds to dwell upon the former ease of the world without recalling therewith the dangers of sin.

Jehovah, as before, directed Moses to take the rod, and, having assembled the people, he was to speak to the rock, and water would come forth. This time Moses, aggravated by the continual complaints, said:

14

"Hear now, ye rebels; shall we bring you forth water out of this rock?"[1]   And he smote the rock twice. Notice he said "Shall *we*," etc.   For this Jehovah issued the decree: "Because ye believed not in me, to sanctify me in the eyes of the children of Israel, therefore ye shall not bring this assembly into the land which I have given them."[2]

It was not a small thing for Moses and Aaron to assume the power within themselves, for this would tend to the exaltation of man above God, and to the bowing down before human authority.   It is likewise a matter of grave consequences that men have given their allegiance to great reformers—often wearing their names —rather than to the God whom these great religious teachers proclaimed.   That the language of men, incorporated in creeds and confessions of faith, should have precedence in authority over the word of God, is just as flagrant a sin as that the word of Moses should supersede that of God.   Much of the weakness of the church to-day has come about by the people drinking of the waters of Meribah (waters of strife).   May the spirit of the church be, "Speak, for thy servant heareth."[3]

Having failed to enter the land of Canaan from the south, Israel essayed to pass eastward from Kadesh, rounding the Dead Sea.   Here they encountered the Edomites, who occupied a narrow strip of territory extending from the Dead Sea to the Gulf of Akabah, known as Mt. Seir.   When Israel made application for passage through their land, the Edomites refused and made preparations to offer military resistance. This forced Israel to turn southward to pass around this unfriendly nation.   On the journey southward they came to Mt. Hor, where Aaron died, and was succeeded in the office of high priest by Eleazar, whose two older brothers, Nadab and Abihu, had been

---

[1] Num. 20: 10.
[2] Num. 20: 12.
[3] 1 Sam. 3: 10.

slain because they offered strange fire upon the altar; that is, fire not obtained from the great altar.

Upon being forced to go around the land of Edom, the people murmured because of the wearisome journey, a journey necessitated by their own lack of faith. This time they were plagued with fiery serpents. Upon the repentance of the people and the confession of their sin, Jehovah directed Moses to construct a brazen serpent and raise it up on a pole to the end that every one bitten might look upon this serpent of brass and be healed.

Thus by an image of that which was producing death, through faith in Jehovah manifested by their looking upon the medium provided, they were healed. In like manner God took upon Himself the form of sinful man, was "made sin" and made a "curse" for us, that whosoever looketh upon Him might be saved. "And as Moses lifted up the serpent in the wilderness, even so must the Son of man be lifted up; that whosoever believeth may in him have eternal life."[1] This brazen serpent was preserved, no doubt, as a memento of their salvation from the plague, and in after years, when idolatry had crept into the hearts of the people, King Hezekiah found the worshipers offering incense to it. He therefore broke it in pieces and called it Nehushtan; that is, a piece of brass. This is another illustration of the danger of images.

The Israelites, having encompassed the land of Edom, now moved northward, passing between Moab and Ammon, into the territory east of the Jordan originally held by the Ammonites, but now occupied by the Amorites, who had come from west of the Jordan, expelling the Ammonites. Here the Israelites were met in battle by Sihon, king of Heshbon, and later by Og, the king of Bashan, each of whom they defeated, and thus came to occupy the territory east of the Jordan.

---

[1] John 3: 14, 15.

Now, the Moabites occupied territory to the east of
the Dead Sea. They became fearful of this great
army, and appealed to their neighbors, the Midianites.
Together they joined in an appeal to the prophet
Balaam to come and curse this people. But upon
consulting Jehovah, Balaam was forced to refuse the
request. Upon continued solicitation it was evident
Balaam desired to respond, and Jehovah told him to
go. In the way, at three different points, an angel
of Jehovah blocked the road so that Balaam's beast
was forced to turn aside, at which the prophet grew
very angry. Then the Lord made Himself known
to him and showed him how much more were his
ways perverse to Jehovah than the acts of the beast
were to Balaam.

Here is a case of a man being called upon to
deliver the message according to the desire of the
king, and not according to the will of God. Four
different prophecies did Balaam utter before Balak
and his people, but not one cursing the people of
Israel. "How shall I curse whom God hath not
cursed? And how shall I defy whom Jehovah hath
not defied?"[1] How, in any generation, can man
cause to prosper that which God opposes, or how shall
he bring to naught that which is purposed of God
to be and which has the Lord's blessing?

Now comes the sad message to Moses that his leadership is about to end. Jehovah invites him to
climb the mountain, and from there view the land
which he is not allowed to enter. Here, again, Moses
shows the marks of greatness in that he wastes no
time nor thought upon useless regrets as to entering Canaan, but begins to plan for his successor. To
him it was a matter of supreme importance that the
work to which he had given so many years of his
life should go on to a successful consummation. Men
are tested to-day by very similar circumstances. One

[1] Num. 23: 8.

man may lay the foundation for a great work, but be called upon to step aside and see another build thereon. Can one shift the cloak of authority, power or popularity to another at the proper time and do it gracefully? That is the test.

No doubt, all these years Moses had been tutoring Joshua for a purpose. Especially since the day it was made known to him that he should not enter Canaan, he knew a leader would be needed. Every Moses should have a Joshua. It is not enough to do one's own part in forwarding the cause of Christ or any useful service, but there is the responsibility of seeing that there are faithful men to whom we can consign the Word, "who will be able to teach others also."

Again, the experience of Moses has its spiritual lesson for us in that he climbed the mount, and from it viewed the promised land. So with the elderly Christian who has been climbing the spiritual heights; he has come to have an anticipatory view, in a way, of the heavenly Canaan. He has been drawing nearer and nearer to the ideals held out by our Lord, until he comes to see more and more of the meaning of the Lord's message, for spiritual things are spiritually discerned. "Blessed are the pure in heart: for they shall see God." It is altogether a matter of what kind of eye we look with as to what we see.

Because of the attempt of the Midianites to obstruct the way of God's people, Moses sent the armies of Israel against them and defeated them in a very decisive manner. In this battle were slain the five kings of Midian; also Balaam, the prophet, who lent his services to Moab and Midian against the will of Jehovah.

After the conquest of the territory east of the Jordan, there came a request from Reuben, Gad and the half-tribe of Manasseh to be allowed to take this land as their possession. This request was granted with the provision that they send their

men of war over with the other tribes to help conquer the land of Canaan. This they readily agreed
to do. Later, having fulfilled their promise, they
were allowed to occupy the land of their choice.
Reuben to the south, then Gad and Manasseh to the
north, was their order of occupation.

In the thirty-third chapter of Numbers is given
a list of the points visited in the journeyings of
Israel in the wilderness march. Some have been
identified in our own time, but many have not. Many,
no doubt, were named because of some event connected with that particular stop. Thus many points
are of but little significance. How like the many insignificant points in our journey to-day! How small
of import, how little in value, the many things we
do! Therefore, the call to make important points,
and to make points important. Some men are known
by the places they visited, while some places are known
because certain men visited them. Jesus could do a
great work in the great city Jerusalem. He could
also make the well of Samaria great because of His
sermon to the woman there.

What was accomplished in the forty long, weary
years of the wilderness march? It seems to the
writer, among other things, there were developed three
essential characteristics, characteristics that were
necessary to make of the Israelites a nation capable
of conquering the land to which Jehovah was leading
them. These were faith, courage and obedience. These
characteristics were necessary not only to Israel, but
are necessary to the church to-day, of which the
wilderness march was a type.

Faith is not a static, definite thing, but is subject
to growth and development. The Israelites believed
Moses and Aaron preaching the message of Jehovah,
and, under the added stimulus of their discontent in
Egypt, the people turned from their homes and
followed them out of the land. They did not have
faith enough in Jehovah's promise to feed them day

by day, and hence gathered more manna than was permitted. They believed Moses was to receive the law from God, but their faith was not strong enough to stand forty days of waiting. They believed Moses, by direction of God, was leading them to the promised land of Canaan, but they did not have faith enough to make the attempt to conquer it. Thus years must be spent in deepening the faith of the people in Jehovah. So the Christian's march to-day affords that opportunity to deepen his faith. He may have had faith enough to lead him out of the "Egypt of sin," but he needs yet more to conquer the territory in which he exercises the freedom of will.

The next characteristic is courage. Many a man, no doubt, believes in Christ. with sufficient faith, but has not the courage to follow his convictions. It took courage for the Israelites to turn from their home and material plenty to face the anger of a Pharaoh and defy his authority. It took yet more courage to face the difficulties of the wilderness, the lack of food, the scarcity of water, and the warlike tribes that met them on the way. Many a person can make the start under all the enthusiasm of the contemplation, but when the long, weary day brings the rays of the hot sun, the dust, the steep and stony pathway; when the enthusiasm of the start has lost its force and the goal is not yet in sight to lend its appealing influence—then do the weary feet lag in the journey and courage is needed to keep plodding on. The sorry sight in the church to-day is the travelers that have sat down by the roadside. They say they believe, but they haven't the courage to travel on.

Last, but not least, is obedience. It is not enough to believe nor yet to be courageous. What made the Israelites an efficient army was implicit obedience to Jehovah and their leaders. There is the true way to do a thing, and for things spiritual we are wholly dependent upon God to know what the true way is. Having been shown that way which is Christ, it can be only by obedience to Him that we can have hope of eternal life. The Israelites' greatest sin was that of disobedience, and time after time they were brought to a recognition of this fact only after great loss of life. But they could not have many leaders leading them with various laws in many directions. That would have defeated the very purpose they started out to realize. As Israel had but one head and one authority, so Christ is the Head of the church, and all authority is centered in Him. What the church needs besides faith and courage is an unquestioning obedience to its Head. "It is not ours to reason why. It is ours to do and die."

CHAPTER XII.

POSSESSING THE LAND

THE work of Moses closed with the great discourse in which he gave a recapitulation of the law and exhorted the people to faithful obedience. These discourses are recorded in the Book of Deuteronomy. Moses gave the final charge and commission unto Joshua, his successor. Moses gave commandment to the Levites to put the "book of the law" by the side of the Ark of the Covenant, to be a witness against them.

After producing the song which Jehovah bade him write and teach to the people, Moses was called up unto Mount Nebo, to the top of Pisgah, which is opposite Jericho. From there God showed him the land which He had promised to give to the tribes of Israel. Then it is said that Moses died there, and God attended to the burial. It was not left to man, lest perhaps too much thought and attention be given to Moses, and not enough unto Jehovah, whose new leader was Joshua.

Jehovah now renews His promises with Joshua, and exhorts him to be strong and courageous. All connection with Moses now broken by his death, the people turn to their new leader. With the promised presence and help of Jehovah, Joshua enters upon the duties of his office by instructing the people to prepare for themselves three days' rations, for within that time it is purposed to cross Jordan.

Having sent out two spies who returned with a favorable report, Joshua moved the people from Shittim to the banks of the Jordan, and instructed them to follow the priests who were bearing the ark, allowing a space between of about two thousand cubits. The time chosen by the Lord for the children of Israel to enter Canaan was the time of harvest, when the Jordan overflowed its banks. Here, again, as in the crossing of the Red Sea, it seems the purpose of God to teach man's dependence upon Him for salvation. Here, again, is the materialist and skeptic challenged with the claim of the miraculous power of God manifest among men.

The people stood facing the overflowing Jordan, waiting for the priests to move forward with the ark. The waters ceased not to flow until the priests, by faith, bathed their feet in the swollen current. The people must be ready to follow their leaders, but it takes men of faith to lead the multitude through the waters of difficulty on to the heights beyond. In science it has been the faith of a Columbus, a Galileo, a Newton, a Marconi, an Edison, that has led us on; the faith of American patriots led on through political difficulties; it was the faith of Luther, Calvin, Zwingle, Knox, the Wesleys, the Campbells and others that led us through the troubled religious waters.

As Israel needed the faith of its leaders, as the church in the past made progress when led by men of faith, so to-day it depends on the men who are willing to take God at His word and move forward. While many leaders are tarrying under the influence of materialistic science, waiting for everything to be demonstrated, denying the miraculous, and even questioning the deity of Jesus, no wonder that the waters of difficulty obstructing progress continue to flow, and the church can not move forward.

The faith of Israel's leadership was tested further in that the priests were required to stand in the midst of the stream until the whole congregation had passed over. It was not enough to have faith sufficient to begin the task, but they must abide in faith until the last man passed over. How like this was the faith of Moses during the forty years of the wilderness march. While the faith of the people wavered, Moses stood stedfastly. How like Luther at the Diet of Worms! How like Knox as he defied the Queen of Scotland! How like the Campbells as they stood out for the great principles of Christian unity! Are the leaders of to-day willing to stand by faith in the midst of difficulties, bearing the appeal for the answer to the Lord's prayer that we might all be one, until God's people shall have passed over into organic union? Or shall we drop the "ark of unity" to run out and federate with those who see not clearly the way out of sectarian confusion? Let it be repeated that the church, of all organizations, needs men of faith as its leaders.

Having crossed the Jordan, the people set up a pillar commemorating their passage. They renewed the observance of the feast of the Passover at that time. The manna ceased, and thus God added the further stimulant of necessity to their purpose to make a conquest of the land. In brief, they must now forage in the land or starve.

The first city confronting them was Jericho. Here the Lord further added His testimony to Israel and to the inhabitants of the land that He was directing and helping His own people. The city was not to be taken under ordinary military procedure, but by Jehovah's instructions. The city was to be encompassed once each day for six days, and on the seventh day seven times, ending with a blast of trumpets and a shout by the people. In this manner was the city taken. Israel could now be assured that Jehovah was with them, and by the same evidence the native tribes were driven to fear Israel's approach.

The next city to be taken was Ai. Here God left the people of Israel to the ordinary processes of war. To the consternation of Joshua and his aids, they were defeated. What could be wrong? Joshua sought Jehovah. This was and is the true method. Does the cause of God fail to make progress; then seek Jehovah, not in prayer alone, but seek His word, for it was the word of Jehovah that made known to Joshua the hindrance to success. It was the sin of Achan. Contrary to the command of God, he had taken of the devoted things, a wedge of gold and some Babylonian garments. Had this practice—that of appropriating the booty to individual use—been tolerated, Israel would have broken up into insignificant pillaging parties, and the whole movement would have failed. Their unity must be maintained, and their true goal kept in view. The act of discipline was severe, but the sin was a grievous one. Following the cleansing from this act of disobedience, the army of Israel was victorious in the second attempt against Ai.

Joshua now records and reads the law to the people at Mounts Ebal and Gerizim, as Moses had commanded. On hearing the news of the fall of Jericho and Ai, the native kings began to prepare for war with the Israelites. The Gibeonites undertook, instead, to make a covenant of peace with them, and, by a nice piece of strategy, they accomplished their desire. Dressing in old clothing and carrying stale bread in their knapsacks, they represented themselves as having journeyed a long distance to make a covenant with Israel. Flattered by the thought that their fame had traveled so far, and not consulting Jehovah, Joshua and the people made a covenant with them, only to find out after three days that their visitors lived but a short distance away. Thus did Israel early begin to transgress the will of God by making compromises with the tribes round about.

The other tribes, being angered by the separate move for peace made by their neighbors, the Gibeonites, proceeded to war against them. The Gibeonites, in distress, called on Joshua for help, and in this way Israel was drawn into the battle because of the unholy alliance. While the action of Israel had not been in accord with the will of Jehovah, yet this became an occasion by which He could give His people a victory over the co-alition of kings. It was in this battle that our text says the day was lengthened by Jehovah on the petition of Joshua in order that the battle might be waged to a successful conclusion.

Having utterly routed the combined armies of the five kings, Joshua turned southward with his forces and entered upon a campaign of conquest city by city. In turn, there fell before his attack the strongholds of Libnah, Lachish, Eglon, Hebron, Debir and others, until Joshua had conquered all the south country, even from Kadesh-barnea to Gaza. This successful campaign being finished, he returned with his forces to their old camp at Gilgal.

The tribes of the north, hearing of the successful invasion being made by the army of Israel in the south, became alarmed, and the various kings called forth their forces and combined them in a vast army near the waters of Merom. Jehovah instructed Joshua to go against them in battle without fear, for He would give him victory. This Joshua did, and was completely victorious, utterly routing the enemy. This was a decisive battle, since it was an engagement against such a representative force. This victory left Joshua in control of all the northern section of Palestine. Thus, with a central campaign, a southern campaign, and the battle with the combined forces of the north, Joshua had put in subjection the entire land.

But the question is sometimes raised, How can God be justified in helping Israel to conquer this land, expelling, by force, and with much bloodshed, the people who had peaceful possession? In order to answer this question the reader must be referred again to the purpose of God in the world which the writer claims is the development of righteous character in man. As the only means to this end, God purposed to send His Son into the world, who, in the likeness of sinful flesh, would offer salvation to every man. For Christ to become a God-man, He must have a human lineage, and for this purpose Abraham was chosen, and the covenant made with him that through his seed should all the nations of the earth be blessed. Abraham's seed must have a home, a land and country, and this must be such a location as will best suit the purpose of reaching the nations of the earth.

Again the same principle is involved as was used in the test put to the barren fig-tree—"Why cumbereth it the ground?" The test of a fruit-tree is the fruit it bears. If year after year it bears no fruit, it is cut down and cast into the fire and another tree is put in its place.

Some have sentimentally bemoaned the fate of the American Indian. Suppose these tribes had been allowed to roam through the centuries over the vast prairies and in the great forests of North America unmolested, engaging their time in hunting the wild animals and making war upon one another, what contribution would they have made to the world's progress? Some one asks, Have they not a right to live? Why? Why should any one live unless by his living he renders some service? Why should he "cumber the ground"?

By this test the unfruitful plants are weeded out; by this rule the unserviceable animal is eliminated; and by this same principle is the unfruitful nation pushed aside to give room to the one that serves. While not championing cruel methods and unnecessary bloodshed, it is claimed that the great and progressive people known as the United States of America, standing out as a world leader, is to-day a justification of the displacement of the Indian.

Although the native tribes of Canaan were not completely driven out, yet such conquest had been made of the land as enabled Joshua to make an allotment to the several tribes of Israel. And this Jehovah commanded Joshua to do. According to previous arrangements mentioned above, Reuben, Gad and the half-tribe of Manasseh were given the territory on the east side of the Jordan. This left the territory west of the Jordan to be divided among nine and a half tribes. Levi, having been taken for the priesthood, was given no territory, but was placed in cities instead. Forty-eight cities, with their suburbs, were assigned unto the Levites throughout the whole territory. Six of these were designated Refuge Cities: Bezer, Ramoth-Gilead, and Golan on the east of the Jordan, and He-bron, Shechem and Kadesh of Naphtali on the west.

A double portion being given to the descendants of Joseph in the tribes of Ephraim and Manasseh, together with the elimination of Levi, maintained the original number of twelve tribes among whom the land was divided. On the west of the Jordan assignments made were in the order of Simeon to the south, then Judah, Benjamin, Dan, Ephraim, Manasseh, Issachar, Zebulun and Naphtali. Later, Dan, being hard pressed by the natives who had not been expelled, sought and obtained some territory in the extreme north, giving to the principal city the name of the tribe. Thus Dan in the north and the city of Beer-sheba, in Simeon, gave rise to the measuring-rod of the country, "From Dan to Beer-sheba."

The goal held before a people for nearly fifty years had been reached. A feat without parallel in history had been accomplished. Moses' guiding hand had been withdrawn at Nebo, but Joshua, his able successor, completed the task. Two of the items of the covenant God made with Abraham had now been fulfilled. He had made of Abraham's seed a great nation; He had given them a land for a possession. There remained to be fulfilled the third and greatest item of the contract: "In thee and thy seed shall all the nations of the earth be blessed." Slowly, but surely, the plan of God moved on toward its consummation, that of bringing Christ into the world, that through Him all men might have the offer of eternal life.

Following the division of the land and the death of Joshua, the people entered upon their possessions and became more or less engrossed with their own individual affairs. They had not completely driven out the peoples of the land, and these soon recovered strength enough to begin to make inroads into Israel's possessions. While the law seems to imply that all civil, as well as religious, matters would be taken care of by the priesthood and judges whom they appointed to sit at the gates of the cities, yet there arose emergencies, such as the invasion of the land by foreign and native tribes, which called for special leadership. Those selected for this work were called judges. Hence, the period from the death of Joshua to the setting up of the kingdom is called the period or reign of the judges.

There were fifteen judges, beginning with Othniel, and ending with Samuel. They judged Israel, but, in the main, as suggested above, they acted as military leaders when Israel's territory was being invaded by some foe. Their work seems mostly to have been confined to some particular tribe or region. Their term of office was irregular, and depended largely upon the circumstances of the time and the strength and personality of the judge.

Moses warned the people in his last exhortation that if they would be faithful to Jehovah, He would protect and preserve them; but if they began to go after the strange gods of the people round about them, Jehovah would sell them into the hands of these nations. This warning was repeated by Joshua, and the people pledged themselves each time to faithful and continued obedience. On the side of natural interpretation we can see how necessary it is to the unity, and, therefore, to the strength, of a nation to follow after the higher ideals that are given to men by God. When these are lost sight of there is a sinking into the sordid depths of selfishness and materialism; and the unity of the nation is broken up. Then it becomes a prey to every invading foe. Just so it was with Israel. When following Jehovah the nation was united

and strong, but when it deserted Him it became dis-
united and weak.

"And the children of Israel did that which was
evil in the sight of Jehovah, and forgot Jehovah their
God, and served Baalim and the Ashteroth. Therefore
the anger of Jehovah was kindled against Israel, and
He sold them into the hand of Cushan-rishathaim, king
of Mesopotamia; and the children of Israel served
Cushan-rishathaim eight years."[1] Thus the narrator
relates Jehovah's interpretation of the events. While
all this occurred in a natural way, it is here revealed
how the purpose of God was working through it all.

Upon petition of the people in their distress, Jehovah raised up a leader in the person of Othniel, nephew
of Caleb, and gave him victory over the king of Mesopotamia, so that the land had rest for forty years.
This invasion was evidently made by the Mesopotamians
coming down the east side of the Jordan, rounding
the Dead Sea and invading the territory of Judah
from the south. Hence Othniel, of the tribe of Judah,
became the first judge.

Upon the further sin and disaffection of the Israelites, Jehovah strengthened Eglon, the king of Moab,
to come up against them. Eglon was assisted by
the tribes of Ammon and Amalek. This combined
army crossed the Jordan and took Jericho. From this
strategic position they were able to hold parts of
Israel, presumably territory of Judah and Benjamin,
for eighteen years.

Ehud, of the tribe of Benjamin, was then called
to the leadership. He visited King Eglon, under pretense of paying him tribute, and assassinated him.
Hurrying back to his country, and quickly gathering
together an army, he took possession of the fords of the
Jordan. The Moabites, hearing of the death of their
king, began a hurried retreat to their own country, and
were slain in great numbers at the crossing of the Jor-

---

[1] Judg. 3: 7, 8.

15

dan. Following the defeat of the Moabites, the land
had rest for eighty years. Following Ehud was Sham-
gar, of the tribe of Judah, who slew six hundred
men with an ox-goad, and delivered Israel from the
Philistines.

The next oppressor of Israel was Jabin, king of
Canaan, who reigned in Hazor, and whose captain was
Sisera. He oppressed Israel twenty years. The leader
chosen to deliver Israel on this occasion was Deborah,
a prophetess, of the tribe of Ephraim. She called,
as the captain of her army, Barak. She gave orders
to Barak to meet the hosts of Sisera, and assured him
that Jehovah would grant him a victory. But Barak
refused to go except Deborah accompany him. She
went, but warned him that the credit of victory would
go to a woman. When the armies joined in battle
the hosts of Sisera were discomfited, and he fled for
his life, coming to the tent of Heber, the Kenite.
There, while asleep, Sisera was slain with a tent-pin by
the hand of Jael, the wife of Heber. Now the Kenites
were of the same people as Jethro, the father-in-law
of Moses, and some of them had followed Israel into
the land of Canaan. The land had rest for forty years.

The next oppression was by the Midianites. This
time Jehovah called Gideon, of the tribe of Manasseh,
west of the Jordan. Gideon was cautious, and called
on the Lord for a sign, which was given him by the
dew on the fleece and not on the ground, and another
sign of the dew on the ground and not on the fleece.
When Gideon called out an army, thirty-two thousand
men responded, but God said it was too many, and
the fearful were excused, leaving ten thousand men.
Still God told Gideon there were too many. The next
test was made by taking the men down to the brook to
drink. All that bowed down to drink were rejected,
while those who lapped like a dog—the water being,
presumably, dipped up in their hands—were chosen,
being three hundred in number. These were armed
with pitchers, torches and trumpets. Having pre-

viously heard a dream related by a Midianite to his
fellow, Gideon was given confidence. He divided his
men and stationed them about the camp of Midian
during the night, and at a given signal they broke
their pitchers, displaying their torches, and blew a blast
on their trumpets. At this the Midianites, believing
they were surrounded by an innumerable host, were
thrown into rout and began slaying one another. The
fleeing army was pursued with great slaughter.

Following this great victory, the people besought
Gideon to be their king. This Gideon refused to do,
but he succumbed to temptation to the extent of taking
the jewelry given him by the people, and of this he
made an ephod. Now God had instructed Moses in the
beginning to make an ephod as one of the distinctive garments to be worn by the high priest. On this was fas-
tened the breastplate with twelve stones, one for each
tribe, emblematic of all Israel, whose cause the high priest
should bear before Jehovah. Because there was given
with the ephod the Urim and Thummim, with which the
priest divined the will of Jehovah, no doubt Gideon was
thus undertaking to command the presence of God. This
act of Gideon was condemned in that it is said: "All
Israel played the harlot after it there." [1] The land had
rest, after the defeat of the Midianites, forty years.

Abimelech, son of Gideon by a concubine, was not
only tempted, but sought to become king by slaying
seventy sons of Gideon and making himself ruler at
Shechem. When the people declared Abimelech king,
Jotham, the only son of Gideon to escape the bloody
hand of his brother, stood on Mount Gerizim and spoke
the famous fable of the bramble-bush. In this fable the
olive-tree, the fig-tree and the vine all declared themselves too busy rendering real service to go and rule
over the trees; but the bramble, which was not rendering
service, was only too ready to become king. In this
fable Jotham predicted the autocratic rule of Abime-

---

[1] Judg. 8: 27.

lech and the consequent rebellion of the people. How true this is to life, that the element of mankind, not rendering any useful service to society, is only too ready to obtain places of power to use for greedy and selfish aggrandizement. After a brief reign of three years, the people rose up in rebellion against Abimelech's tyrannical rule, and he was slain.

After Abimelech came Tola of Issachar, then Jair, the Gileadite. Then followed the invasion of Israel by the Ammonites, who claimed Israel had taken from them the territory east of the Jordan. This was not true, since they had been dispossessed by the Amorites. For a leader in this emergency, the people sought Jephthah, the son of a harlot, who had been ostracized socially because of his parentage. Upon being assured of his restoration, he agreed to become their leader.

Now, the victory of Jephthah is overshadowed in interest by the rash vow he made. He vowed to Jehovah to make a sacrifice of whatever came first from his house to meet him, if Jehovah would give him victory. The first to meet him was his daughter. We must remember that Jephthah had for years been estranged from his own people; that he lived in Gilead near to the tribes of Ammon and Moab, who practiced human sacrifice. The fact that he rashly made this vow did in no way command the approval of Jehovah or stamp it as a sample of the common practice of Israel. On the other hand, there was the specific law of God forbidding such practice, and condemnation is made of others—Manasseh, for instance—for such action.

After Jephthah followed three obscure judges—Ibzan, Elon and Abdon. Then followed the character perhaps most unique among all mentioned in Old Testament times—Samson, son of Manoah. Samson's mother took upon herself, at the direction of God, the Nazarite vow, and Samson became a Nazarite from birth. All the freakish feats of strength which Samson did will be passed over to come to his seduction by the wily

Delilah. At her repeated solicitation he gave her the secret of his strength, and she cut off the locks of his hair. Then followed his capture by the Philistines, and his servitude in prison.

The church, like Samson, was tested by the green withes of Judaism, the strong ropes of Greek and Roman paganism, but was able to break them. In turn, her locks were interwoven with the state in the days of Constantine in the strongest form of ecclesiasticism. But Luther and his colaborers were able to break this mighty power. In our own time the inroads of "higher criticism," evolution, etc., are causing the very vow of faith to be broken. To the extent that her locks of faith are shorn the church is weakened. Let us hold on to God, keeping intact our vows of faith, and we shall go on to mighty victories for His cause.

It is said that the Philistines put out the eyes of Samson and made him grind in the prison-house. As his hair grew his strength returned, but it was made to serve the purpose of the Philistines. How often we see men of our own day endowed with mighty power, physical or intellectual, but because of wrong ideals their strength is consumed in turning Philistine mills rather than in helping to forward the purpose of God.

The next judge, Eli, combined that office with the office of high priest. Regardless of the responsible positions held by them, the sons of Eli were very corrupt, being guilty of the grossest immorality while engaged in the duties of their office. Now, when the people of Israel were defeated in battle with the Philistines, they thought to command the presence and blessing of Jehovah by carrying the ark of the covenant with them. This unholy act was performed by the wicked sons of Eli. God allowed the ark to be taken into battle, but refused to give Israel the victory. The result was that Israel was defeated, the sons of Eli were killed, and Eli himself, receiving word of the capture of the ark by the Philistines, fell over and died.

The Philistines placed the ark in the house of Dagon, their god. The presence of Jehovah in the symbol of the ark was too much for the idol, and it fell. Just so to-day, wherever the gospel of Christ goes the images of idolatry begin to fall. The Philistines found the presence of the ark a curse to them, so they sent it back to Israel. It came eventually to the house of Abinadab, where it remained until removed by David to Jerusalem.

The last judge, the one who was also the head of the school of prophets, was Samuel. He was the gift of God to a very devout woman who sought of Him a child. Samuel, when old enough to be separated from his mother, was taken to the home of the high priest, Eli, where he was to be trained in the religion of Jehovah. Samuel was a good and faithful servant of Jehovah, and judged Israel justly. But his sons were corrupt.

When he became old the administration of his sons was so corrupt that the people besought him to give them a king that they might be like the nations round about them. Samuel felt the sting of his rejection, taking it as a reflection upon himself, but Jehovah told him that they had rejected their God, not their judge. Whereupon He instructed Samuel to grant their wish, but to warn them of the consequences.

Thus it was that by constantly falling under the influences of idolatry about them, and having to struggle against the growing power of those whom they had not driven out of the land, the Israelites sought a solution after the ways of men, and not after the way of God. They thought to become a great power if they but had a king like the other nations. So figure the militarists of to-day. They say we must have a big army and navy like the other nations of the world; but the truth is "righteousness," not militarism, "exalteth a nation."

CHAPTER XIII.

THE KINGDOM

LET it be kept in mind that the Israelites rejected Jehovah and asked for a king that they might be like the nations round about them. Nations, like children, can learn some things only by experience. So God granted the request of Israel and gave the nation a king. Since it was the people's idea, the first king chosen was, according to the human estimate, what a king ought to be.

Samuel was directed by Jehovah to anoint one Saul, son of Kish, a man from the shoulders up taller than other men, to be the first king. The idea of the people was that which many have to-day: success depends upon physical power and military might. Thus a man, almost a giant in stature, would make the ideal king. He would be the embodiment of power, and, when heading their armies, would be able to lead them to victory.

Saul was a very promising youth. To begin with, he was humble. He had great physical strength, and seemed gifted with intellectual power. But his character had not the proper spiritual balance, and when the test days came, he failed. Saul, upon becoming king, became infatuated with power and with the admiration of his subjects. Because of this idol enthroned in his heart, he could not tolerate a rival.

Saul started out auspiciously by defeating the Ammonites, and received the praise of the people, who thereupon declared him king. But just before entering into war with the Philistines, Saul grew impatient at the delay of Samuel, and himself offered sacrifice. Thus did Saul start on his career of the usurpation of authority, and a disregard of the will of Jehovah.

Saul was ordered by the Lord in a campaign against the Amalekites, to destroy them and their property utterly, but he returned with Agag, the king, and the best of the sheep and the oxen. Then did Samuel utter that profound dictum of the Lord: ''Behold, to obey is better than sacrifice, and to hearken than the fat of rams.''[1] Not the opinion of men, but the word of God, is the only safe guide.

The supreme test for Saul came when he was confronted by the Philistines, led by the giant Goliath. Saul, the man of great stature and physical strength, was then confronted by one greater than he, and he and his people were dismayed. Then did the Lord teach them the lesson of the superiority of him who relied upon Jehovah, when David, the youthful musician, disdaining the armor of the king, went forth with his sling-shot and slew the giant leader of the Philistines.

This feat of David, while bringing to him the praises of the people, also called down upon him the jealousy and anger of the king. From this time forward, David was a fugitive until the death of the king, his life being brightened only by the beautiful friendship of Jonathan, the king's son. Saul went on in his mad career of disobedience until Jehovah entirely rejected him. During his last days, in desperation, he called on the witch of Endor, only to have Samuel pronounce his doom. He and Jonathan were slain in battle at Mount Gilboa.

At the death of Saul, David was chosen to be king. Now, Abner, captain of Saul's host, thinking to retain power for himself, made Ishbosheth, the only surviving son of Saul, king over the northern tribes. Hence, David ruled over Judah, with his capital at Hebron, for seven years and six months.

---

[1] 1 Sam. 15: 22.

Ishbosheth was a weakling, depending upon the power of Abner to retain his throne; and when he accused Abner of usurping his power, the captain revolted to David. This left Ishbosheth helpless, and his power soon waned. His subjects grew discontented and assassinated him. Then all the tribes looked to David as their king. Here it was that the prophecy of Jacob began to be fulfilled in that the sceptre was given to David, who was of the tribe of Judah.

The first act of David of importance was the taking of the Jebusite stronghold, Jerusalem, which he immediately made his capital. From that time on Jerusalem has been one of the most renowned cities of the world. "For out of Zion shall go forth the law, and the word of Jehovah from Jerusalem."[1]

David, with the high compliment of being designated as a man after God's own heart, combined in his character the traits of a great military leader with those of deep devotion and spirituality. He had also an artistic temperament, being a musician and a poet. Thus was he able to extend the borders of his kingdom by military prowess, and strengthen his nation internally by contributions to the worship of Jehovah. The leader is always great who can guide the people and at the same time follow God.

David conducted successful campaigns against the Philistines on the southwest, Edom to the south, and Moab, Ammon and Syria to the east. He pushed on to the north until it is said his kingdom extended from the great river, the river Euphrates, to the little river of Egypt on the south. This was the greatest extent ever reached by the kingdom of Israel, and the reigns of David and Solomon marked the height of her civil power.

Not only was King David interested in strengthening the civil power of Israel, but he desired to see the worship of Jehovah restored to its proper status. See-

[1] Isa. 2: 3.

ing that the ark of the covenant was not in its accustomed and legal position, he sent men and had it brought up to Jerusalem and placed in a tabernacle which he had erected for that purpose. David made the mistake that many do, in that his zeal was not directed by knowledge. He loaded the ark on an ox-cart, and Uzzah, an attendant, fearful of its falling therefrom, sought to steady it with his hand. This error was fatal, for when he touched the ark he fell dead.

The death of Uzzah caused David to delay the removal of the ark, and it may be presumed that in the interim he consulted the "book of the law," and there learned the instructions that were given concerning the handling of this sacred piece of furniture. The next time he had the priests carry it, and all went well. The ark was then removed to Jerusalem and placed in the tabernacle. Having now restored the ark, he proceeded to reorganize the worship. Being himself a musician, he organized the choirs, and, no doubt, wrote many of the psalms which they used.

But very often great men are not without their faults. In an hour of weakness David committed the great sin of adultery with the wife of Uriah the Hittite. Since one sin usually brings on others, so David was guilty of having Uriah put in the forefront of the battle that he might be killed. Upon the death of Uriah, David took Bath-sheba to wife. Then Nathan the prophet stood before David and spoke to him the famous parable of the man who had but one little ewe lamb, and the rich man passed by his own numerous herds and flocks to take the poor man's lamb to make a feast for his guests. Not discerning the parable, David's anger and sense of justice were stirred, leading him to pass sentence of death on the one who should be guilty of such a deed. Then spoke the prophet, "Thou art the man." How easy to condemn others for that of which we ourselves are guilty.

As in the life of Jacob, so in that of David, his sin came home to him many-fold in the sins of his children. This often bowed his aged head in sorrow. First, there was the death of Bathsheba's child. Then came the sin of rape committed by Amnon against his sister Tamar, both children of David. This was followed by the revenge of Absalom in slaying Amnon. The murder of Amnon, of necessity, drove Absalom into exile and estrangement from his father's house.

By the friendly offices of Joab, the captain of David's host, Absalom was restored, but began immediately an insidious propaganda which culminated in a rebellion. Under pretense of going to Hebron to fulfill a vow, he sent spies out into all the country, and, at a given signal, sprang his coup. David, desirous of saving Jerusalem from the destruction of battle, fled to the east of Jordan until he could organize an army. When Absalom followed and joined him in battle, the rebel was killed and his army defeated, leaving David free to return to the throne. But at what cost was such a victory.

Suffice it to say in this brief statement of the life of David that he gave evidence in the Psalms he wrote of his sincere repentance, and, being humbled by his sorrow, he strove faithfully to do the will of Jehovah. He respected at all times the Lord's anointed, and punished severely those who did not. He sought justice and equity for the people, and prosperity for the kingdom. David attained to a high place among the seed of Abraham.

In the closing days of the life of David, Adonijah attempted to gain the throne. By the quick action of Nathan and other close friends of the king, this movement was forestalled, and Solomon was made the successor of David.

One of the most outstanding acts for which Solomon was noted was the building of the temple. This David assayed to do, but Jehovah refused the work from hands so bloody with war and reserved it unto his son. This structure was built, in the main, on the plan of the tabernacle, but with the dimensions doubled.

Seven years were used in its construction, and hundreds of men served in the gathering and preparation of its material. Very much gold was used in overlaying its wooden parts, and the most delicate handwork was required for its furnishings. So that, though small, it was one of the most magnificent buildings ever erected in ancient times.

When Jehovah offered to give Solomon the desire of his heart, he chose wisdom. With the inheritance of a great kingdom, together with the wealth he was able, by his power, to acquire, and the gift of wisdom from Jehovah, Solomon became the most renowned monarch of his day. He increased his national prestige by marrying the daughter of Pharaoh, and women from other neighboring peoples. But these unholy alliances in the end brought trouble, as it led him into the worship of idols. "For it came to pass when Solomon was old that his wives turned away his heart after other gods."[1]

As God had warned the people by Samuel the prophet, they found a king to be an expensive luxury. He who goes to Tarshish must pay the fare. Taxes became high and burdensome, and discontent grew among the people. Leaders who sought some relief were looked upon as rebels, and had to flee the country, as, for instance, Hadad, Rezon and Jeroboam. While there was the outer glamor of wealth and power, inwardly Solomon's kingdom was in a state of disintegration.

At the death of Solomon the discontent of the tribes crystallized into a definite movement. Jeroboam, who had been in exile in Egypt, returned and headed a delegation who visited Rehoboam, son and successor to Solomon, asking relief from the heavy yoke of his father. Rehoboam, rejecting the counsel of the old men, and accepting that of his young advisers, because it pleased him, refused the petition of Jeroboam and

---

[1] 1 Kings 11: 4.

his companions. This led to civil war, in which Rehoboam was defeated and the kingdom was divided. Ten tribes to the north followed Jeroboam, leaving Judah and Benjamin to Rehoboam.

Jeroboam, in order to hold his following, and break completely with the southern tribes, established altars of worship at Bethel in the south, and at Dan in the north. The images used were golden calves, an idea he, no doubt, obtained while in exile in Egypt. He realized he could not hold his subjects if they went to Jerusalem to worship, for man's religion is his dominating force. Thus, through the disregard by Solomon of the will of Jehovah, his following strange gods and taxing the people to maintain a luxurious court for worldly display, the kingdom was divided and a false religion set up by the ambitious Jeroboam. The people were indeed paying for a king.

Jeroboam, by his force of personality, continued as king for twenty-two years, but his son, Nadab, could rule only two years. Since the people had turned to idolatry they could not maintain a high standard of morals, which, without an extraordinary personality at the head, is necessary to the maintenance of unity.

Baasha, having assassinated Nadab, took the throne and carried on the civil war with the king of Judah. He had a reign of twenty-four years, but continued the policy of "Jeroboam, son of Nebat, who caused Israel to sin." His son, Elah, reigned only two years. Zimri, the captain of his host, took advantage of the king when he found him drunk with wine, and slew him. Thus, in a brief time, ended two dynasties of two kings each in Israel, a strong proof of their moral weakness caused by rejecting Jehovah.

Zimri reigned the brief period of seven days. The people revolted at his usurpation of the throne, and made Omri, captain of the host, king. Omri then besieged Tirzah, the temporary capital, and Zimri, realizing his defeat, shut himself up within the king's house and set it on fire.

With Omri began one of the most powerful, as well as the most wicked, dynasties of the kings of Israel. It is said of Omri that he dealt wickedly above all that were before him. He was followed by the notorious Ahab, who took to wife the wicked Jezebel, a Baal-worshiper of the Sidonians. It was not enough that the people were led by Jeroboam into the Apis worship of Egypt. There was further introduced, by the wicked Jezebel, the immoral and degrading worship of Baal and the Ashteroth. The patience of God is wonderful. One would expect Him to reject utterly this people who were so willful and headstrong in their disobedience. Jezebel was a strong personality, and Ahab was but a tool in her hands. Baal-worship grew and flourished. At Mt. Carmel, Elijah, the prophet of God, was in contest with four hundred and fifty prophets of Baal. In this contest Jehovah made His power known to the people by consuming with fire the offering of Elijah, even to the altar and the water round about. But Jezebel ceased not her activity, and Elijah fled to the south to escape her wrath. Here in his gloom and discouragement he asked God to take him, thinking he stood alone in the battle with wickedness, but the Lord made known to him that there were yet seven thousand who had not bowed the knee to Baal.

Jehovah continued his warning to Ahab by the prophet Elijah, but the king heeded it not. In alliance with Jehoshaphat, king of Judah, he went to war against Syria, and was mortally wounded in battle. His son Ahaziah succeeded him, and reigned but two years. He was succeeded in turn by Jehoram, another son of Ahab. During his reign Elijah was translated, and his mantle fell to Elisha. When Elisha returned from the east side of the Jordan, relating the story of Elijah's ascension, some youths mocked him, saying, "Go up, thou baldhead, go up." Some have criticized this event, saying the punishment inflicted on the lads was too severe for so slight an offense. But the offense was not slight. It represented the thought of the people, for the youth speaks openly what is said more guardedly at home. The taunt, "Go up," was a challenge to the truth of the prophet's statement concerning Elijah and his translation and the challenge of the prophet was a rejection of Jehovah. So to-day those who hold lightly the word of God challenge the truthfulness of the Holy Spirit, which is a grave offense, if not, in fact, the unpardonable sin itself.

Jehu now conspired against Jehoram, slaying him and also Ahaziah, king of Judah. Thus ended the mighty dynasty of Omri. The dynasty of Jehu had the longest reign in the kingdom of Israel, having five kings: Jehu, Jehoahaz, Jehoash, Jeroboam and Zechariah. Of these Jeroboam had the longest reign. Under him the adjacent nations were defeated in battle, and the boundaries of the kingdom enlarged. Under his forceful leadership a period of material prosperity obtained, but the secure foundation of a nation was neglected—that of worship and service to the true God.

Following Jeroboam the kingdom deteriorated rapidly under the weak kings Shallum, Menahem, Pekahiah, Pekah and Hoshea. The Assyrian kingdom of the east had been reorganized and strengthened under Tiglath-pileser, and was making campaigns into the west-land. Israel, weakened by idolatry and dissension, became an easy prey, and, under Menahem, Israel was forced to pay tribute to this eastern monarch. Pekah, in alliance with Syria, rebelled, but was dethroned, and Hoshea put in his place. Now, Hoshea sought alliance with So, of Egypt, and ceased to pay tribute, whereupon Shalmaneser, king of Assyria, came up and besieged Samaria, Israel's capital city. It seems that Shalmaneser must have died during the siege, as his successor, Sargon, completed the task by carrying large numbers of the Israelites into captivity, and placed them in "Halah, and on the Habor, the river of Gozan, and in the cities of the Medes."[1] In this way the ten

[1] 2 Kings 17: 6.

tribes became the "lost tribes of Israel." Those whom Jehovah can not save, He must cast off.

Now, to return for a brief sketch of some of the high points in the history of the kingdom of Judah; for only such a brief account will the confines of the present treatise admit.

Rehoboam weakened his kingdom by a fruitless civil war with Israel, and was, therefore an easier prey to the invading armies of Egypt under Shishak. Shishak despoiled the temple, carrying off the treasures of the house of Jehovah and those of the king's house. Abijah, the son of Rehoboam, was more successful in war against Jeroboam, but he waxed mighty in his own sight, and reigned but three years. Asa, his son, inaugurated a reform by pulling down the pillars and foreign altars and hewing down the Asherim. Though Asa had a long and prosperous reign, he began, in his last days, to make a league with foreign kings to the displeasure of Jehovah.

Jehoshaphat, his son, continued the religious reform by taking away the high places and the Asherim out of Judah. He had peace from the nations round about, and built up the industrial and commercial side of his kingdom. He sent teachers throughout the land teaching the book of the law to the people. Hence the kingdom grew mighty and strong. But Jehoshaphat made league with Ahab, and went with him to war against Syria. He further made league with the house of Ahab by marrying his son Jehoram to Athaliah, daughter of Ahab and Jezebel.

Jehoram, upon ascending the throne of Judah, slew all his brethren, and it is said of him that he walked in the ways of the kings of Israel. No doubt, through the influence of his wife, Athaliah, he introduced idolatrous worship and caused the people to play the harlot after false gods. His kingdom was weakened, and suffered invasion by the Philistines and the Arabians. He was cursed of Jehovah, and died, having reigned eight years. He was buried in Jerusalem, but not in the tomb of his fathers.

Ahaziah continued the wickedness of his father, and reigned but one year. At his death his mother, Athaliah, had, as she supposed, all the heirs to the throne killed in order that she might reign. Thus, by one of the wicked house of Ahab and Jezebel, the prophecy of Jacob, that the sceptre should not depart from Judah, seemed about to fail of fulfillment.

Joash, the one to escape the wicked hand of his grandmother, was hidden away by his aunt, wife of Jehoiada, the priest. When Joash was seven years of age, Jehoiada, by secret arrangement with the people, brought him into the temple and had him crowned king. Athaliah, hearing the noise of shouting, went to see the cause, and was slain at the entrance of the horse-gate. The reign of Joash was directed by his uncle in reformation of the worship. In his latter years Joash remembered not the kindness of Jehoiada, and led the people astray, so that he was stoned to death in a conspiracy made by his own subjects.

Amaziah started his reign in the favor of Jehovah, and did that which was right. But later he brought up the gods of Seir, taken in a campaign against Edom, and caused Judah to bow down before them. He, too, fell at the hands of conspirators.

Under Uzziah, whose reign was contemporary with that of Jeroboam II., Judah had an era of great prosperity. Uzziah was successful in war, defeating the nations about him and causing them to pay him tribute. He fortified the cities, built cisterns, established vineyards and looked after the matter of stock-raising. In brief, he stimulated every line of industry, while keeping up the military standards. But Uzziah, intoxicated with power, sought to burn incense in the temple, a privilege reserved only to the priests. For this transgression he was stricken with leprosy, and Jotham, his son, became king. Jotham continued the good

16

work of his father, and brought further prosperity to his country during the sixteen years of his reign.

Ahaz, son and successor of Jotham, was besieged by the combined forces of Rezin, king of Syria, and Pekah, king of Israel. Instead of going to Jehovah for help and to His prophets for counsel, he offered himself a vassal to Tiglath-pileser, king of Assyria. Having made a trip to Damascus to meet Tiglath-pileser, Ahaz sent to the priest Urijah the pattern of an altar he saw there and had the priest make one like it. Thus Ahaz introduced the worship of strange gods.

Hezekiah, the son of Ahaz, instituted reforms by removing the high places, breaking the pillars, cutting down the Asherim and breaking in pieces the old brazen serpent which he found the people worshiping. When Sennacherib, king of Assyria, came up against Jerusalem, Hezekiah first paid the tribute demanded by the Assyrians, but, this failing to prevent an attack, he sent messengers to Isaiah, the prophet. Upon the further prayer of Hezekiah to Jehovah, Isaiah gave to him Jehovah's message, assuring him of protection. In answer to the boastful defiance of the Assyrians, God sent the angel of death to their camp, and the next morning there were found dead one hundred and eighty-five thousand.

Sennacherib hastily returned to his own country, and was there slain by his own sons, while worshiping in the temple. Hezekiah was later visited by the king of Babylon. Flattered by his presence, he showed him all his wealth, for which very indiscreet act he was reprimanded by the prophet of God.

Manasseh, son of Hezekiah, reigned fifty-five years in Jerusalem. His was the most wicked reign of all the kings of Judah. He built the high places; he reared up altars to Baal; he made an Asherah, and worshiped all the host of heaven. Not content with this, he brought the altars of idols into the very house of God. He even offered his own children as human sacrifices. He shed much innocent blood. Being taken captive to Babylon by an invading army, Manasseh cried unto Jehovah, and because of his repentance he was restored to his place. Manasseh spent his last days trying to undo some of the evil he had brought upon the kingdom. He reformed, but only after he had been guilty of much wickedness.

Amon followed in the evil ways of his father for the two years he ruled. Then Josiah, his son, began to reign, being eight years of age, and he reigned for thirty-two years. Josiah was a real reformer, and he restored the worship of Jehovah, having destroyed the altars and images of foreign gods. In the eighteenth year of his reign the book of the law was found by Hilkiah, the priest, in the temple, while the house of God was being cleansed and repaired. Upon hearing the contents of the book, the king rent his clothes and gave order to have the people assembled that they might hear the reading of God's word. Now that he had access to the law, Josiah made his reform more orderly and complete. He restored the worship as therein directed. How the people of God have been handicapped from time to time as they have lost sight of their Bible.

Now, Josiah interposed himself in a campaign Pharaoh-Neco was making against Carchemish, and was killed. The people thereupon put Jehoahaz, Josiah's son, on the throne. Neco, returning three months after from his campaign in the north, deposed him and made Jehoiakim king, carrying Jehoahaz into Egypt. Jehoiakim reigned eleven years. He did that which was evil in the sight of Jehovah, and he was taken captive by the invading army of Nebuchadnezzar.

Jehoiachin, the son of Jehoiakim, reigned but three months, until the king of Babylon, fearing his efforts of rebellion, sent and had him brought to Babylon, leaving Zedekiah, his brother, on the throne. During these last years God sent his prophet Jeremiah, in a last desperate effort to regain His people, but they disregarded Him and persecuted His prophet. The reform of Josiah was forgotten, the word of Jehovah was unheeded, and the kingdom went to decay. God sold them into the hands of Nebuchadnezzar. The Babylonian army reduced Jerusalem, destroyed the temple and carried off its rich furnishings and golden vessels. Those who escaped the sword were carried captive to Babylon and held in bondage to the king.

Some of the poor were left in the land, for it was the policy of the eastern kings not to depopulate a country completely, but to leave some of the inhabitants and then import others from distant provinces. In this way the power of production was preserved, but there was not enough unity to furnish military strength which might be used in rebellion. Over the ones left, Gedaliah was made governor. During an insurrection the governor and the Jews and Chaldeans that were with them were slain. This made many fear the wrath of the Babylonian king, so they fled into exile in Egypt. Tradition has it that Jeremiah visited these exiles, and while exhorting them to return to their own land, they became angered at him and slew him. Thus ended for a period of seventy years the once mighty kingdom of Israel.

CHAPTER XIV.

THE CAPTIVITY AND RETURN

HAVING entirely cast off the ten tribes of Israel, God purposed by the Babylonian captivity to cure Judah of idolatry. If persecution and trouble at home were not enough, then, in bondage to a foreign people, they would have opportunity to repent of their ways. The consequences of sin must often bear heavily upon man before he will turn to the Lord.

The two outstanding figures in the Babylonian exile are Ezekiel and Daniel. The name "Ezekiel" means "God strengtheneth." Ezekiel was a priest, perhaps of the lineage of Zadok. During the invasion made by the army of Nebuchadnezzar on Jerusalem, about 597 B. C., ten thousand captives were taken to Babylon, including the king Jehoiachin. Ezekiel was among this number. Being a priest, he was acquainted with the law, and therefore was especially fitted as a teacher.

The first task of Ezekiel was to destroy the false hopes in the hearts of these early exiles of an early return to Palestine. The people were inclined to sit around in inactivity, pining at their misfortune, and looking forward to their return home. This Ezekiel condemned, portraying to them in the words of Jehovah the coming destruction of Jerusalem and the overthrow of their government. He urged them to be resigned to their fate, to go to work and make their life permanent in their new surroundings.

After the destruction of Jerusalem, and the coming of the last exiles, it was his task to keep them from complete resignation and utter despair. He therefore gave them words of comfort, telling them of the coming downfall of the nations which had harassed them. He predicted to them the consummation of God's blessings. He gave them a vision of the restored temple and rehabilitated land.

Being now away from Jerusalem, they established the synagogue as a place of worship. Or, perhaps, from assembling to read the Scriptures such a gathering was so called, and afterward the building used for the place of meeting came to be known as a synagogue, just as our word "church" is used to-day. It is thought that the synagogue was also used as a school where the children were taught, as well as a place of worship, for such seems to have been the practice in later years.

Daniel's mission was different from that of Ezekiel, in that he was called to give some contributions to the affairs of state, as he was at the court of the king, and, further, in apocalyptical style, he was called to portray future events. Daniel interpreted the king's dream, in which there was a prediction of the rise in turn of four great kingdoms—the Babylonian, the Medo-Persian, the Macedonian and the Roman, which last kingdom was to be broken in pieces by the stone cut out of the mountain, evidently the church, or kingdom of Christ.

Daniel and his companions fell under the anger of Nebuchadnezzar because they would not worship the golden image which the king set up, and were cast into the fiery furnace, but Jehovah preserved them alive.

While the new Babylonian empire was being hard pressed by the armies of Cyrus, Nabonidus, the king, being in charge of the army in the field, left his son, Belshazzar, as acting king. Belshazzar, with a thousand of his lords, was drinking himself drunk in the palace when all were startled by a handwriting on the wall. Daniel was called and gave the interpretation that God had numbered his kingdom and had brought it to an end. The king had been weighed and found

to be wanting, therefore his kingdom was to be divided
between the Medes and Persians. That night Belshazzar was slain.

Jealous satraps sought to overthrow the influence
of Daniel, and, finding no fault in his conduct, they
struck at his religion. So they obtained a decree from
the king that any man asking a petition of any god
or man save the king himself for thirty days should
be cast into the den of lions. When Daniel, having
violated the decree by praying unto Jehovah, was
brought before the king for sentence, the king would
have relented but for the inexorable law of the Medes
and Persians. The king came early in the morning
from a sleepless couch, and found Daniel safe, for he
had been protected by an angel of the Lord.

The remainder of the Book of Daniel is taken up
with visions portraying in symbolic figures the movements of empires and the shifting of scenes in the history that was to be. Among these the most significant
is the vision of the seventy weeks in which the prophet
so clearly predicts the coming of Christ. From the
going forth of the decree to restore and build Jerusalem
(457 B. C.) seven weeks, or forty-nine years, it shall
he built again with street and moat even in troublous
times (408 B. C.). And after threescore and two
weeks, or 434 years (26 A. D., with correction, 30 A. D.),
shall the anointed one be cut off. And in the midst
of the week (33½ A. D., crucifixion of Christ) He
shall cause the sacrifice and the oblation to cease. Thus,
starting with the decree of Artaxerxes to rebuild Jerusalem, which was given 457 B. C., the figures point
directly to the death of Christ. (For fuller explanation
see "King of Kings," by E. V. Zollars.)

In this way the Lord preserved His people through
the remainder of the years of the new Babylonian
empire. By the teaching of the priest Ezekiel, together
with his portrayal of the return and rebuilding of Jerusalem and the temple, and the mighty sweep of prophetic
vision given by Daniel, exhibiting the hand of God in

the disposition of nations, the people were kept encouraged and made ready for the day when the man, whom God had designated by the mouth of the prophet Isaiah, even Cyrus, should come into power and issue the decree for their return.

In 626 B. C. the rising power of new Babylonia was joined by the Medes in the overthrow of the Assyrian Empire, and the territory was divided btween them. The capital city of Nineveh held out twenty years longer under the last two kings of that once mighty power. About this time there arose in Elam a military force headed by a man destined to be famous in history. This man was Cyrus. He enlarged his power and increased his forces until, in 558 B. C., he went against the Medes, but these refused to battle and joined his forces. Then, in 538 B. C., Cyrus overthrew the Babylonian Empire, and became sole ruler in all that region.

As predicted by the prophet, Cyrus issued a decree for the return of the Jews to their own land. This was immediately acted upon, and under the leadership of Zerubbabel forty-odd thousand of them made the journey to Palestine. What joy must have filled their hearts in contemplating the time when once again they should be at home sitting under their own vine and fig-tree, yet with what sorrow they looked upon the desolate ruins of their once beautiful temple and beloved Jerusalem. So far as this material world is concerned, the returning ''prodigal son'' does not always find a loving father ready to receive him with plenty of new raiment in the wardrobe and fatted calves in the stall, but he often comes back to the ugly desolation—the result of his own evil-doing.

As previously stated, some of the poor had been left in the land, and people from other countries brought in, thus causing, by mixed marriages, an amalgamated race. These became known as the Samaritans. Having been furnished with priests, they had preserved to some extent their former religion, and when the Jews began to rebuild the temple they asked for the privilege of helping in the work. This the Jews refused, for had they not just been rendering a servitude of seventy years for their loose conduct in relation to other people and their religion?

Upon their refusal to let the Samaritans have part with them in the rebuilding of the temple, the Jews incurred the enmity and opposition of the Samaritans. This opposition took form in a letter to the Persian king, calling his attention to the military power of the Israelites in former days, and warning him of their attempt to regain such power. Upon this petition an order was given for the work to cease.

The prophets Haggai and Zechariah were prophesying unto the Jews that were in Judah and Jerusalem. These prophets kept urging the people to go forward with the building of the temple. So in the second year of Darius, king of Persia, petition was made to the king asking that search be made for the former decree of Cyrus. This was done and the decree was found. Darius gave orders commanding the Samaritans not to interfere with the Jews in the privilege granted by the decree, and, furthermore, orders were given to assist in every way possible its fulfillment. So the temple was completed in the sixth year of the reign of Darius.

Zerubbabel led the first return in the latter part of the first year of Cyrus the king, or probably in the second year, which was 537 B. C. In the second year of their return they laid the foundation of the temple, 535 B. C. They were then delayed about fifteen years, resuming the work in the second year of Darius, 520 B. C., and completing it in the sixth year of Darius, 515 B. C. The fall of Jerusalem under Nebuchadnezzar occurred about 586 B. C., so that the prophecy of Jeremiah, that the captivity would last seventy years, was fulfilled.

In the seventh year of Artaxerxes, king of Persia (457 B. C.), Ezra, a priest and scribe, obtained permission of the king to go to Jerusalem. This request was granted, and Ezra, with another company of priests,

Levites, singers, porters and others, made the journey
to Jerusalem. It seems to have been the purpose and
work of Ezra to restore the worship of Jehovah, making
known the law to the people, for the scribes were well
versed in the Holy Scriptures.

Ezra found upon his arrival and investigation of
affairs that the men were taking wives of the people
of the land. This he condemned, and, having prayed
unto God, he required of the men on oath that they would
forsake this practice. Ezra recognized and confessed
to Jehovah that by such practices had they lost their
former greatness, having been forced into captivity,
and now they could only hope to secure the blessings
of their God by strict obedience to His word. By a
return to the will of Jehovah, under the direction and
guidance of Ezra, the nation was saved from idolatry,
absorption and decay.

In the twentieth year of Artaxerxes (457 B. C.),
Nehemiah, cupbearer to the king, was waited upon
by a delegation of his people from Jerusalem, making known to him the waste condition of their city
and asking for help. Then Nehemiah went to the
king and obtained permission to visit Jerusalem and
aid in its reconstruction. The king gave him a letter,
embodying these privileges, together with instructions
to the governors of the provinces.

Nehemiah entered upon his task by first making a
secret survey of conditions, going by night to view
the broken walls and burned gates. He made his plans
and then made his appeal to the people. As soon as
they began to build, the inhabitants of the land, under
the leadership of Sanballat, Tobiah and Geshem, began their opposition. First they made fun of their
efforts, then undertook to frighten them. Later they
sought to inveigle them into some sort of compromise
by means of a council in the plains of Ono. But Nehemiah was adamant in his disregard of their every move
and kept on building. He had the men armed while
they worked and a trumpeter ready to call them to-

gether to meet any sudden attack. So the walls were built.

Nehemiah acted as governor of Judah for twelve years (444-432 B. C.). He appointed his brother governor of Jerusalem and gave strict orders concerning the keeping of the gates. The people were divided by lot, every tenth one residing in Jerusalem and the nine-tenths in the other cities.

The people were then numbered, and gifts were made for the use of the sanctuary. Then they were assembled to hear the reading of the law. Ezra the scribe stood upon a pulpit of wood with helpers on either hand, and instructed the people from the word of God. The feast-days were observed again. The Levites offered prayer, making confession of national sin. The people covenanted to keep the law. "They clave to their brethren, their nobles, and entered into a curse, and into an oath, to walk in God's law, which was given by Moses the servant of God, and to observe and do all the commandments of Jehovah our Lord, and his ordinances and his statutes." [1]

With the restoration of the law of Jehovah they began its enforcement. Foreigners were excluded from the assembly, the payment of tithes was enjoined, Sabbath-breaking was suppressed, and mixed marriages condemned. Having learned a lesson by the severe experience of bondage, the leaders now sought to draw the people near to Jehovah.

A part of the history of the captive Jews is given in the beautiful story of the heroine Queen Esther, in the book bearing her name. In contrast with the ignoble and wicked Queen Jezebel, it is refreshing and comforting to have a glimpse into the life and character of Esther, who was ready, unselfishly, to make the supreme sacrifice for the deliverance of her people.

In the third year of King Ahasuerus, who has been satisfactorily identified with the Persian Khshayarsha

---

[1] Neh. 10: 29.

(which name the Greeks and Romans rendered by the word ''Xerxes''), he made a feast unto all his princes and servants. The third year of the reign of Xerxes was 482 B. C., and since his famous campaign in Greece was made in 480 B. C., this was, no doubt, an occasion for securing the help and assistance of the satraps and governors of his various provinces.

While the king was drunken with wine he ordered Vashti, the beautiful queen, to come in and exhibit herself before the carnal eyes of his intoxicated guests. Much to the credit of Vashti, she refused thus to be a party to such immoral practices. This made the king very angry and he consulted his lords as to what should be done with Vashti. They answered that her example would cause rebellion among all the women of Persia and Media, therefore she should be deposed from being queen.

''After these things'' in the second chapter of Esther may refer to a time subsequent to the king's campaign in Greece, in which his army was defeated. Having returned home now, he took up the matter of filling the place of the deposed Vashti. For this purpose young maidens were brought in to Sushan, the palace, and, having been purified, they made up the group from which the king chose a queen. Of the number gathered, the king favored Esther and made her queen.

Esther, being an orphan, was reared by her cousin Mordecai. Mordecai, while sitting at the king's gate, overheard a conspiracy formed against the king and made it known to Esther, who in turn informed the king, and he had the conspirators hanged and record made of the affair.

Haman, an officer of the king, was angered at Mordecai because he refused to bow to the king's appointee. Learning that Mordecai was a Jew, he sought revenge by having his whole people destroyed. The king, not knowing the cause of Haman's wrath, or the nature of the plot he was forming, was easily persuaded to issue a decree for the slaughter of the Jews. The king, being reminded by his record that he had not shown his gratitude to the one disclosing the plot against him, asked Haman what he should do for the one whom the king should delight to honor. Then it was that Haman's anger was further stirred by having to lead the king's horse while Mordecai rode thereon and all the people did him obeisance, since he had thought that he himself was the one whom the king would delight to honor.

Mordecai, learning of the plot to slay the Jews, made appeal to Esther, asking her to put the matter before the king. To appear unbidden before the king was to risk one's own life, so Esther took the matter under advisement. Mordecai further urged her to act, using the famous words: "And who knoweth whether thou art not come to the kingdom for such a time as this?"[1] Esther sent word to Mordecai to have all the Jews fast, and she and her maidens would do likewise. Then Esther resolved to give herself for her people.

Fortunately, when Esther entered the presence of the king he extended the golden sceptre and bade her state her petition. She thereupon invited the king and Haman to banquet with her. This they did. She did not then state her message, but invited them to a second banquet. At this time she told the matter to the king, who was deeply incensed at such a plot and ordered Haman to be hanged on the gallows fifty cubits high which he had made for Mordecai. He further issued a decree and had it sent by hurried post to all outlying provinces giving the Jews authority to protect themselves and their families against any who should make assault upon them. By unselfish service were the Jews saved from an awful massacre, by the beautiful Queen Esther.

Because Haman cast lot (Pur) every day for a year to find an auspicious day on which to massacre the Jews, and because they were delivered from the murderous hand of Haman, Mordecai called upon all the Jews to observe the fourteenth and fifteenth days of Adar as

[1] Esth. 4:14.

days of feasting and gladness because of their deliverance. From the Persian word for lot (Pur) this feast
became known as the Feast of Purim.

The Jews now being re-established in Canaan, with
their temple rebuilt and the worship of Jehovah restored, God sends them one more prophet, Malachi, and
with his ministry leaves them to await a voice which
should announce the near approach of the new dispensation. The throne of David has continued and the sceptre has not departed from Judah. Four hundred years
more and the last element of the Abrahamic covenant
will be fulfilled: "In thee and in thy seed shall all the
nations of the earth be blessed."

CHAPTER XV.

PSALTER AND WISDOM LITERATURE

THE religion of Israel had its appeal to the intellect in the great messages of the prophets; it called for a bowing of the will in the ritualism conducted by the priest; it contained also the element which would feed the emotions, the devotional part of the worship. It is only natural to conclude that God, being the author of man's being, would provide, in the religion given to him, for every part of man's nature, that he might have a systematic and all-round development. In the record preserved to us in the Old Testament we have that agency represented which was used to develop the emotional nature of man; namely, the Psalter.

The wisdom literature of the Old Testament is found particularly in the four books of Job, Proverbs, Ecclesiastes and Song of Solomon. In these same books are also found, to a considerable extent, the devotional element, and they are therefore commonly referred to as the devotional books of the Old Testament. It is not the purpose of this thesis to treat them technically as wisdom literature or as devotion, but to suggest briefly some of the part they played in helping work out the purpose of God.

Because the Israelites were receiving the blessings of Jehovah in return for faithful obedience, which blessings resulted in their material welfare, it was easy for them to draw the conclusion that the two were inseparable; that if a man was righteous he was naturally prosperous as a consequence, and *vice versa*. This conclusion, coupled with God's blessing of Israel, would cause men to lose sight of the end and purpose God had in view in His use of Israel as a nation. For if that conclusion were true, God could not give particular help to Israel, and yet be universal in His love.

Evidently, then, to stem the progress of this fallacy God gave to His people, and through them to us, the history of His dealing with Job, which became a test case. Now, Job was a model man, one that loved God and forsook evil. But Job was prosperous, having about him a large family, with high rank and immense possessions. Were Job's loyalty and love to God dependent on his worldly prosperity? Is God obligated to-day to prosper materially the man who serves Him? Or, rather, does it rain on the unjust as well as the just?

This question may come to the paid worker of the church, or be raised concerning him by others. Does the preacher go to church because he wants to worship, or is he going because he is employed to preach? What would we do if the material consequences were changed? This is not exactly the same problem, but a similar one. It suggests to the Christian that every paid worker should so keep himself in the devotional and worshipful spirit as to be above the material rewards.

Jehovah, in opposing the charge of Satan, claimed that without regard to material prosperity, and even in affliction, Job would be true. The test was made. The friends of Job delivered their arguments and Job gave his answers. Then came the message of Jehovah challenging the power of Job, showing him how futile was his puny strength, and how mighty was the power of the Almighty. It taught Job that he should refrain from criticizing God, and should recognize his own dependence.

The object of the book has been summed up in the following able manner: "But the direct object of the whole work is stated at the outset, and pervades every portion of the dialogue; it is to show that although goodness, by virtue of the divine appointment, and as a result of divine governance, has a natural tendency

to secure a full measure of temporal happiness, yet that
in its essence it is independent of such a result. Goodness consists in the fear of God, depending upon a
loving appreciation of what a good man instinctively
feels to be His essential characteristics; and in the hatred
of evil, not merely for its effect upon human happiness,
but as in itself abhorrent to a mind conscious of the
difference between right and wrong."[1]

While the laws of God are in harmony and all truth
is one; that a life lived in harmony with the will of
Christ makes naturally for better health; that Christian
principles will succeed in business; yet Christian
ethics is not utilitarian, and men must not be bribed
to follow Christ for the loaves and fishes. Just so the
people of Israel were taught by this lesson of Job that
though blessings were bestowed upon them because of
their obedience, yet these blessings were in the end bestowed to make it possible to bring through Israel the
Christ who was to bless all mankind. In like manner
now these blessings of God are not inseparable with our
righteous acts. They are but means to the end, even the
higher blessing of eternal life God desires to bestow
upon us.

Only the most exalted themes have been worthy of
being the subjects for the lyrical expressions of man.
When he writes his poetry or sings his songs it is about
the matters of greatest interest and value. Themes of
love, patriotism and virtue; of God, eternity, and the
boundless universe; of sacrifice, suffering and death—
these occupy the center of thought in man's emotional
moods. It is so in the Hebrew Psalms. Perhaps there
has yet been no book in all history which has furnished
such true expression of the human heart in its ideas
of God and His universe, or has reflected such a wide
and perfect sympathy for man in his weakness, in his
strength, in his joy, and in his sorrow, as has the Book
of Psalms.

---

[1] "Bible Commentary"—Job.

17

Ethically, the Psalms teach "single-heartedness, transparent truthfulness, utter absence of guile, purity of heart as the center and mainspring of moral life." They teach justice, rectitude, self-control, fortitude in man's dealing with man, sympathy in suffering; warm and tender friendship; loyalty of subjects to kings, and unselfish and sacrificing love of princes for the people. It is particularly noticeable that in a higher degree than ever before the grace of humility is emphasized. This is a near approach to the Christian ideal: "A broken and contrite heart, O God, thou wilt not despise." [1] "For thou wilt save the afflicted people" [2] indicates God's love and care for the poor and humble.

While the ethical ideal is not yet perfect, it is certainly a near approach to the Christian standard, and a preparation for the New Testament idea.

As to the exaltation of the power and glory of God there is a wealth of expression, so much so that a large amount of the hymnody of the church has been taken from the Psalms. Almost any desired form in the expression of praise to Jehovah, and such moods as reflect all the varying emotions of man, may here be found.

While there is very little given in Israel's literature up to the time of the Psalms concerning another life, and even here it is not altogether specific, yet there is much to be found that implies a future state. No doubt, what obscurity is found here, as elsewhere in the Old Testament concerning a future state, is in harmony with God's plan to hold revelation concerning this matter in reserve for the fuller revelation of all things in Christ. Notwithstanding, such hope would be held forth as would keep men from the gloom of despair. And in the hymns of the Israelites there was given that necessary reliance upon God.

The most important feature of the Psalms to be considered here is their Messianic character. What part did the Psalms play in pointing to Him who was to

---

[1] Ps. 51: 17.
[2] Ps. 18: 27.

fulfill the third and last item of the Abrahamic covenant? While Israel sang of the glory of God, of the grandeur of His power, and of the sins and iniquities of man, did they sing of the coming Messiah?

In answer to the question three Psalms are cited as especially significant—the twenty-second, the forty-fifth and the 110th. The twenty-second begins with the words used by Jesus while on the cross: "My God, my God, why hast thou forsaken me?" Then follows an exaltation of God and His protection of Israel. Then a description is given of the scorn of the people, and the lowliness of His deep humiliation. The picture darkens as the malicious forces close in on Him to take away His life. Here is a prophetic message uttered: "They part my garments among them, and upon my vesture do they cast lots." And again: "They pierced my hands and my feet."

As to the forty-fifth Psalm the writer of the letter to the Hebrews says, "Of the Son he saith," and then quotes the language of this Psalm, thus giving the stamp of authority of inspiration itself, that the language quoted from the forty-fifth Psalm refers to Christ. There is a further conformity of the contents of this Psalm with the person and kingdom of Christ, which could not be found with any person or institution at the time the Psalm was written.

Psalm 110 begins with the language: "Jehovah said unto the Lord, Sit thou at my right hand, until I make thine enemies thy footstool." In Matt. 22:44 Jesus quotes this as the language of David, and applies it to Himself. No higher testimony than this could be had for the Messianic character of this Psalm.

"Such, in broad outline, appears to be the Christology of the Psalter; bearing throughout a reference to the ultimate purpose of God, for which both the sufferings and preservation of His faithful servants were preparatory; in a considerable portion bringing into light the characteristics of the Saviour both in His humiliation and triumph, and at least in three Psalms, probably in

others of similar import, setting forth all the graces of
His human nature in combination with the attributes
of God.'' [1]

This book not only served its day and time as a
hymnal for the assembly of Israel, but added its part
to the greater scheme of holding before the people the
fulfillment of the promise of God.

The root meaning of the Hebrew word *mashal,* translated "proverb," was to liken, or to make like, hence
the wise sayings known as proverbs were in a wider sense
known to the Israelites as comparisons. Yet their use
of the word shows that they, too, included the idea of
proverb. It seems to be one of the natural tendencies
of the human mind to put into a brief form some bits
of wisdom. They have greater force and usableness because of their brevity. The more significance or meaning that can be put into a few words the more it attracts
the attention. Seemingly the ingenuity of making a few
words convey much thought calls forth the admiration
of mind, and is therefore effective.

Israel, like other nations, had its proverbs. Because
of the extraordinary wisdom of Solomon, and the large
number of proverbs that issued from his pen, those
collected and preserved in the second book of the wisdom
literature are attributed to him as the author; just as
the activity of David as a writer of Psalms gave to him
the authorship of the book by that name.

1 Kings 4:32 says: "And he spake three thousand
proverbs; and his songs were a thousand and five."
This statement shows that many more proverbs were
in use than have been preserved to us in this book.

In the law Israel was directed in the matter of worship, sacrifices, feasts, and the duties of priests; they
found there also instructions covering the handling of
property, the duties of citizenship, etc. The prophets
brought the message of God as He wished to warn them
of impending danger, or to exhort them as a people

---

[1] "Bible Commentary"—Introduction to Psalms.

to faithful obedience. Since the people had other books of instruction covering the concrete acts of life, the wisdom literature presented the principles of life, which would help to build up in the hearts of the people a love of right, justice and truth, which in turn would become the mainspring to spur them on to right living.

Much is said in Proverbs of wisdom. This is that knowledge that puts one in right relation to God. It may therefore be said to be practical knowledge, since to be in right relation to God is to make for one's welfare here and hereafter. "The fear of Jehovah is the beginning of wisdom." Thus it is taught at the very outset of life that man must come to realize his utter dependence upon a higher power, and that this power is Jehovah. He can not begin to act in his own best interests until he recognizes the source of all strength. The favor of Jehovah is the greatest of all blessings and the curse of Jehovah is the severest of all penalties. Therefore those who keep His commandments are, ultimately, to bask in His favor.

Men are urged to seek after wisdom, since wisdom includes a knowledge of the will of God, and would lead man in the way of His grace. This wisdom was more than earthly prudence, and so led to a reward above that of material prosperity. "Righteousness delivereth from death" (11:4). It is said of the righteous that he hath hope in his death (14:32).

Regarding the social life, the young were warned with oft-repeated earnestness against the dangers of extravagance, indebtedness, drunkenness and impurity. There is held up before them the dark picture of the harlot and the money-lender. They are exhorted to obedience to parents and respect to the aged.

As a group the nation is exhorted to education as a cure for many of its ills. The individual might find the proper training and restraint in the family, but the nation needed for its ruler a righteous king who would administer justice. To this end the king should surround himself with wise and just counselors. At last it is by the wisdom of God that kings rule with justice to the satisfaction of their subjects.

Because of the fundamental place of the home in every social group and of the importance of woman in the home, no ethical system is complete that does not give full consideration to the place of woman. It is not strange, then, that we find in the Book of Proverbs much concerning the home, the place of woman and the relations of the members of the household. The "prudent wife" is one of God's best gifts. "She buildeth her own house on a sure foundation." Her influence upon the children is recognized as being as great as that of the father. Their shortcomings bring her to grief. They owe her loving obedience. The virtue of the wife becomes the anchor of the home and the moral standard of society, for the children owe their goodness to her loving persuasion.

These short, pithy sayings, then, could not, by their very nature, incorporate a long and connected message such as the prophets were called upon to give. Neither were they fitted to embody the law that should govern their civil and religious life. But they did preserve to Israel, in a forcible way, the great principles of life, such as the relation of man to Jehovah, of child to parent, of people to king and of king to people, and of the proper relations in the moral realm. These all helped to stabilize the inner life of men and enabled the law of God to function properly. In this way, then, even the "wise sayings" of the seers of Israel helped to bring about that day when He, who was God in the flesh, should teach as no other man taught.

The third book of the wisdom literature begins, "The words of the preacher, the son of David, king in Jerusalem," words which plainly describe Solomon as the author. To see more clearly the thought expressed in this book we should keep in mind the main features in the life and experience of this famous man. It is recalled that upon his choice God gave to him wisdom and added therewith wealth, glory and power. Solomon allied himself with the royal families of neighboring kingdoms by marriage and made for himself the largest harem known in history. Through these foreign wives he was led to worship idols and to build to them luxurious shrines of worship. He also built dwellings for these foreign princesses. His fame brought him much honor, which no doubt intensified his desire to display his wealth, his wisdom and his power. Wealth and luxury tend to indulgence, and Solomon not only tasted, but drank deep of, all the sordid things of life. He tested thoroughly the ability of this world to satisfy the desires of the soul.

A second key to the understanding of the book is the frequent use of the word "vanity," which occurs thirty-seven times. Now, vanity means that which passes away quickly, leaves no result or none of consequence, and fails to satisfy the human mind. The frequent use of this word as applied to the various fields of human endeavor, together with the wide range of the experience of Solomon, is fraught with great significance. It gives value to the book in the warning given to others who might be looking to the things of this life as ends in themselves, or as means to satisfy the deep needs of the soul.

The author cites the endless cycles of physical forces, the coming and going of the generations of men in a ceaseless monotony, which overwhelms the mind of man as he contemplates the stupendous quantity of physical force and his insignificance in the midst of it all. He cites how he failed to find satisfaction in wisdom. "For in much wisdom is much grief." He turned to wine "and to lay hold on folly," he builded houses, he made great works, he tried horticulture, agriculture and stock-raising. He gathered much wealth, so that there were none so great in all that were before him. He looked upon all these, the works of his hands, and declared: "All was vanity and vexation of spirit, and there was no profit under the sun."

The author seems, at times, to reflect the thought of a fatalist when he says that that which befalleth men befalleth beasts, "so that a man hath no pre-eminence above a beast." Wherefore he praises the dead as better off than the living. And for him who loses sight of the life hereafter and centers his attention upon this world alone, we can readily see how he would come to such a conclusion.

The author continues his gloomy, pessimistic picture of man in the world seeking this activity or that experience, only to find, at last, that all is vanity. It is not necessary, then, to follow in detail the narrative, but it is enough for the present purpose to see the general course of the author's mind. Let us now look at the closing thought of the book. After all his meanderings through the experiences of life the author comes at last to give this advice to youth: "Remember also thy Creator in the days of thy youth, before the evil days come, and the years draw nigh, when thou shalt say, I have no pleasure in them." Then, after giving one of the most beautiful pictures of the creeping on of old age, the author sums up the whole of life: "This is the end of the matter; all hath been heard; fear God, and keep his commandments; for this is the whole duty of man. For God will bring every work into judgment, with every hidden thing, whether it be good, or whether it be evil."

When the people of Israel were inclined to look to the things of this world for satisfaction, or to experience the disappointment of carnal rewards, the words of the preacher came as a great admonition. The message called men to depend upon Jehovah and keep His commandments, and to look to the reward that comes only to him who lives righteously in this present world.

In the Song of Songs Solomon is pictured as taking a Shulamite maiden away from her rustic and humble home, and bringing her to Jerusalem to raise her to the heights of felicity and honor by making her his wife. Then, after many expressions of mutual praise and love, the bride entreats the king to go with her to her former home, where vows of invincible love are proclaimed. In a literal way true love and marriage are here shown to be a great leveler of humanity. This song exalts the marriage tie, and shows forth the sacredness of its vows of love.

Figuratively, the Song has been construed to forecast the time when Jesus, the King of kings, would come to earth, stooping from His divine station to lift up fallen humanity unto heavenly places. He then awaits the day when the bride, His church, shall invite Him to return to earth to take her unto Himself.

Thus Hebrew poetry, wisdom and song are made to play their part in working out the great purpose of God.

CHAPTER XVI.

PROPHECY

IN the law given to Israel by Jehovah through Moses the office of priest was provided for, and its duties stipulated. He was to administer the law and conduct the ritual. This routine of ritualism tended to make him conservative, and cause him to think it was enough to fulfill the formalities of the law. Since Jehovah's plan was a progressive one it was necessary that the nation be moved onward and upward toward the goal He had set for it. While the priestly office was essential in its conserving power, it would not be an ideal instrument for the introduction of new teaching that would be necessary, therefore God used also the office of prophet in the working out of His plan.

The Hebrew word for prophet means one inspired or moved to communicate the mind of God. The prophet was the one standing in the place of God to give to the people Jehovah's message. Aaron was Moses' prophet because he was to deliver the message of Moses. The Greek word from which we derive the word "prophet" means one who has insight into divine things, and speaks them forth to others. The prophet, then, was one who in some manner received his message direct from Jehovah, and gave it to the people as the word of God.

In all the ages preceding Moses the purpose of God seems to have been merely to direct the people of the time in their acts of worship and manner of living, therefore He used the patriarchs as mouthpieces. They were the representatives of Jehovah, speaking to their families and tribes. This was in keeping with the time when writing was but little used, and when the purpose was to preserve a righteous line which might consist of a family only. But when in the lineage of Abraham God had raised up a nation, the office and work of the prophet became more specific and distinct.

Following the death of Joseph, God seems to have left His people for several centuries without any divine communication. And then when oppression became severe, when the people were crying out for help, He sent His prophet Moses. Because of the long silence and because of their dire distress, it was all the more probable they would be willing to listen to the message of God.

Now that Israel is to be preserved as a nation, they are unified under the leadership of Moses. They are given one prophet to be the mouthpiece of God to all. Moses is also commanded early in his administration to begin writing down in a book the things Jehovah wanted preserved. The laws He was now giving them would continue in their application, and hence could be made a matter of record. Further, these dealings with Israel looking toward the fulfillment of the Abrahamic covenant would be significant for all future time, and therefore should be recorded.

Written prophecy, so far as it has been preserved to us, began with Moses. Verbal prophecy continued, perhaps, through the whole period of revelation, and was used even in the early church in the Christian dispensation. Written prophecy served the double purpose of being a message of the day and time in which it was given and a message also to future times; while verbal prophecy was limited to the time in which it was given.

Not all written prophecy has been included in the Old Testament canon. Mention is made in Jude of the prophecies of Enoch, and in Joshua reference is made to the Book of Jasher. These and other instances show that no doubt much was written which, though valuable, was not essential to the purpose of God as that purpose was to be worked out by His word. It is reasonable to suppose that the Lord guided in the preservation of such books as would meet His purpose. Not all the doings of Jesus were recorded, but all that was necessary to present completely the plan of salvation. "Many other signs, therefore, did Jesus in the presence of the disciples which are not written in this book; but these are written that ye may believe that Jesus is the Christ, the Son of God, and that believing ye may have life in his name." [1]

A further division of prophecy, other than written and oral, may be made first as to manner of impartation; second, as to subject-matter, and, third, as to form. The manner of impartation was by visions, dreams, supernatural illumination and direct communication. Since this subject was considered in the chapter on revelation and inspiration, it will be passed over here.

As to subject-matter, prophecy contains instruction, warning, exhortation and prediction. In recent times the word "prophecy" is used, in the main, with the restricted *sense of prediction*. Not so in Old Testament times. Whatever the message of God, that was prophecy, and the one delivering it was a prophet. If God saw fit by the mouth of His representative to warn the people of impending dangers, or to instruct them as to right forms of worship and living, or to exhort them to obedience, that was as much a part of His will to men as the prediction of future events, and therefore was prophecy. Even the recording of events of the dealings of God with His people would furnish a warning to future generations, and therefore the historical element could in the most general sense be classed as prophecy.

No doubt, with this idea in mind, Jesus spoke of the Old Testament books as the Law, the Prophets and the Psalms: the Law, the writings of Moses; the historical and prophetical books as the Prophets, and the remainder as the devotional element or Psalms. Since the historical books are plainly distinguished in form and in time from the prophets proper, they have been referred

---

[1] John 20: 30, 31.

to under the division of the "Former Prophets," and the prophetical books as the "Latter Prophets."

Under form, prophecy may be classified as verbal and pictorial. Verbal prophecy is that form in which God gave to the prophet His message in direct speech, which, in turn, was delivered to the people in the language of the prophet or in the language of God, or partly of each. Such inspiration and conveyance of thought would be used as would insure the deliverance of Jehovah's message to the people.

Under pictorial prophecy we have the figures of the visions and dreams, which, in their parts and as a whole, are typical of the essential points in the Lord's message. Bits of history are likewise used in a typical way. Thus the message is clothed with figures of speech, suggestive types and meaningful symbols which may or may not be followed with a key of explanation. This form of prophecy was a sort of linguistic code which furnished a sufficient guide to those able to "spiritually discern," but meaningless to the "carnal-minded."

The seventeen books known as the "Latter Prophets" are classified for convenience of study into the Major and Minor Prophets. Major, referring to the larger books, includes, of course, Isaiah, Jeremiah, Lamentations, Ezekiel and Daniel; while the remaining twelve smaller books are called the Minor Prophets. Another classification, based upon the time and circumstances in which the prophets labored, is as follows: First, the prophets of Israel, Jonah, Amos and Hosea; second, the early prophets of Judah, Obadiah, Joel, Isaiah and Micah; third, the later prophets of Judah, Nahum, Zephaniah, Jeremiah and Habakkuk; fourth, the prophets of the captivity, Ezekiel and Daniel, and fifth, the post-exilic prophets, Haggai, Zechariah and Malachi. Since it is the design of the present brief treatise to consider the part the prophets played in working out the purpose of God, the chronological order, as nearly as we can determine it, will be followed. This method will lend some historical value.

Obadiah, who probably prophesied about 840 B. C., has for the burden of his prophecy the kingdom of Edom and its relation to Israel. The theme of part one may be stated as the destruction of Edom and the cause thereof. This part may be divided into three sections, whose contents may be thus summarized. (Sec. 1.) The heathen nations are summoned to take vengeance on Edom. In spite of her impregnable position, they shall bring her low and strip her of her wealth, being aided and encouraged by her allies. (Sec. 2.) This punishment falls upon her as the result of the malice and unfriendliness which she has displayed towards Israel in the time of Israel's calamity in that she rejoiced at her sister's disaster and took part with her enemies. (Sec. 3.) For this cause Edom shall be remembered in the day of the Lord; she shall suffer at the hands of the heathen what she inflicted on others.

The theme of part two is the restoration of Israel. The house of Jacob shall be delivered and shall add to its possessions and spread far and wide. Salvation shall come to Zion and "the kingdom shall be the Lord's." Thus the purpose of God is shown to be that of continuing Israel as a nation, that through them salvation shall be offered to all the nations of the world.

Jonah, a prophet of Israel in the ninth century B. C., was called upon by the Lord to go and give a message to the Ninevites. This message was a warning of destruction. But Jonah, like many of to-day, fled from the call of duty. Jehovah, by supernatural agencies, brought him back and he delivered the message as directed, only to sink into a sulking attitude when God spared the city because of the people's repentance.

In the special care and favor bestowed upon Israel they grew selfish and narrow, forgetting the terms of the contract containing the universality of the love of God. Jonah, representative of this attitude, was rebuked for his bigotry, and through the Lord's rebuke the whole nation was arraigned for its narrowness. The Book of Jonah teaches the brotherhood of man and foreshadows the preaching of the gospel to the Gentile nations, and their repentance.

Joel, a native of Judah and probably living in, or near, Jerusalem, prophesied in the southern kingdom in the latter part of the ninth century B. C. The burden of his prophecy was, impending dangers to Judah by the invasion of foreign armies. In the plague of locusts and drought, which was the occasion of his prophecy, he saw a sign and a presage of the great day of judgment and redemption—the day of Jehovah. The outpouring of the Spirit of Jehovah quoted by Peter (Acts 2:14), the judgment of the nations, the reward of the righteous and the punishment of the wicked constitute the kernel of his message.

Amos, a shepherd and horticulturist, was a native of Tekoa, south of Jerusalem. He was called by Jehovah to go and prophesy to the northern kingdom in the days of Jeroboam II. Israel and Judah enjoyed great prosperity during the reigns of Jeroboam II. and Uzziah. But this prosperity brought on a state of great internal corruption, which condition was the occasion of the prophetic ministry of Amos. This is seen particularly in his scathing denunciation of the profligacy of the rich, and their indifference to the suffering of the poor.

Amos holds out as his central doctrine the sovereignty of Jehovah. God is the God of all nations and the director of their destinies. He teaches that every nation has a standard of right and wrong, and that to this standard they are held responsible. But especially is Israel responsible, to whom He has given a law. He rebukes in strong terms the sins of the nation, and in figurative language predicts the invasion of foreign armies. The northern kingdom will be overthrown, but a remnant will be saved. He gave no direct Messianic prophecy, but connected the hope of the future with the house of David, which house, of course, gave to the world the Saviour of men.

Hosea, sometimes called the Jeremiah of the northern kingdom, gave forth the message of God for nearly

seventy years to that apostate people. By the mouth
of Hosea did Jehovah make His final appeal to Israel
in a last supreme effort to save the nation from destruction. The prosperous reign of Jeroboam II. was followed by a rapid decline, in which the kings sought the
aid of heathen monarchs and became vassals, in turn, of
Assyria and Egypt, rather than servants of Jehovah,
obeying His law.

The family of Hosea is used in picturing the sins of
Israel. His wife, taken from whoredom, symbolizes the
apostasy and profligacy of the kingdom. He purchased
his wife after he had cast her away and held her in
probation; her full restoration was subject to her
reformation. The names of his children portray the
relation of Israel to Jehovah.

In the second division of his book, the sins of the
people in all ranks of life are exposed and censured.
He gives forth warnings as to what such conduct will
bring upon them. Yet Jehovah is ready to pardon, and
one day Israel will return, repent and be restored, no
doubt referring to the remnant who would return with
Judah. "And the children of Judah and the children
of Israel shall be gathered together, and they shall ap-
point themselves one head, and shall go up from the
land; for great shall be the day of Israel."[1]

Isaiah of Judah, like Hosea of Israel, had a long
ministry; he prophesied in the days of Uzziah, Jotham,
Ahaz and Hezekiah. It is thought that he lived in
Jerusalem and was of royal blood, acquainted with kings
and associated with nobles, while his contemporary,
Micah, was of the common people. The ministry of
Isaiah followed the prosperous reign of Uzziah, and
therefore he was called upon to rebuke the people for
their sins. He strongly opposed the inclination of
Judah's kings to make alliances with foreign potentates.

Besides his message to Judah, Isaiah gives the relation of the kingdom of Jehovah to the nations in ten
burdens. Thus Isaiah, like other prophets, holds up

[1] Hos. 1: 11.

before the world the supremacy of Jehovah's kingdom,
for through His people is to come the promised blessing
to all mankind. He follows by showing the consummation of the preceding prophecies and their everlasting
issues. Then the course of the change from universal
judgments to eternal glory is given, followed by the
prophet's view of the end. The first part (chaps.
2-32) of Isaiah treats of Ahaz in the Syro-Ephraimitic
war, and the second division (chaps. 33-36) deals with
Hezekiah in the Assyrian wars. In this latter division
he gives his five woes and their outcome. Then follows
an historical section. Chapters 40-66 are a parallel to
chapters 24-27, containing the great theme, "The Servant of Jehovah."

Isaiah is known as the Messianic prophet because of
his plain references to the coming Messiah. The fifty-
third chapter contains almost a perfect picture of Him
who was to be the consummation of all prophecies. By
the mouth of Isaiah God not only gave rebuke to sin and
warning to disobedience, but pictured in the plainest
terms yet used the One who was to be the fulfillment
of the Abrahamic covenant.

Micah, a contemporary of Isaiah, lived at Moresheth,
southwest of Jerusalem, and was called the Morasthite.
He preached universal judgment to come, especially
upon Samaria and Jerusalem. He predicted the sin and
misery of the people, the exile and the restoration, saying: "Jerusalem shall be plowed as a field." He fore-
told the ruin of the state and the temple, its restoration
and the universal reign of righteousness and peace
under Messiah, born at Bethlehem, at the end of a period
of exile, suffering and degradation. He further portrayed His victories abroad, and His purifying chas-
tisements at home. In his closing section he showed
how hopes are deferred, and drew lessons from the past
both of sin with consequent sufferings, and of redemption which shall yet be complete. Micah likewise pictured
the victorious kingdom of Jehovah in the coming of
the Lord.

18

Nahum calls himself the Elkoshite, but nothing certain is known of the location of Elkosh. "Nahum probably migrated from his native place before the overthrow of Israel to Judah, and there lived and prophesied, at the same time, or soon after that, of Isaiah." [1] Nahum's prophecy was directed at the wicked city of Nineveh. "Nahum describes the fate of the vast city in images which human imagination or human language has never surpassed." He said nothing of Messiah or His kingdom, but preached the destruction of this world's kingdoms built on the foundation of force and fraud. He declared the purpose of Jehovah to judge and destroy the rival and oppressor of His people Israel, and made known how He would commission powerful ministers of vengeance who would sweep away the city, leaving no trace of its former existence. This was to be done because of Nineveh's extraordinary wickedness.

The Book of Zephaniah has been called a "compendium of all prophecy." He is thought to have been a descendant of King Hezekiah. He prophesied in the days of Josiah. In section one (chap. 1) of his book he declares a judicial sentence on the whole world, and especially on God's professing people gathered at Jerusalem. In section two (chap. 2) a respite is granted to Jerusalem while the sentence is being carried out on the nations. In section three (chap. 3: 1-8) the respite is declared to be at an end, and Jerusalem must take her place among the nations on whom the universal sentence is executed. In the last section the prophet speaks well of God's people: "The Lord hath taken away thy judgments, he hath cast out thine enemy; the King of Israel, even the Lord, is in the midst of thee; thou shalt not see evil any more." [2] "At that time will I bring you again, even in the time that I gather you; for I will make you a name and a praise among all

---

[1] "Bible Commentary."
[2] Zeph. 3: 15.

people of the earth, when I turn back your captivity before your eyes, saith the Lord."[1]

Very little is known of the prophet Habakkuk. Probably he was a Levite who had charge of the temple music, since his poem bears such a close relation to the Book of Psalms. He was a writer, not a preacher, and was commanded to write his message upon tablets of stone, no doubt to be placed where the public might read. His message is a complaint of existing conditions, and a cry for immediate retribution. God is guiding the nations, and will punish in His own way and time. Faith and repentance are the gist and essence of Habakkuk's message.

Jeremiah, the "weeping prophet," began his ministry in the thirteenth year of the reign of Josiah, and continued until the Babylonian captivity. Concerning the character of Jeremiah, the "Bible Commentary" says: "We find him sensitive to a most painful degree, timid, shy, hopeless, desponding, constantly complaining and dissatisfied with the course of events, with the office which has been thrust upon him, and with the manner of the Divine Providence, but never flinching from his duty."

As by the ministry of Hosea God made a last desperate effort to save the kingdom of Israel, so by the ministry of Jeremiah He made a last effort to save Judah from captivity, but failed. Following the reformation made by Josiah and his death in battle with Neco, the kingdom of Judah rapidly declined under the vassal kings who succeeded him. In undertaking to avoid the burdens imposed by the Assyrian kings, the kings of Judah sought alliances with the Pharaohs of Egypt. It was in these days of storm and stress that Jeremiah sounded the warnings of Jehovah.

In his introductory prophecy Jeremiah gives an account of his call. His second prophecy is an arraignment of Judah for her apostasy. The third is a call

---

[1] Zeph. 3: 20.

to repentance. The fourth prophecy, or group of prophecies, is God's judgment upon the unrepentant, followed by a sermon in the temple upon the fast-day. The sixth prophecy contains the curse of the broken covenant. Next Jeremiah shows forth the discipline of Jehovah to be brought upon His people by the illustration of the linen girdle. He then predicts a drought and the punishment of Judah by pestilence and exile. Next follows a reiteration of the law of the Sabbath. The power and authority of God are emphasized by the figure of the potter and his wheel. By breaking a vessel in the sight of the people, the prophet illustrates how Jehovah will destroy Jerusalem.

Jeremiah now turns upon King Zedekiah with the severe warnings of God. He tells of the exile of His people, but promises them deliverance. This is followed by a delineation of the wine-cup of fury, and then he tells of the attacks made upon himself. Jeremiah then urges the king and the people to bow to the inevitable, even the yoke of Babylon. In the thirty-first chapter the prophet clearly sets forth the hope of Israel, yes, the hope of the whole world, in giving the terms of the new covenant, as contrasted with the old, in which he pointedly refers to the new dispensation in Christ. Then he follows with a statement of Zedekiah's fate, the emancipation of the Hebrew slaves, the shaming of Judah by the faithfulness of the Rechabites to their standards, some historical events, Baruch's disappointment, and prophecies against the nations. His closing prophecy is a setting forth of the destruction of Babylon, and the return of Israel from captivity. Jeremiah's message in the main is a call to repentance and a warning of judgment.

The prophets of the exile—Ezekiel and Daniel—were considered in connection with the captivity. The post-exilic prophets—Haggai and Zechariah—were mentioned as having an important work in the return to Canaan, in that they continually urged the people to go on with the rebuilding of the temple. It remains to give

some of the other teachings of Zechariah. He set forth
two general principles: first, that the moral law is above
the ceremonial law; and, secondly, that Jehovah's
promises are conditioned upon obedience to His precepts. Hence fasts are to be turned into feasts, and
the Gentiles are to be brought in. He closes by fore-
casting the overthrow of the heathen powers, the coming
of Messiah, and the establishment of His kingdom.

Malachi, whose book closes the Old Testament canon,
prophesied about 431 B. C. He, perhaps, stood in the
same relation to Nehemiah in the latter part of his work
that Haggai and Zechariah bore to Zerubbabel. He
gives an arraignment of Israel for unkindness, irre-
ligiousness and profaneness. He reproved the priests
for neglecting the covenant, and the people for idolatry,
adultery and infidelity. He portrays the messenger,
majesty and grace of Christ, the rebellion of the people,
and the promise of blessing to those who fear God.
His closing message is a warning of the day of judgment, the promise of the coming of Christ preceded by
the appearance of Elijah. "But unto you that fear
my name shall the sun of righteousness arise with healing in its wings; and ye shall go forth, and gambol as
calves of the stall."[1]

By the mouth of His prophets the Lord sought to
guide His people in the way of holiness. He warned
them of the dangers of idolatry, and continually called
on them for faithful obedience. He rebuked the other
nations for their wickedness, and held them responsible
for interference with the plan being worked out through
Israel. Above all, He gave from time to time clearer
pictures of Him who was to come in the lineage of
Abraham, through whom the families of the earth were
to be blessed.

---

[1] Mal. 4: 2.

CHAPTER XVII.

"CRITICISM"

THE nature of the present thesis being along the line of an apologetic interpretation of the Old Testament, it seems to the writer appropriate to give a chapter to a brief consideration of "higher criticism." This subject is now demanding our most serious consideration because of the destructive effects on faith of the radical theories that have come from this branch of study. Higher criticism is a legitimate study, and many writers on this subject are men of true faith. Yet so much of a destructive nature has come from the pen of critics that the words "critic," or "higher critic" and "higher criticism," have come to be used in a popular way to denote the destructive critic or destructive criticism. These terms, therefore, imply a position antagonistic to the faith of the church. Such will be their use in the following pages.

The beginning of the critical movement is generally associated with a profligate French physician by the name of Astruc. Astruc, in his "Conjectures," in 1753, advanced the idea that the Book of Genesis was composed of two documents, the one using for the name of God the Hebrew word "Elohim," and the other using the word "Jehovah." This idea was enlarged upon by Eichhorn, who said that the two documents might be traced, not only by the use of the two words "Elohim" and "Jehovah," but also by a difference of style; that the authors of the two documents used different vocabularies, which were easily traced in their writings. The third main step in the critical theory was taken by

De Wette (1805-06) when he claimed that the style and character of Deuteronomy was such that it could not have been written prior to the reformation period in the reign of Josiah.

This lead was followed by others who added from time to time other items of disintegration, until the Bible became broken up into an innumerable number of fragments. In fact, the process of disintegration went to such an extreme as to become suicidal in its effect, and reaction set in. Out of all the various theories that have been propounded it will be the purpose here to give in a simple statement what comes nearest to being now the fundamental elements of the critical claims.

In making a statement of the critical theory the condensed form given by J. W. McGarvey, in the introduction of his work, "The Authorship of Deuteronomy," will be followed.

Critics of the radical type hold that no writing was done by Moses, but the more conservative ones allow that Moses wrote "The Book of the Covenant," meaning Exodus 20-22. With this possible exception, Israel had no written law or history until the eighth or ninth centuries, about the time of Elijah and Elisha, or the time of Amos and Hosea. About this time there appeared in Israel, the northern kingdom, a document which included much of what we have in the Pentateuch. It uniformly used the Hebrew word "Elohim" for God. About the same time a similar document appeared in Judah, the southern kingdom, likewise giving a portion of the present Pentateuch, but using the word "Jehovah" for God. The former document is referred to as E, or the Elohistic, and the latter J, or the Jehovistic document.

At a later period, but earlier than the appearance of the Book of Deuteronomy, some third person took these two documents, E and J, and combined them into one by taking first of one and then of the other. Sometimes, seemingly uncertain which to use, he copied the records of both. He occasionally added material of his own. This person is referred to as a redactor, the German word for editor. The document resulting from this combination is called JE.

The critical theory goes on further to claim that in the days of Josiah the Israelites were so enticed by the idolatry which was all about them that it occurred to the author, or authors, of Deuteronomy, to write a book which, in the name of Moses, would condemn what had hitherto been considered lawful; that is, to worship "on every high hill and under every green tree." As a substitute they desired to concentrate the worship at the central altar in Jerusalem. This would not only tend to suppress idolatry, but would enrich the treasury of the priests at Jerusalem. Hence this book was written and hidden in the temple "to be found." This book, "found" by Hilkiah the priest in the temple in the eighteenth year of the reign of Josiah, is referred to as D.

Between the time of the writing of Deuteronomy and the Babylonian captivity, a portion of Leviticus was written, which is known as the "law of holiness," and is represented by the letter H. This contained chapters 17-22 of the Book of Leviticus.

At the time of the captivity Judah had the book of the covenant (JE), the legal part of Deuteronomy (D) and H, the "law of holiness." Near the close of the exile another writer known as P, because he is said to have been a priest, wrote other parts of Genesis and the main body of Exodus, Leviticus and Numbers. By this writer the first chapter of Genesis was composed, about one thousand years after the death of Moses.

It fell to still another redactor to take JE, D, H and P, and combine them into the books of the Pentateuch as we have them to-day. When Ezra took this new compilation (about 457) and read it to the people, it was its first publication to the world. Now, concerning the writers of these various documents, or the documents themselves, there is no claim made that there is the least historical evidence. All the argument produced to support the theory is purely inferential. When first known, the books of the Pentateuch, so far as history is concerned, existed in the same form as we have them to-day. The whole critical structure stands on the claim that the writings can thus be separated, and proved to have had separate authorship by the peculiarities of style and subject-matter. Upon so slender a foundation as this, then, the whole superstructure of the critical theory is builded; and this is the theory that, because of its destructive influence on faith, is so "troubling Israel" to-day.

Now it is the claim of the critics that we should, without bias, study the Bible, as to date, authorship, credibility, and literary characteristics, as we do any other book. This, in the opinion of the writer, can not be done without in a manner prejudging the Bible; for to put it on the plane with other books is to put it in the class of man-made books, which eliminates inspiration at the very beginning. This is, by competent witnesses, shown to be the case with the critical writers, therefore substantiating the claim. The language of James Orr ("The Problem of the Old Testament," p. 12) quoted above is repeated: "For now the fact becomes apparent—there is, indeed, not the least attempt to disguise it—that, to a large and influential school of critical inquirers—those, moreover, who have had most to do with the shaping of the current critical theories—this question of a supernatural origin for the religion of Israel is already foreclosed; is ruled out at the start as *a priori* inadmissible." We have on this point the following language from William Henry Green ("The Higher Criticism of the Pentateuch," p. 157): "All the acknowledged leaders of the movement have, without exception, scouted the reality of miracles and prophecy and immediate divine revelation in their genuine and evangelical sense. Their theories are all inwrought with naturalistic presuppositions, which can not be disentangled from them without their falling to pieces." It

19

is no wonder, then, that the critics come to a certain conclusion when they start out to prove that very thing.

Since the critics assume there was no miracle, they base their theory upon the claim that religion came to man by an evolutionary process, and that all peoples went through practically the same stages of development in their religious thought. Therefore Israel must have passed through the same stages of development as they assume for other peoples.

Let us consider first that part of the theory which says that Moses wrote nothing, or at most four chapters of Exodus. According to the theory of evolution as applied by the critics, Israel could not have been at the time of Moses far enough advanced in culture to have produced such writings as the books of the Pentateuch. But what are the facts? The Bible tells us that Israel was in Egypt, and Moses was educated at the court of Pharaoh. Was there sufficient learning in that day to prepare Moses for so great a work? Here, fortunately, we have the testimony of ancient documents, made accessible by the spade of the archæologist. Discussing the Tel-el-Amarna tablets found in Egypt, A. H. Sayce, an authority on the monuments, says: "The Mosaic age, therefore, instead of being an illiterate one, was an age of high literary activity and education throughout the civilized East. Not only was there a widespread literary culture in both Egypt and Babylonia, which had its roots in a remote past, but this culture was shared by Mesopotamia and Asia Minor, and more especially by Syria and Palestine."[1] Further on Professor Sayce says: "The civilized world was a world of books, and a knowledge of writing extended even to the classes of the population who were engaged in manual labor."[2] Again he says: "We have learnt many things of late years from archæology, but its chiefest lesson has been that the age of Moses, and even the

---

[1] "Monument Facts and Higher Critical Fancies," p. 40.
[2] *Ibid.*, p. 43.

age of Abraham, was almost as literary as our own." [1]
M. G. Kyle ("Deciding Voice of the Monuments,"
p. 84) says: "Evidence has been found of the establishment of a postal system in Babylonia extending to its
Palestine province in the days of Naram-Sin, about
seventeen hundred and fifty years before the time of
Abraham." Hence we conclude that rather than think
Moses could not know how to write it would be a greater
wonder to us if he did not have such knowledge.

Next we are asked to believe that though Moses
wrote very little, if anything, yet those who wrote the
contents of the Pentateuch attributed their work to
Moses, and the people received it as such. This forces
us to believe that men in our day, removed by thousands of years, can know that Moses did not write these
books, yet people living in the day when the books first
appeared were led to think that they were written by
the ancient patriarch. Again, if Moses was so lacking
in ability, so low in the scale of development, why should
the writers think that using the name of such a semi-
barbarous leader would lend weight to what they had
written?

Not only did Israel believe that Moses wrote the law,
but Jesus gave His approval to that belief by saying:
"Did not Moses give you the law?" [2] John the Baptist
so testified: "For the law was given through Moses." [3]

The basic principle in the critical theory, and the
one that gave rise, seemingly, to the whole critical
procession, is the claim that two documents can be
traced in Genesis by the use of the two names "Elohim"
and "Jehovah," and that this documentary hypothesis
is further supported by differences of style even to the
use of different vocabularies. The truth is that the
word "Elohim" is repeatedly found in the sections
attributed to J, where only Jehovah ought to be found;
also Jehovah is found in sections attributed to E, where

---

[1] "Monument Facts and Higher Critical Fancies," p. 43.
[2] John 7: 19.
[3] John 1: 17.

only Elohim ought to be found. The critics explain this by saying that at times the author used both names as occasion demanded. They thus surrender their own most vital contention, for this is the true explanation that *Moses* used both words as occasion demanded. "Elohim" was the name used for God in the most general sense—God of all the nations, creator of heaven and earth. But as the God of Israel He was known as "Jehovah." In identifying Jehovah as the God of all the world the words were combined in the phrase "Jehovah God."

According to the argument of the critics, if a man was to write an article to-day, using the words "God," "Lord," "Jehovah," "The Deity," and like terms, the article would be declared to be composed of as many documents, written by as many different persons, as there were terms used in reference to God. This, of course, is absurd. That most any narrative can be divided into different documents has been illustrated by William Henry Green,[1] by dividing the well-known parables, the prodigal son and the good Samaritan, each into two parts. On the similar ground of difference in style the Epistle to the Romans has been dissected into four parts as an illustration of the futility of this argument of the critics. Since any brief, simple narrative, whose unity is not questioned, can be similarly dissected, the argument based on this contention falls.

Further, we are called upon by the critical theory to believe that up to the time of Elijah, or even to the time of Amos (eighth or ninth century), Israel had no writings, with the possible exception of four chapters of Exodus, and no law until the eighteenth year of the reign of Josiah (621 B. C.). We are to think of all the work of Moses as a leader; that of his successor, Joshua, in the conquest and division of Canaan; the administration of the fifteen judges; the reigns of Saul, David and Solomon, with the extension of the

---

[1] "The Higher Criticism of the Pentateuch," p. 119f.

kingdom, the organization of the kingdom, the building of the temple and its consequent use, to say nothing of the following events through a long period of years— with scarcely any writings, much less any written law. This goes beyond man's natural credulity, to say nothing of reason.

Then, in the eighteenth year of Josiah's reign the priests found a book, or pretended to have done so, which they brought to the king. While this book was never seen or heard of before by king or people, they hastened to accept it as genuine, and changed the whole tenor of their lives to fit its mandates. Surely Israel liked to be deceived and made an easy mark for the fakir. This is not the nature of their descendants. With this perversion of facts, and its consequent irrational conclusions, we can see that the critical theory is not built upon the facts, but that the facts are perverted to fit the theory, showing, again, that the critic formed his conclusion at the beginning of his inquiry, and not, as he would have us believe, at the close of his investigation.

According to the critical theory, the ten tribes of Israel passed out of history (722 B. C.) at the fall of Samaria, their capital city, not having had any other writings than the document E, and later the document JE, with possibly some knowledge of H (the law of holiness). No wonder they declined so rapidly. Judah had, besides J, JE and H, the Book of Deuteronomy from Josiah's time (621 B. C.) to the fall of Jerusalem (586 B. C.). "There had been, of course, a temple, priesthood, religious institutions, sacrificial ritual, priestly rules and technique. Still, the law, as elaborated in the exile, was practically a new thing."[1] That is, the bulk of the laws found in Exodus, Leviticus and Numbers was written by the priestly writer (P) near the close of the captivity, and attributed to Moses. It is surpassingly strange that a nation surrounded as

---

[1] "The Problem of the Old Testament," Jas. Orr, p. 288.

Israel was all the centuries of its history by well-developed and cultured peoples, should continue its extensive religious ritual, to say nothing of the government, with so little written law.

We must keep in mind that the priestly writer (P), writing near the close of the Babylonian captivity, and giving us the bulk of the law found in Exodus, Leviticus and Numbers, attributed his work to Moses, though writing nearly a thousand years after the lawgiver's time. Is it reasonable to suppose that a people would believe that writings had thus been preserved among them for such an enormous length of time, and yet had never been known? Where had they been secreted for all these centuries? On the other hand, how meek would be the man who had ability to write as this man did, and yet would purposely conceal his identity and give the glory to another. This practice (that of attributing their work to others), claimed by the critics to have been practiced so extensively by writers of Biblical documents, is unknown among any people. Authentic history records no such practice anywhere.

Again we are called upon to believe that a nation, after passing its golden age of power and influence, such as Israel experienced in the reigns of David and Solomon, and having declined to that point of weakness which made it a prey for other nations, and having been taken into captivity and held in slavery, came back from that decline to only a shadow of its former power, and produced its greatest literature. The greater part of the law was written, according to the critical theory, just as Judah was emerging from Babylonian captivity and servitude. The greater part of the Psalms was written during and after the exile. The loftiest part of Isaiah was also written following the captivity. This was not true of the literature of the Greeks and Romans. Their golden age of literature was contemporaneous with the golden age of the empires. The English, in the days of Elizabeth, wrote largely just as they were coming to be a great nation, not after their collapse, for they have had none. American literature came at the time when the United States was coming into being as a great nation.

That the critics are trying to explain everything on naturalistic principles, setting aside the miraculous, is evidenced further by the fact that when the date of any book is being considered, and that book contains the predictive element, the book is given a date late enough to make the predictive portion mere history. If it does not seem wise to move the whole book to a later period, then the book is divided and attributed to different authors. Isaiah is thus divided into two or more Isaiahs. Daniel is given a late date. Jonah is declared to be unhistorical. In brief, such arrangement must be made as will dispose of the miraculous. The dividing-line in the controversy is the miracle. The line of distinction between the Christian religion and its opponents to-day is the supernatural element. Take the supernatural element out of Christianity, and you take Christ out; and to take Christ out is to destroy the whole system. At this point Christianity stands or falls. Consideration has been given in a previous chapter to the question of the possibility of miracles, which justifies passing it by at this time.

The Bible, while thought of as one book, is really a collection of books—"a divine library," Jerome named it. It was written by about forty different persons, through a period of about fourteen hundred years, yet these writings when taken together form a homogeneous whole, with complete unity. This unity is seen in purpose and plan. It is one history, one movement, toward one end. This can not be said of the Koran or of the Buddhist or Zoroastrian Scriptures. How could this unity obtain through so many writers, and over such a long period of time, except the whole be directed by one mind, and that mind be God's?

Again, there is a wonderful fulfillment of the Old Testament in the New. Constantly one is reminded in the Old Testament of the incompleteness; that things are not permanent, but a shadow of things to come. "Jehovah thy God will raise up unto thee a prophet from the midst of thee, of thy brethren, like unto me; unto him ye shall hearken."[1] Thus Moses cites the people to some one ahead, of whom he himself was but a type. Take the picture drawn in the fifty-third chapter of Isaiah, and then see how beautifully it is fulfilled in the Gospels. But predictive prophecy is miracle.

From the call of Abram of Ur of the Chaldees, to whom God said, "In thee and in thy seed shall all the the families of the earth be blessed," there is a steady connected movement onward for the carrying out of that covenant. Though Jacob and his family went into Egypt, and became involved in servitude, yet God led them out to the *promised* land. Though they did not continue faithful, and were again sent into exile, yet He brought them back. Nothing is clearer than the theological character of this history. Prophets were raised up from time to time to aid in the execution of the one great plan. The religious ritual was arranged to forecast it. The songs of Zion proclaimed it. All eyes were turned toward the coming Messiah. Even the erroneous idea of the orthodox Jew of to-day, in that he is still looking for the Messiah's coming, is proof of our contention.

Again, as James Orr says, "a unique religion will display its character equally by what it has and by what it wants."[2] Many things that are found in Israel's religion are found in others, but there are things found in other religions not found here. Take the spirit worship and the magic of Babylon, the animal worship and the ancestor worship of Egypt, the stone worship, fetishism, tree worship, serpent worship, human sacrifice and lustful rites that are found in other religions— these are not found in the religion of Israel, but are specifically forbidden. If the religion of Israel had the same evolutionary origin and development that the

---

[1] Deut. 18: 15.
[2] "The Problem of the Old Testament," p. 39.

critics claim for these other religions, then why are these practices absent from Israel? All the other religions are polytheistic, but Israel's is monotheistic. "The Old Testament knows of no time when the people of Israel were without the knowledge of the one God as the Creator and providential Ruler of the whole world."[1]

The doctrine of grace is peculiar to the Biblical religion. While there is the condemnation of sin, yet from the very beginning there appears the developing plan of God for the salvation of man. In this plan it is the purpose of God that men shall be holy; and here it is found as a distinctive feature that the idea of the connection of morality and religion is a dominant one. The Biblical religion is distinctly an ethical one.

The interpretation of the "modern" viewpoint is that the writings of Paul, Isaiah or Peter are the thoughts of these men about God. The Bible claims to be inspired. These writings are the record of what God has done, and of His revelation to man. "For no prophecy ever came by the will of man: but men spake from God, being moved by the Holy Spirit."[2]

Now, the critical theory, which W. H. Green says originated among the enemies of Christianity, brings us, instead of the Bible, a heap of scraps or fragments thrown together by men according to their own whims or fancies, uninspired and unhistorical; without purpose or end, save to meet the needs of the passing day. This leaves us without any Old Testament support for the deity of Jesus; in fact, without any revelation from God. On the other hand, all archæological discovery is supporting the Biblical narrative, proving its credibility. The Bible meets all the tests of historicity, authenticity and credibility, and gives that basis of faith in Christ that leads to life eternal. "But these are written that ye may believe that Jesus is the Christ, the Son of God, and that believing ye may have life in his name."[3]

---

[1] "The Problem of the Old Testament," Jas. Orr, p. 41.
[2] 2 Pet. 1:21.
[3] John 20:31.

CHAPTER XVIII.

CONCLUSION

THE Bible is such a book in its content, in its claim, in its age, and in its past influence, as to demand the serious consideration of any thinking person. It meets us with the claim that it stands out apart and alone, distinct from all other books in that it is the word of God given to man by revelation, and by faithful men handed on from generation to generation. It seemed logical, in starting in to make a study of the Old Testament first, to look into the question of revelation and inspiration. We find nothing in the claims of revelation and inspiration contrary to the work and power of a being who could bring into existence this material universe, including man, but, on the other hand, it would seem a necessary procedure by an all-powerful being who is responsible for man's existence, and who would therefore be responsible for making known to him the divine purpose.

In trying to comprehend the purpose of God recorded in the Old Testament, it seemed well first to look into the nature and being of God. For how could God have a purpose at all except He be a living personality with ability to reason and power to carry out a plan when instituted? From all the possible theories concerning the existence or non-existence of God, the most reasonable conclusion is that the world must have had an adequate cause. To-day, and each moment of time, the world needs the same adequate cause to sustain it. Further, that cause must be all-powerful, all-wise, holy and good. Being righteous, and, of course, intelligent,

God would have a purpose, and in His revelation to man He would portray that purpose.

Since early in the Old Testament narrative it is made clear that in man particularly is that purpose to be centered, it appeared necessary to look into the nature and possibilities of man. What, by his nature, is his relation to all other life, and what is his relation to God? The purpose of any thing, or of any life, depends not only upon Him who made it, but will be limited by the nature of the thing itself. When it is found that man by nature is intelligent, moral, religious and free, it is seen that he of all creatures of the earth can develop, or make progress, morally. He alone can become righteous. This leads us to decide that since the purpose of God in the world centers in man, it must be found in the moral or religious side of his nature. This is further emphasized by a consideration of sin as opposed to righteousness, and the relation of the former to law.

Then a study is made of religion and its relation to the nature of man. If man is to become righteous, he must be not only a moral being knowing right and wrong, but he must have a conception of a being who is perfect in goodness. There being no assurance that man can ever discover for himself the way of righteousness (and if he did, it would be long after millions had passed from earth without a chance to try it), there must come from the perfect One that guidance which leads to a higher life. The brevity of this life has never satisfied man; he has, without exception, looked for another existence. So man is found to be a being who by nature looks to a higher power for guidance and help, and bears in his breast the hope eternal.

With this view of God as Creator, and man as the creature made in His image, which image is to be developed still more like the Creator, we are ready to see more of the meaning of the material world, the stage of action set for man in whom the purpose of God is to be carried out. The material world is, then, not an end in itself, but a means to bring about the true end. Since the stage is so large and the actors so small, and the appearance of each so brief in time, we are apt to commit the error of substituting the means for the end. We lose sight of the actors, and think that the stage is the thing of supreme importance.

When we make the proper comparison between mind and matter, we see that mind can exist aside from matter, but how matter can be apart from mind is an enigma. This leads us at last to conclude that matter is, in the ultimate, but the manifestation of mind. Where there is no mind there is no purpose, but if we hold that back of the existence of all things is a supreme mind, then we can assume that there is a purpose in all things, and that these purposes are all subordinate to one great purpose. Hence, to read the true purpose or meaning of anything we must read back to the one great purpose to which it is subordinate. A rod may have as its immediate purpose that of conveying motion or power from piston-head to wheel, but its greater meaning is that it is a part of a great machine that moves freight in the interests of humanity, and the supreme interest of humanity is to become in character more like God.

This idea of the development of character we see takes precedence from the beginning. God takes cognizance of the moral acts of man. In the garden it is the conduct of man which leads to a moral state that is given prominence in the narrative. After expulsion from Eden it is the religious and moral practices that have chief consideration. Abel secured the favor of God, not alone because he was a good shepherd, but because he offered an acceptable sacrifice. It was the sin of Cain that drove him into wandering, not his lack of skill as an agriculturist, or lack of skill in the trades on the part of his descendants.

So in the days of Noah God was concerned with the fact that all the world was becoming corrupt. But it is in the days of Abraham that the plan of God is brought more clearly to view. It is here that we find the promise: "In thee and in thy seed shall all the families of the earth be blessed." It is that blessedness that the Father desires for His children. But this blessedness can not be separate from righteousness, and righteousness must result from the choice and act of man together with the love and help of God. Abraham believed God, and it was accounted to him for righteousness. It was through Abraham that the Lord planned to raise up a particular nation, and in Abraham's seed He would send His Son into the world. For this reason He led him into the land of Canaan. To this same end God renewed the covenant with Isaac. To this same end was Esau, the unambitious, shiftless character, rejected for the industrious, though imperfect, character of Jacob.

Having this covenant of God with Abraham, Isaac and Jacob before us, containing the clause, "I will make of you a great nation," we can follow intelligently the movements of God's people in Egypt. We can see how here, under the protecting care of a friendly monarch, this clause of the contract was being worked out to its full and complete issue.

With the further item of the contract in mind, "I will give you a land for inheritance," we are ready properly to interpret the calling of Moses, the exodus, and the wilderness march. We are further able to see how Israel is justified in entering and taking possession of the land of Canaan.

Then in the last and most important item of the contract, "In thee and in thy seed shall all the nations of the earth be blessed," are we able to find justification for God in giving help to Israel against the other nations. Since through Israel salvation was to be brought to all men, God was justified in protecting and preserving that nation at any cost.

To be blessed would mean to have salvation in Christ. But what was required of man as a condition on his part? In the very beginning God demanded obedience as one virtue of man, to the extent that death was made the penalty of disobedience. Outside the garden, God called for faithful obedience unto whatever plan of worship He had provided him. In His rejection of Cain, His purifying the world by flood, His commendation of the righteous acts and corresponding condemnation of the wicked acts of Abraham, Isaac, Jacob, Joseph, Moses and others, does God speak clearly His demands for a righteous character.

In the law given through Moses to Israel there is a high ethical standard. God required not only the obedience of man, but an undivided love, such as would prompt the best of actions. He required such regulation of the conduct of man toward his fellow as not only contributed to the general welfare of society, but such as would build up the proper condition of mind and heart in the individual. An instance of such was the law against covetousness; man was forbidden, not only to steal, but to covet his neighbor's goods.

In the religious ritual the priests who stood highest in example and influence were required to be men physically without blemish, to abstain from the use of intoxicating liquors, and to lead a pure life. Disregard of these rules by the priests, as in the case of the sons of Eli, was noted and condemned; and the priesthood was changed to another line because of their wickedness.

God withheld not His condemnation of wickedness even in high places. Abraham's act of lying to Pharaoh and Abimelech, Moses' sin in failing to give the glory to God when he smote the rock, David's sin of adultery, and Solomon's idolatry, were each the occasion for God to make known His unalterable opposition to sin and hatred of evil. In fact, it is not the concern of God that man be a senseless, meaningless machine, doing His bidding as a selfish satisfaction to Himself, but that man develop honesty, purity, justice, and all those moral characteristics which are to be found in God's own activities toward man. We are to assume that God, having created man in His likeness, desires that man develop that image to a greater approximation of the perfect pattern.

These moral characteristics God required of king and of peasant, of prince and of pauper, of the priest and of the people. His demands were embodied in the law. They constituted the fabric of the religious ritual. They were the principles that fired the prophets to such exalted and holy zeal. They furnished the themes for the lyrical poetry used by the temple choirs. Nothing, then, can be clearer than that God has made known in the Old Testament message His desire that man become righteous.

Then we conclude that from the very nature we must assume God to have, He would desire that quality in His creatures which would be most like Himself, and therefore most nearly in harmony with His character and will. This we further conclude could be made possible only through moral beings with freedom of choice. Hence, man to become virtuous must be created with a potential moral nature. He, then, must be an intelligent, moral being, with the power of choice. But choice can not come from one alone, so in order to have righteousness we must have the possibility of evil. With evil there is sin, and sin leads to death. Since man could not lift himself from sin and death, God provided a way of escape by sending His Son as a sacrifice for sin, that through faith in and obedience to Him man might be saved.

Toward this end, that of bringing His Son into the world as Redeemer, God chose Abraham to head a people or nation who shall furnish the necessary religious setting or background for such an important event. Then we see that the immediate purpose of God as made known in the Old Testament is to arrange for the coming of Christ into the world. He was to be the center of all history. Everything, therefore, before Him was but pointing the way to Him, as that which has followed points back to Him as the great mountain peak of all history.

As this was the immediate purpose of God, so salvation through Christ, or the building of a righteous character made possible by His gospel, was the mediate or ultimate purpose. God therefore desires that all men be righteous. "Whosoever doeth not righteousness is not of God."[1] "If ye know that he is righteous, ye know that every one also that doeth righteousness is begotten of him."[2]

This, then, is the purpose of God as we see it idealized in the Old Testament Scriptures. To see how that purpose is realized we must turn to a study of the New Testament.

---

[1] 1 John 3: 10.
[2] 1 John 2: 29.

THE END.